Russia & Central Asia
by Road

THE BRADT STORY

In 1974, my former husband George Bradt and I spent three days sitting on a river barge in Bolivia writing our first guide for like-minded travellers: *Backpacking along Ancient Ways in Peru and Bolivia*. The 'little yellow book', as it became known, is now in its sixth edition and continues to sell to travellers throughout the world. Since 1980, with the establishment of Bradt Publications, I have continued to publish guides for the discerning traveller, covering more than 100 countries and all six continents, and winning the 1997 *Sunday Times* Small Publisher of the Year Award. *Russia and Central Asia by Road* is the 134th Bradt title to be published.

The company continues to develop new titles and new series, but in the forefront of my mind there remains our original ethos – responsible travel with an emphasis on the culture and natural history of the region. I hope that you will get the most out of your trip, and perhaps have the opportunity to give something in return.

Travel guides are by their nature continuously evolving. If you experience anything which you would like to share with us, or if you have any amendments to make to this guide, please write; all your letters are read and passed on to the author. Most importantly, do remember to travel with an open mind and to respect the customs of your hosts – it will add immeasurably to your enjoyment.

Happy travelling!

Hilary Bradt

41 Nortoft Road, Chalfont St Peter, Bucks SL9 0LA, England
Tel/fax: 01494 873478 Email: bradtpublications@compuserve.com

Russia & Central Asia by Road

4WD • MOTORBIKE • BICYCLE

Hazel Barker

with David Thurlow

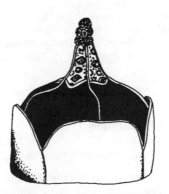

Bradt Publications, UK
The Globe Pequot Press Inc, USA

Published in 1997 by Bradt Publications,
41 Nortoft Road, Chalfont St Peter, Bucks SL9 0LA, England
Published in the USA by The Globe Pequot Press Inc, 6 Business Park Road,
PO Box 833, Old Saybrook, Connecticut 06475-0833

British Library Cataloguing in Publication Data
A catalogue record for this book is available from the British Library
ISBN 1 898323 61 5

Library of Congress Cataloging-in-Publication Data
Barker, Hazel
Russia and Central Asia by Road: 4WD, motorbike, bicycle / Hazel
Barker with David Thurlow.
p. cm.
Includes index.
ISBN 1-898323-61-5
1, Asia, Central – Description and travel. 2. Russia (Federation) –
Description and travel. 3. Barker, Hazel – Journeys – Asia, Central.
4. Barker, Hazel – Journeys – Russia (Federation) 5. Thurlow,
David – Journeys – Asia, Central 6. Thurlow, David – Journeys,
Russia (Federation). I. Thurlow, David. II. Title.
DK854.B338 1997
915.804'429—dc21   97-22761
                                                                            CIP

Photographs Hazel Barker
Front cover: Khulans, Mongolia
Back cover: Motorbike outside a *ger*

Illustrations Wendy Dison
Maps *Inside cover:* Steve Munns
Others: Hans van Well, from originals supplied by the author and Athol Yates

Typeset from the author's disc by Wakewing Ltd, High Wycombe HP13 7QA
Printed and bound in Spain by Grafo SA, Bilbao

CONTENTS

Introduction   IX

PART ONE   BEFORE YOU GO   1

Chapter One   **Planning and Preparation**   3
                When to go 3, Group travel or going it alone 3,
                Vehicle choice and preparation 4,
                Motorcycle preparations 8, Camping equipment 12,
                Telephone 14, Photography 14, Computers 15,
                What to take 16, Maps 17, Documentation 18,
                Getting your vehicle to Russia 23,
                Customs and immigration 24, Health 25,
                Safety 27, Money 28, Accommodation 29

PART TWO   RUSSIA AND MONGOLIA   33

Chapter Two   **Russian Federation**   35
                Facts and figures 35, Geography 38, Climate 38,
                Natural history and conservation 39,
                Historical outline 41,
                Politics and government 49, Economy 49,
                People 50, Language 51, Religion 51,
                Culture and the arts 52

Chapter Three   **In Russia**   55
                Communications 55, Electricity 57,
                Driving in Russia 57, Cycling in Russia 60,
                Public holidays 63, Shopping 64,
                Food and drink 64, Tips and tipping 66,
                Accommodation and camping 66

Chapter Four   **Russian Routes**   69
                Vyborg 69, St Petersburg 69, Novgorod 74,
                Moscow 79, The Golden Ring 86, Suzdal 86,
                Cheboksary 90, Kazan 90, Perm 91,
                Ekaterinburg 92, Kurgan 97, Petropavl 97,
                Omsk 97, Kuibishev 98, Novosibirsk 99,
                Barnaul 103, Kemerovo 103, Krasnoyarsk 104,
                Nizhneudinsk 105, Irkutsk 105,
                Excursions from Irkutsk 110, Buryatia 112,
                Ulan Ude 112, Kyakhta 115, Naushki 115,
                Chita 116, Skovorodino 119, Taldan 119,
                Magdagachi 120, Blagoveshchensk 120,
                Birobidzhan 122, Khabarovsk 123, Gaivoron 130,
                Vladivostok 130, Pushing the boundaries 136

Chapter Five   **Mongolia**   **139**
Facts and figures 139, Geography 141,
Climate 141, Natural history and conservation 141,
Historical outline 143, Politics 145, Economy 145,
People 146, Language 146, Religion 146,
Culture and the arts 147,
Planning and preparation 149, In Mongolia 153,
Getting there and away 157, Suhbaatar 158,
Darhan 158, Ulaanbaatar 160, Arvaiheer 163,
Bayanhongor 164, Altai 165, Takhiin Tal 167,
Khovd 169, Olgii 170, Altanbulag 173

PART THREE   **THE 'STANS**   **175**
Getting to and from the 'Stans 177

Chapter Six   **Kazakstan**   **179**
Facts and figures 179, Geography 179,
Climate 180, Natural history and conservation 180,
Historical outline 181, Politics 182, Economy 182,
People 182, Language 182, Religion 183,
Culture and the arts 183,
Planning and preparation 183,
In Kazakstan 186, Getting there and away 188,
Semey 188, Taldy-Qorghan 189, Almaty 190,
Medeu and Shymbulaq 193

Chapter Seven   **Kyrgyzstan**   **197**
Facts and figures 197, Geography 197,
Climate 198, Historical outline 198, Politics 198,
Economy 199, People 199, Language 199,
Religion 199, Culture and the arts 199,
Planning and preparation 200, In Kyrgyzstan 201,
Getting there and away 205, Bishkek 206,
Lake Issyk-Kul 209, Tamchi 209,
Cholpon-Ata 210, Karakol 210,
Cycling in Kyrgyzstan 214

Chapter Eight   **Uzbekistan**   **221**
Facts and figures 221, Geography 221,
Climate 223, Natural history and conservation 223,
Historical outline 223, Politics 225, Economy 226,
People 226, Language 226, Religion 226,
Culture and the arts 226,
Planning and preparation 228, In Uzbekistan 230,
Getting there and away 233, Tashkent 234,
Samarkand 238, Bukhara 240, Khiva 243,
Nukus 244

Chapter Nine   **Turkmenistan**   **245**
Facts and figures 245, Geography 245,
Climate 245, Natural history and conservation 247,
Historical outline 247, Politics 248, Economy 248,
People 248, Language 248, Religion 249,
Culture and the arts 249,
Planning and preparation 249,
In Turkmenistan 251, Getting there and away 253,
Charjou 254, Mary 254, Merv 255, Ashgabat 256,
Nisa 258, Turkmenbashi 258

Appendix One   **Language**   **259**

Appendix Two   **Vehicle Agency Addresses**   **263**

Appendix Three   **Further Reading**   **265**

Index   **270**

Maps

Ekaterinburg	94
Irkutsk	106
Kazakstan	178
Khabarovsk	126
Kyrgyzstan	176
Mongolia	140
Moscow Metro	80
Novgorod	76
Novosibirsk	100
Russia	36
St Petersburg Region	68
St Petersburg Metro	70
The 'Stans	176
Suzdal	90
Turkmenistan	246
Ulaanbaatar	160
Uzbekistan	222
Vladivostok	132

AUTHORS

Hazel Barker, librarian, and lawyer, David Thurlow, retired from their first careers in 1992 and set off around the world. After a trial run of 16,000km around Australia they shipped their LandCruiser to Durban and spent nine months driving south to north through Africa. Their route zigzagged through 16 countries, covering 47,000km, and resulted in *African Adventure ... a senile safari.*

Having reached the UK they decided, against all advice, to return to Australia via Norway, Finland and Russia. Safely home in Sydney, Hazel began to write for the motoring magazine *4Wheeler*, travel magazines and newspapers. Looking for another adventure they decided to return to Russia to write *Russia by Road*; as they poured over maps, the trip grew to cover Mongolia and the 'Stans and so *Russia and Central Asia by Road* was born.

This year they plan to go, in comparative comfort, to Ushuaia and the Antarctic, but who knows where next year will take them?

ACKNOWLEDGEMENTS

Many thanks are due to our family and friends, in Australia and England, who encouraged us on each escapade and listened to interminable tales of derring do on our return. Special thanks to Rosemary and Colin Lewis who twice welcomed us and our filthy truck when we reached England from Africa and Russia and waved us off on our next adventure despite thinking we were quite mad.

Special thanks to Sergei Chekov and Tanya Chekova, for helping us with our vehicle problems; to Sveta and Sasha Volobyev; and to all the other wonderful Russian, Mongolian, Kazak, Kyrgyz, Uzbek, Turkmen and Iranian people for their hospitality, help and friendship which are, after all, what make our travels memorable.

Thanks for their contributions to Athol Yates, Helen Zak, Rohan Pigott and Marc Llewellyn, Erik Korevaar, David McGonigal, John Lee, Gary and Monika Wescott, Margaret and John Willard, and Ross Mackenzie. Also to Neil Taylor and Lucia Wilde of Regent Holidays for their helpful comments.

For help with consular and other information we must thank Mr Sean Hinton, Hon Mongolian Consul, Sydney; Mr Ermek K Saudabaev, Consul of the Republic of Kazakstan, Sydney; Mr Victor Rodionov, Russian Consul, Sydney; Mr Gavriluk, Hon Australian Consul and Mr Vladimir S Gorokhov, Trade Representative, Australian Consulate, Vladivostok; and many other consular officers in Sydney.

Introduction

'Don't do it! You'll be mugged! Your car will be stolen! What if you are ill?'

If you have ever travelled off the beaten track then the above refrain will be familiar to you. However brave and bold you are, it's bound to have an effect – with us it usually reinforces our determination to go whilst increasing our anxiety levels, particularly if the speaker hails from the country we plan to visit.

On the first day of our first trip across Russia we were threading our way through the crowds on Nevsky Prospekt in St Petersburg, heading for the Hermitage, when David was surrounded by a group of muscular young gypsy girls intent on extracting his wallet from him. Fortunately, being well travelled, he had buttoned it securely into his shirt pocket inside his zipped-up jacket and we had time to haul them off. Nevertheless it was a scary moment and for a few days our boundless confidence was shaken – was it possible our Russian friends in Sydney were right?

Perhaps we were lucky or, more likely, the dangers were greatly exaggerated and, apart from that one incident, we experienced nothing but kindness from the Russians we met, many of whom became our friends.

On our next expedition through Russia, Mongolia and the 'Stans we had similar experiences. The only sad thing is that we rarely get the chance to return the hospitality we receive, but even sending photos back pleases our new friends and makes them realise we haven't forgotten them.

So – if you are looking for adventure in a continent rarely traversed by car, go to it and enjoy the wonderful people and sights as yet unspoilt by tourism.

Since returning to our home in Sydney from our first trans-Russia drive in 1994 we have had numerous phone calls, letters, faxes and email from people who plan a similar trip but are experiencing all the problems we had in trying to get first-hand up-to-date information. This book is written for them and all the other people who are wondering if it is possible. Take this as a guide but go out and enjoy your own adventures, find your own special places and make new friends.

At the same time we stress again that the situation is changing all the time and we would love to hear from anyone who has current information.

NOTES

Russia is, of course, part of the Commonwealth of Independent States (CIS) so it may seem strange that we sometimes refer to Russia and the CIS as if they were separate. Throughout the guide we refer to Kazakstan, Kyrgyzstan, Tajikistan, Uzbekistan and Turkmenistan collectively as the 'Stans, an expression first coined, I believe, by David McGonigal in the *Sydney Morning Herald*.

Siberia is the vast area stretching from the Ural Mountains in the west to a line going north from Khabarovsk. Land and islands east of Khabarovsk are known as the Russian Far East.

Names

Place-names and road names have a habit of changing throughout the CIS and Mongolia. We have tried to use the most recent one in common usage but, as even maps published locally may differ, it can be confusing. Editions of the *Automobile Road Atlas* published before 1993 use place-names from the communist era which have since been changed, such as Sverdlovsk for Ekaterinburg. Even from 1993 onwards place-names in the 'Stans use the Russian spelling, for example Taldy-Kurgan in place of the Kazak spelling Taldy-Qorghan.

Money

As US dollars are the most commonly used foreign currency in the CIS and Mongolia we have used these throughout unless otherwise stated, eg A$ = Australian dollars.

Costs

As in all the most interesting destinations, conditions and costs in Russia and Central Asia change almost daily. All prices, opening hours and so on are therefore only a guide. Most of the currencies seem to have stabilised but who knows what will have happened by the time this goes to press?

Part One

BEFORE YOU GO

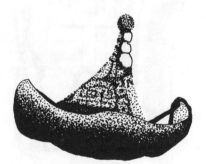

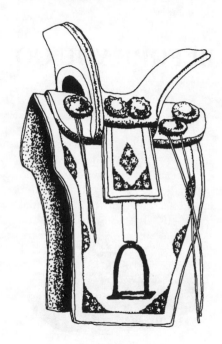

Chapter One

Planning and Preparation

Much of the information in this chapter applies to Russia, Mongolia and the 'Stans – for more specific information refer to the appropriate chapters.

WHEN TO GO

If you are looking for an interesting adventure then the northern summer is the best time to go to the CIS and Mongolia. Whether driving west to east or east to west you will find travelling easiest and most pleasant from May to September; but if, like American couple Gary and Monika Wescott, you fancy a challenge and can afford all the extra gear, ship your vehicle to Magadan and head west in winter. You may need an ice breaker to get the ship into port but what a start to the journey.

GROUP TRAVEL OR GOING IT ALONE

If, like me, the very thought of group travel fills you with horror then skip this section; but if you have an open mind here are some pros and cons from an Australian who, with her husband, was part of a Toyota Club expedition.

Pros

The three most obvious points in favour of group travel are combined mechanical expertise, security and company. Four vehicles is probably the maximum and all should be in similar good condition to avoid irritating delays. With a group of five or six people there is a pool of talent. With luck and good planning there will be a mix of mechanical skill, knowledge of the language, navigating skills including a good sense of direction (especially useful when entering and leaving towns), people management (especially useful when dealing with bureaucrats), knowledge of first aid and – almost the most important – someone with a sense of humour for those inevitable tense moments.

However, the size and composition of the convoy are important. A group of friends travelling together is very different from a convoy of strangers so it is important to get to know each other before setting off.

You can avoid taking excess equipment and spares: for instance, one easily accessible high-lift jack is sufficient for everyone. If the vehicles are the same model, as may happen in a 4WD club expedition, then a pool of spares is feasible.

Two 4WDs will fit on one railway bogie which saves much money.

Different interests and knowledge shared among the group can add to everyone's enjoyment.

Cons

One of the worst things about group travel is the different driving speeds of members and length of time spent on the road each day. Some people like to get going early in the morning and set up camp in the afternoon, while others like a leisurely start to the day and are happy to drive into the evening – it is light until late in the Siberian summer. These things must be sorted out early in the trip before they become a source of frustration and irritation.

When driving in less developed areas where road conditions and other factors may be unknown, it is almost impossible to suggest a rendezvous which allows members to go at their own pace. This inevitably means travelling in convoy. If the last driver wants a break or sees a track he or she wants to explore, then everyone must stop.

One car breaking down means everyone is held up.

A large group of people is less likely to feel relaxed about accepting hospitality along the route.

A compromise

A few companies specialise in putting together itineraries for independent travellers:

Regent Holidays, 15 John Street, Bristol BS21 2HR, England, tel: (0117) 921 1711; fax: 925 4866; email: 106041.1470@compuserve.com; http://www.regent-holidays.co.uk, offer discount air fares to the Baltic States, Russia and Central Asia. They can also book hotels in all these countries and specialise in bookings for the trans-Siberian railway.

The Russia Experience, Research House, Fraser Road, Perivale, Middx UB6 7AQ, England; tel: (0181) 566 8846; fax: 566 8843; email:100604.764@compuserve.com; http://travel.world.co.uk/russiaexp, prepares independent intineraries for Russia, Siberia, Mongolia and Central Asia. Experts in Trans-Siberian routings, they can offer stopovers in St Petersburg, Moscow, Siberia and Mongolia; Russia à la carte, family homestays, Russian buddies. More adventurous options include trekking, rafting and scuba in Siberia; camel trekking and cycling in Uzbekistan; and mountaineering in Kyrgyzstan.

VEHICLE CHOICE AND PREPARATION
Choice

It is possible, in summer, to drive across Russia and the 'Stans in an ordinary saloon – in 1996, Noel and Bill MacIntosh drove their 1913

Vauxhall from London to Vladivostok – but a 4WD vehicle is preferable if you want to get off the main roads. Whatever vehicle you choose you will probably have to put it on the train for a few hundred kilometres in eastern Siberia.

Summers tend to be wet in Siberia causing some roads to become quagmires, with trucks and cars sliding into deep ditches or simply bogging down in the deep ruts caused by tractors and heavy vehicles. Whilst an enormous amount of road building is being carried out in Siberia and the Russian Far East, the road between Chernyshcvsk and Blagoveshchensk is still problematic after rain. As for Mongolia, unless you intend to stay within a 400km radius of Ulaanbaatar, a 4WD is essential.

Choice of vehicle is a very personal thing but the most important points are reliability and availability of spares. Diesel and leaded petrol of various octane ratings are readily available in most of Russia, Mongolia and the 'Stans but unleaded petrol is not, as yet. In some parts of the Russian Far East and Siberia Japanese vehicles almost outnumber Nivas and Ladas. Toyota, Mitsubishi and Nissan 4WDs are very popular – Toyota and Nissan have a number of modern workshops throughout the CIS (see *Appendix Three*) but, be warned, they do not hold stocks of spare parts and may not even have oil filters in stock. In Mongolia Russian military-type jeeps predominate and there are very few Japanese or European vehicles on the roads.

If you prefer to use a saloon make sure you choose a model with a strong suspension and good clearance. Both Peugeot and Subaru have good reputations in developing countries for strength and reliability.

Preparation

Unless your vehicle is brand new have a thorough service before you leave home. If you have a diesel model make sure the **fuel injectors** are working efficiently – black smoke from the exhaust often means problems with the injectors. A properly tuned engine means optimum fuel consumption.

Equipment

Bear in mind that there are quite long distances between fuel stations so you should be able to carry fuel for up to 1,000km (620 miles) although, as more vehicles begin to cover longer distances, more fuel stations are opening. Toyota LandCruisers have **long-range tanks** (95+45 litres) as standard and Land Rover, Nissan and Mitsubishi have them available as optional extras. Most other makes of 4WD vehicles can be fitted with extra tanks. Carrying **jerry-cans** of fuel is not recommended, even if they do look impressive, as they tend to unbalance the vehicle. If you must use them don't put full ones on the roof-rack; it is safer to have a bracket made over the front or rear bumper. Use only metal jerry-cans for fuel. Empty them before loading your vehicle on to the train otherwise the inspectors are likely to do it for you and possibly charge you for the service.

Built-in **water tanks** are a good idea if you plan to cross the Karakum Desert in Turkmenistan or the Gobi in Mongolia although you will not need to carry large quantities of water for most of Russia and Central Asia.

Steel baffle plates to protect the sump and other vulnerable parts are standard on many 4WD vehicles – check this before buying and have them fitted if necessary.

Make sure you have good **tow points**, fore and aft – even if you never need a tow yourself you are likely to help other people along the way.

Roof-racks can be a trap – it's so easy to overload them – but are very useful for light bulky items such as camping equipment. For our trans-Africa and first trans-Russia trip we used a rooftop tent – it folds down neatly with sleeping bags, pillows and clothes inside. For the last Russia trip we took a small tent and used the roof-rack for extra tyres and camping gear.

A **snorkel**, or raised air intake, is not really necessary for Russia and the CIS unless you intend to do a lot of desert driving or to ford deep rivers in Siberia.

Headlight protectors – remember to wash them regularly when travelling over unsealed roads or you will wonder why your lights are so poor.

A second heavy-duty, deep-cycle **battery** and **split charge system** is essential if you take a refrigerator. The split charge system enables both batteries to be charged simultaneously but they can be discharged separately. A neat alternative, if you just want a back-up for a flat battery, is a power pack which can be recharged through the cigarette lighter as you travel or from a main electrical supply. We make do with this and a cool box which saves weight.

Tie-down straps – use heavy-duty for external use, lighter ones for holding gear in place inside the vehicle.

Security equipment

Vehicle security is very important. Some people put metal grilles on their windows and bolts and padlocks across their doors. We find the number of padlocks securing equipment on the outside of our vehicle enough of a hassle and don't want to look like a security van. However, curtains across the windows are a good idea, keeping prying eyes out and the vehicle cool when parked in the sun.

We have sheet steel drawers bolted into the back of our vehicle which act as a safe for cash, camera equipment and other valuables. By the time you have locked the drawer and padlocked the spare wheel bracket across the locked rear doors it is unlikely to be broken into. It is surprising how cool food keeps in these drawers, and items are out of sight. It is also possible to build in small 'safes' into the body of the vehicle.

A set of padlocks with a common key is convenient for securing items, such as jerry-cans, ladders and spare wheels, on the outside of the vehicle.

Alarm systems which immobilise the ignition system, or an isolator between the ignition switch and the fuel pump stopping fuel flow, prevent thieves driving the vehicle away and are a good investment. Be sure to find out how to reset the alarm should a mechanic disconnect the battery of the vehicle during servicing or repairs.

Spares and consumables

Whatever your choice of vehicle you will still need to take as many spares as you can afford and have space for. Even if you know there are agents for your brand of vehicle throughout Russia it is unlikely that the agent will have a large stock of spares (or, indeed, any) and it is both infuriating and expensive to be held up while they are flown in. Consult your agent as to what spares you are most likely to need but do take the following:

- Filters, (oil, fuel and air), brake pads/linings and fluid, clutch fluid, coolant
- Oils, including gear and transmission oil. Diesel engineer John Willard recommends using synthetic engine oil, which means you have to change the oil only every 10,000km instead of every 5,000km. This also cuts down on the number of oil filters and amount of oil carried. John suggests carrying 20 litres for a 20,000km trip for LandCruisers, plus 10 litres if your engine is 'using' oil.
- Fuses, gaskets, belts, globes
- Insulation tape, electrical wire
- Silicone adhesive and epoxy repair kit for fuel-tank or radiator leaks
- Rain-x rain repellent for windscreens – also makes bugs and grime easier to remove
- Fuel hose, windscreen wipers, radiator hoses, hose clamps
- Thermostat
- Wheel bearings/seals (2 inner + 2 outer + 2 seals)
- Shock absorbers
- Spare leaves, if you have leaf spring suspension, and a full set of replacement shackle bushes
- An assortment of nuts and bolts and wire for emergencies and tying down on the train and in the container if shipping home
- WD40 or other metal-protector and moisture repellent
- Tyres – make sure these are in good condition and take spare tyres and tubes or, better still, two spare wheels plus extra tubes and puncture repair kits. We found many places, including stalls in markets, selling tyres but were unable to find the correct size for our LandCruiser.

Tools

Take a good set of **basic tools**, as even if you have only limited mechanical knowledge, Russian and CIS mechanics can work wonders if they have the right tool.

Likewise workshop and spare-parts **manuals** are essential as 'a picture is worth a thousand words', particularly if your words are in English.

A **compressor**, mounted under the bonnet, is essential as few fuel stations have compressed air. It is useful for blowing dust out of the air filter as well as inflating tyres. We use a Thomas 180psi 12-volt compressor, which is very reliable powered by the battery with the engine running. There are also engine-driven compressors available. Small electric compressors are not strong enough for constant use. Also include:

- Tyre pressure gauge
- Grease gun and grease
- Bolt cutters for cutting the tying-down wire
- Jumper leads
- Fluorescent light which plugs into the cigarette lighter and a big torch
- A fire extinguisher (you are likely to be asked to show this if you put your car on the train) and two warning triangles which are compulsory
- Length of small, high-tensile steel chain and turnbuckle
- Bead breaking pliers, unless you have split rims, and tyre levers.

Recovery gear: a snatch strap (for towing), shovel and axe are essential gear for any long trip. The pros and cons of full recovery gear can be argued for ever. Many drivers consider it necessary if you intend to leave the beaten track or if there is a lot of rain – the roads in Siberia and the Far East get very boggy very quickly. We have driven around Australia, the length of Africa, across Russia, Mongolia and the 'Stans and the only time we were bogged there was nothing to attach a winch to. Yes! We've heard the one about burying the spare tyre or a star post and using that as an anchor – have you tried this particular manoeuvre? A manual winch is a good compromise.

A good **jack**: high-lift jacks are heavy and expensive and tend to be unstable on all but the flattest surfaces but will give you a higher lift (obviously) and can be used to get you out when you're bogged. Take a square of strong wood to use under the jack.

MOTORCYCLE PREPARATIONS
David McGonigal

In exchange for the wonderful feeling of participation that riding provides, motorcyclists face many of the same problems as drivers plus several others specific to riding. When it comes to preparation, motorcyclists must balance needs against weight. Yet I've seen guide books that suggest we should carry a spare ignition system in case the fitted one fails! That's fine – if you have a support truck, a big bank balance, and expect you might need it. Better to take the workshop manual or a parts book for your bike (if you can find one in these days of microfiche) and arrange for a friend or dealer back home to ship parts to you in an emergency. Arrange a system of payment or credit with your dealer, too – and it costs nothing to open an account with an international courier company, in case you ever need it.

Choice of bike

I'm not buying into the argument of what is the best bike to take. I've ridden around the world twice – once on a two stroke, high performance production racing Yamaha RD350 and decades later on a BMW R1100RT. Many would argue neither is the right choice but I've enjoyed both trips and had very few hassles. A light, simple dirt bike is great when the going gets tough or repairs are needed or security is so bad that you want to ride the bike into your hotel room and chain it to your bed (as I have done). And it will always be cheaper to ship. However, it doesn't allow you to carry much and it certainly won't be as comfortable on those days when you are riding hundreds of kilometres on good tar roads. On the other hand, a big touring bike has more parts that aren't user serviceable, it's not as easy to manoeuvre into guest house courtyards and there may be some rough trails it can't follow. The trade off is that it will be more comfortable and can carry more gear. Take whatever bike you like. I'd just suggest reconsidering if your first choice is a cruiser or race replica. Cruisers aren't designed for picking a way across bad roads or running a slalom through a Russian army convoy on a muddy road. And, while a race replica's paint scheme is likely to impress the locals, after 20,000km in race position your aching back and arms are likely to severely restrict your social life.

Spares

The world is not as large as you may think, so, depending on what sort of wear you normally get, you could probably expect to cross Russia and Central Asia on one set of brake pads and one set of tyres. But in stop-start Asian cities and on mountain passes brake pads wear out faster than usual so, unless your calculations show a good margin for error, I'd pack spares.

Tyres are a problem for tourers as even big cities in Russia and Asia are very unlikely to stock replacements. It's fine to calculate that your tyres will carry you across the wilderness to a reliable European or Asian tyre shop but even Mick Doohan would wear his tyres square in the long straights encountered in any transcontinental ride. And damage to either the front or rear tyre's carcass will leave you stranded. But two spare tyres take up a lot of space that you may think can be used to better advantage. However, not taking a spare and relying on shipping in tyres if required may take a large chunk out of your travel budget – I've been quoted several hundred dollars to ship a tyre a few thousand kilometres; and that's on top of the cost of the tyre and any import duty charged.

My experience suggests that it is usually the rear tyre that is damaged (presumably because it carries most of the weight) so if you are only taking one spare, make it a rear. I wouldn't go without one. If you have room to carry a spare front tyre too, do so – it's a good security blanket.

But you'll get very tired of carrying these tyres in and out of tents, hostels and hotel rooms.

You can expect to experience flat tyres along the way and should know how to fix them. However, the danger they can create by leaving you stranded in the middle of nowhere may be worse than the messy hassle of fixing them. If travelling on tubeless tyres (which are much safer in a blow out) I would not do the trip without one of those instant repair kits that includes sealing plugs and glue and compressed gas to reinflate the tyre. In most cases they will have you back on the road in less than half an hour.

Tubeless tyres frequently come on alloy **rims**. The roads of Asia tend to dent these rims in jagged-edged potholes. Just as you should carry a few spare spokes for steel rims, you should be prepared to have your alloy rims straightened when they are dented enough that air starts leaking out. Don't allow Russian mechanics to attempt straightening with a large hammer – a bench press is much less likely to fracture the rim. A better option all round is to consider buying replacement spoked wheels.

Take spare **spark plugs** – they take up little room and replacements are unlikely to be available locally. Also, pack spare **fuel filters** – and fit one if your bike doesn't already have it. You are likely to encounter dodgy fuel so learn how to drain a carburettor float bowl – and how to adjust timing to run on low octane fuel. If you head into the mountains, don't expect other tuning to be necessary – even at 4,000m in the Andes and Himalayas I've never been down on power enough to justify fiddling. If you are considering fitting a long range **fuel tank**, do it. The secure feeling of being able to go 500km or more before refuelling makes it money well spent.

If your bike can take a reusable **air filter**, fit one. Or take a spare **paper filter**. The dust and diesel fumes of Asian roads and traffic will more than halve the normal life of both your lungs and the filter.

A spare set of **cables** (clutch, accelerator and brake, if applicable) is good insurance and takes up no extra room if you tape them in position to the existing cables.

You can expect the bike to fall down or be knocked over along the way. Spare **clutch** and **brake levers** also take up little room and enable you to keep moving after the bike has been dropped. Of course you can also rely on the unlimited ingenuity of Asian mechanics – I've had clutch throw out levers and even a throttle twist grip machined up for me (the latter had the minor problem that it tended to rust to the handlebars in wet weather). But no mechanic can make you a replacement **helmet visor** so you may wish to carry a spare or two to fit after weeks of emergency wiping turns the original screen opaque. I also suggest carrying a small can of wood-furniture polish – it's great as a visor and headlight cleaner and removes sticker and tape residues too.

Security and equipment

The main perceived drawback of motorcycle touring is security. The uniform luggage of international motorcyclists is two panniers, backpack on rack and tank bag. If you are having **panniers** fitted you can expect most plastic panniers to survive everything except road rash but large, well sealed and securely locked aluminium panniers are available and offer much better security and durability. Your backpack is likely to contain camping gear and other light items. Buy a rafters' **sleeping bag cover** as there's nothing worse than finishing a long day of riding through the rain only to open your backpack and find your sleeping bag is soaked. If you take a **stove**, make sure it runs on petrol so you don't have a separate fuel container to lug (and to leak). A length of plastic hose long enough to syphon fuel from one vehicle to another or to refill the stove is also very useful.

The tank bag is likely to have your cameras and other valuables in it so it can be taken off the bike at each stop. At least that's the traditional way of doing things. After months and years in places where theft is a very real risk, I've revised my thinking on this. I generally keep my camera gear in a pannier – it's not much less accessible to me than it is in a tank bag and it's well out of other people's sight. My riding jacket has body armour and I've found that a travel wallet fits inconspicuously within the back pad. I know of other tourers who keep emergency cash within the pages of their invariably filthy owner's manual in the bike ducktail, but that's a risk because if the bike is stolen so is your cash. My tank bag holds only documents I need for the day, maps and low-value items.

It's easy to be too paranoid about crime. The first motorcyclist I ever met in South America (another reportedly high-risk area) was a Japanese rider who had ridden from California to the bottom of Chile. He was on a dirt bike and had all his possessions in a backpack he always left strapped to the bike when he went sightseeing. He reported no problems anywhere along the way. In fact, I never met a motorcyclist in Latin America who had been robbed. However, Robert Felton, author of Fielding's *The World's Most Dangerous Places,* told me that he has spoken to lots of motorcyclists who have toured the world for years 'then get to Russia and after three days have had everything stolen – on the fourth day the bike is stolen'. The advice for car security and overnight parking applies equally to motorcycles (see page 60).

There are various ways of making your bike more secure. A disk **lock** and a cable you can lock to a pole or fence are both worthwhile. They are even better if combined with a bike **alarm**. My suggestion is not to fit an alarm that may require cutting into the bike's wiring harness – you may be creating problems that will only become evident at the worst possible time. Thieves in most of the world aren't sophisticated so an alarm that just connects up to your battery and is triggered if the bike is moved is protection enough. If you can trigger the alarm remotely that's a plus as it can deter children and others from crawling all over your bike. The best feature of an alarm is that you can sleep at night (or go into a restaurant) knowing that you will hear if anyone touches the bike while you're out of sight.

It may be worthwhile taking off (and storing within the bike) any registration label required by your home country (but not number/licence plates of course) as they can be a temptation to souvenir hunters. Similarly I burred the nuts and screws on my country plate and number plate so they are very difficult for the light fingered to remove.

Clothing

Take the best wet weather/riding gear you can afford. After all, you'll be living with them every day and in this part of the world you are likely to encounter everything from searing heat to freezing cold. Keep that in mind when you shop. There are now riding suits that really are windproof and waterproof; they are likely to cost as much as your first bike, but they'll last longer. I've found that breathable waterproof gear is unlikely to be designed for the wind-tunnel blasting motorcyclists experience at touring speeds.

Before you go

The best preparation for the trip is to put some kilometres up at home. It will give you a better idea of what you need and should reveal if the bike has any weaknesses. If you don't service the bike yourself check with the service staff if any special factory tools are required. You'll probably need to augment the very basic tool kit with which most bikes are supplied. Besides basic sockets, spanners and screwdrivers I've found a small multimeter invaluable. For running repairs I've also had considerable use out of a roll of cloth gaffer tape, self-adhesive Velcro patches and two-part flexible glue.

Of course, if you want to see what items I would not recommend carrying on an extended tour just call into almost any hotel or campground around the world and see what I left behind. Striking a balance between overpacking and insecurity is the hallmark of the experienced world rider. By jettisoning items as I go I think I'm almost there now.

David McGonigal has spent five years of his life travelling the world on motorcycles. He became a travel writer after leaving the legal profession to ride around the world in the 1970s. Now the author of some dozen books and hundreds of articles on topics as diverse as crossing the top of Siberia by icebreaker and flying a MiG 21 jet fighter in Slovakia, he has served as president and vice-president of the Australia Society of Travel Writers. He is currently engaged in seeing if he can visit every continent and time zone on a single cycle circumnavigation. He can be found (and contacted) at his website at www.davidmcgonigal.com.au.

CAMPING EQUIPMENT

There are as many advantages and disadvantages as there are sleeping arrangements on long trips. A vehicle converted to a **camper** is a convenient way to go, particularly if you do a lot of one-night stands. There are no organised camping grounds in Siberia or the Far East and you will be more comfortable than in a tent, especially in wet weather.

The snag with this arrangement is that you lose your passenger seats and cannot give lifts.

Alternatively, a **rooftop** tent means you can leave a passenger seat in and still have the back of the vehicle for your gear but you will have to forgo all but the smallest roof-rack. Make sure the one you choose is really quick and easy to erect. The cheapest is a standard tent – it can be carried on the roof-rack and modern ones with external frames are very quick to put up.

Therm-a-Rest self-inflating **mattresses** are surprisingly comfortable, roll up neatly and do not need a pump.

Refrigerators are heavy and have very small capacity. Some people cannot leave home without them and if you feel a cold beer at the end of the day is essential to your well-being then buy the best you can afford. If you take one do have a heavy-duty cigarette lighter connection fitted in the rear of the vehicle – I am assured it can be used to drive a hair-dryer too. We use a cool box for perishables, give up butter, and use powdered and tinned milk and streams to cool the drinks.

Gas is probably the most convenient fuel for cooking but filling gas tanks can be a problem – every country we've travelled in seems to have different connections and pressures. Try to get an adaptor in the first big town. Fortunately Russia and other CIS countries use the same system and gas is readily available even in small towns. **Warning:** an Australian group found **kerosene** very hard to obtain and gave up using their kerosene stove.

Table and chairs – preferably so slim you can clip them under your roof-rack or roof-top tent. It's very annoying if you have to unload the back or scramble on to the roof before you can prepare dinner.

A **portable shower**, though not essential, works well when camping beside rivers. The Twine shower pumps water from a stream, through a heat exchanger under the bonnet of the vehicle (engine running), producing unlimited instantaneous hot water. The Glind shower has a heat exchanger and pump and can thermostatically control the temperature of storage water which is heated while travelling. Solar-heated shower kits are effective in good weather.

A good **short-wave radio** is essential if you want to hear what's going on in the world when travelling in countries where you cannot speak the language fluently – for most of us that includes all of Russia, Mongolia and the CIS. It does not have to be attached to the vehicle – there are excellent small portable ones available which you can slip into your overnight bag when staying in hotels. We use a **Sony ICF-SW7600**, which measures roughly 185mm x 120mm x 30mm and uses four AA alkaline batteries.

Mid-weight down **sleeping bags** are fine for summer, unless you plan to go into the Arctic Circle. It's a good idea to take a set of thermal underwear to sleep in at high altitudes if you feel the cold. We struck a snowstorm in Kyrgyzstan in August.

Tarpaulins – take at least one small, useful to protect your clothes when checking under the car, and one large to use as an awning, to cover gear and so on.

Rope of various thicknesses has many uses; and don't forget a spool of twine.

TELEPHONE

If money's no object and you need to keep in touch with home or business then take a satellite phone with you. John Willard ran his Sydney business from his LandCruiser for four months in Russia, Mongolia and Europe using a Telstra Satcom M. Not cheap – around A$10,000 – but very convenient.

PHOTOGRAPHY

Still cameras and lenses

These are a very personal choice but remember all gear is heavy to carry and easy to lose. UV or skylight filters are vital for high altitudes as well as for protecting your lenses. If you are a serious photographer think about taking two SLR (single lens reflex) bodies in case one develops a problem. Even in capital cities you are unlikely to find a technician capable of repairing a hi-tech electronic camera. If you use an SLR camera and slide rather than print film take a small automatic 35mm camera and print film for people shots. This makes it easy to keep your promises to send your subjects a copy.

Zoom lenses have improved greatly over the last 20 years so a 35–80mm, an 80–200mm plus a 24mm wide angle lens will cover most subjects, unless you are a keen bird photographer. If you can afford a panoramic camera take one along for the magnificent steppe and mountain views.

Many SLR and most small automatic cameras have built-in flash which is sufficient for fill-in flash and close subjects. For indoor architectural photography you will need a separate flash unit. One which can be set on automatic is very convenient.

Film

Do take some high-speed (400 ISO) film as well as your usual 64 or 100 ISO. You are unlikely to be able to buy slide film in the CIS or Mongolia so think how much you may need and then double it.

From 40 years' experience I find Kodachrome 64 ISO does not fade as quickly as other brands although, in fairness, most manufacturers have probably improved the durability of their film. Try comparing Fujichrome and Kodachrome before you leave home, particularly on dull days – you may find you prefer the colour saturation of one over the other. I usually take some of each. If you choose PKR (professional Kodachrome) you will need to keep it in an insulated bag to avoid extremes of temperature but this is a good way of keeping all film dust-free. PKR is more expensive than the process-paid Kodachrome but if you hope to publish your work then it is worth the extra money.

Video cameras

These are, again, a very personal choice and, again, weight has to be an important factor unless you are of herculean build. Take all the cassettes you think you will need with you although you *may* be able to buy them in the bigger cities. Remember local background noise can add to the atmosphere of your film. David recorded our Mongolian friends singing at a picnic on video – it makes us very nostalgic. As a hint, avoid too much panning.

Take a lightweight but stable tripod which you can use for both video and still cameras, for early morning, evening and indoor photography.

Miscellaneous

Take plenty of spare batteries for cameras and flash units. You will need at least three video batteries – one in the camera, one charged ready to use and one charging. Take a 12-volt car battery charger which can be plugged into the cigarette lighter for recharging as you travel.

Do get used to using your camera equipment before you go. If you are buying it duty free on the way spend as much time as possible reading the instruction manual; it will save you grief and frustration if you are familiar with your camera's idiosyncrasies before the pressure to capture that magic moment is upon you.

When taking photographs, always ask people's permission for close-ups. Have a notebook handy to write their addresses in so you can send them prints when you get home. Russia is amazingly relaxed these days but guards are still touchy so it is advisable to ask permission before using your cameras in border zones. Museums often allow photography for an additional fee.

COMPUTERS

Laptop computers are small and comparatively light but, by the time you have added battery adaptors/chargers, manuals and possibly a portable printer, you will find the weight begins to add up as you haul it, plus your camera equipment, plus your overnight bag up three or four flights of stairs to your hotel room. (For some reason, foreigners are always put on the higher floors and there are rarely lifts in small hotels in the country.)

However, despite the state of the telephone service in the CIS and Mongolia, email is the easiest and quickest way to communicate. Unless your computer has a built-in modem, you will need a PC card modem – not cheap but very convenient (the size of a credit card). We got a real buzz when a picture of our newest grandson arrived via email in Ekaterinburg.

WHAT TO TAKE
Clothes
As for most countries, layering is a good idea. Despite Western ideas of Siberia being cold all the year round, the weather in the summer is usually mild but you will need a light jacket and a sweater for early mornings and evenings. Also include:

- Cotton shirts with two breast pockets for putting passport, visa, pen, notebook etc in as you complete endless forms at borders, hotels etc.
- Cotton trousers or jeans and/or cotton skirt (can be more comfortable in hot weather)
- Cotton shorts and T-shirts
- A 'good' outfit (Russians tend to dress up a bit at night in the cities)
- Sweater, cotton or fine wool, or sweatshirt
- Jacket, shower-proof/waterproof and wind-proof
- Boots or comfortable walking shoes
- Flip-flops/thongs for wearing in the shower
- Socks, cotton or wool
- Silk scarf, for women to cover their heads in Orthodox churches and also to wear across the mouth and nose in sand storms in the desert.

If you plan to travel through Iran, before crossing the border women should try to buy Indian-type loose pants and overshirts, reaching over the knees, with long sleeves and high necks – unless they intend to embrace the chador!

Miscellaneous
- Russian phrasebook and several guidebooks (see *Further Reading, Appendix Two*)
- Photographs, extra passport-size for visas etc
- Compass, good hand-held model. You will be surprised how comforting it is to check your route at intervals with a compass, especially in Siberia and Mongolia.
- Adaptors for electrical appliances
- Adaptors to charge your video and computer batteries in the car
- Universal bath plug – perhaps the most vital item – a second one is a good idea in case you lose the first. Trying to wash your socks in a basin without a plug is no fun.
- Elastic clothes line, the twisted type you can sling over the bath or along the side of the tent
- Swiss Army type penknife – the best you can afford
- Small torch, kept in your overnight bag, is essential as bedside lights are not standard in small hotels
- Wet-wipes, or whatever they are called in your local store, great for cleaning muddy, dusty, dieselly, sticky hands and faces

- Cotton gloves, heavy weight, for use when filling up from dirty diesel pumps
- Immersion heaters (possibly two, one to use in the cigarette lighter of the car, one to use in your hotel room) – much quicker and easier than setting up the gas stove for that much-needed cup of coffee or tea
- Pocket-size notebooks
- Small tape recorder
- String or cloth bags for shopping – goods are not automatically put into plastic bags
- Strong plastic garbage bags.

Gifts

It is good to have small gifts for your hosts and for friends you make. We were told that soap was in great demand but when we were in Russia we were embarrassed to give it away as it seemed to imply a need for cleanliness and everyone had soap in their bathrooms. However, good perfumed soap, which comes wrapped in elegant paper, is acceptable. Women like fashion magazines, and paper patterns for making their own clothes; and cosmetics, scarves and costume jewellery are appreciated.

Young people like rock and pop cassettes, or even CDs, T-shirts with motifs of your country, and Body Shop cosmetics. Small badges and stick pins are good for men and children's picture books with simple stories please the smaller children as many schools teach English these days.

Packets of special tea, Earl Grey or Prince of Wales etc, vacuum-packed ground coffee and other 'luxury' goods were a hit with our hosts. Small torches with extra batteries and Swiss Army type penknives make good presents too. Some of the most appreciated presents are books of coloured photos of your country or city.

THANK YOU
On one occasion a friend of our host in Novosibirsk who had worked on our car for two hours firmly refused payment but, when pressed, asked shyly for a souvenir. We dug out a small spotlight he could plug into his car cigarette lighter and he was delighted. Another time a mechanic welded pipes together to make a solid tow and towed us 100km and still refused payment. On our way back past the village we took boxes of chocolates and bunches of bananas as thank-you presents and received warm hugs in return.

MAPS

The *Automobile Road Atlas*, Атлас автомобильных дорог, covering the whole of the former USSR, is vital but not easily available outside Russia and the CIS although it is worth asking your travel bookshop if they can get you a copy. It used to be published in Minsk but may now be produced in Russia. It is for sale in bookshops and on street stalls in St Petersburg, Moscow and Vladivostok and some capital cities in the CIS. Try to find a recently published edition as those published before 1993 use Soviet names which have since been changed, for example Sverdlovsk is now Ekaterinburg.

Try to obtain maps of as many of the big cities as you can before you leave home. Your travel agent should be able to get maps of Moscow, St Petersburg and Vladivostok. The *Automobile Road Atlas* has rudimentary city maps in the back showing major arteries.

If you decide to take a GPS (Global Positioning System), one of the wonders of modern science, it can tell you where you are to within 100m or so, but only if you have accurate maps of the area. If you have good maps and a compass you probably don't need a GPS unless you intend to travel through the north of Siberia.

Map and travel bookshops

Australia
The Travel Bookshop, 6 Bridge Street, Sydney 2000; tel: (02) 9241 3554; fax: 9241 3159

Travel Books, 66 Boundary Street, West End, Brisbane 4101; tel: (07) 3846 5432

United Kingdom
Stanfords, 12-14 Long Acre, London WC2E 9LP;
mail order tel: (0171) 836 1321; fax: 836 0189
Also at British Airways, 156 Regent Street, London W1R 5TA and 29 Corn Street, Bristol BS1 1HT; tel: (0117) 929 9966; fax: 925 3252

Travel Bookshop, 13 Blenheim Crescent, London W11 2EE

United States
The Adventurous Traveler Bookstore; tel: 800 282 3963 (US & Canada), 802 860 6776 (International); fax: 800 677 1821 (USA & Canada), 802 860 6667 (International); email: books@atbook.com or www: http://www.gorp.com./atbook.htm

The Complete Traveler, 199 Madison Avenue, New York 10016; tel: (212) 685 9007

Chessler Books, PO Box 399, 26030 Highway 74, Kettredge CO 80457; tel: 800 654 8502 or 303 670 0093; fax: 670 9727.

DOCUMENTATION
Visas

These are getting easier to obtain but it is still necessary to have some accommodation booked or sponsorship from someone in Russia or the CIS. In 1994 we booked and paid for one night in five different Iris hotels (a chain of hotels attached to Mikof eye hospitals established by Professor Fedorov, the surgeon who pioneered eye microsurgery) across the continent from St Petersburg to Irkutsk, leaving the dates open. This was accepted and Iris

Tours, PO Box 60, Hurstville, Australia 2220 procured our visas for us from the Russian Consul General in Sydney. In 1996 Iris arranged an invitation from Mikof for us and we did not book any accommodation ahead.

Russian visas are not stamped in your passport so a photocopy of your passport is normally acceptable together with completed Form 95, three identical passport size (3cm x 4cm) photographs, a covering letter from your travel agent, proof of medical insurance, proof of negative HIV status and a bank cheque, money order or cash. Applications submitted in the UK must be accompanied by the original passport, not a photocopy.

The maximum period for tourist visas is three months which is not long enough for an extended tour.

Make sure you apply for a double or multiple-entry visa if you want to go into Mongolia and/or other neighbouring states. Double-entry visas should be obtained from the Russian Embassy or Consul. A multiple-entry visa must be applied for via Moscow, is more difficult to procure and takes months. However, it may be necessary if you intend to visit neighbouring countries from Russia on your way. Some Russian embassies and consulates may be prepared to issue two double-entry visas with overlapping dates which would be much quicker, if more expensive, than battling with Moscow bureaucracy. You should take care over your entry and exit dates to make this effective and it would then give you about five months.

In theory a valid Russian or CIS visa gives you a transit visa for the other CIS countries but this is not always so. On the other hand you may drive across some CIS borders without any customs and immigration formalities at all.

Your passport must be valid for at least three months after your scheduled departure date from Russia. One minor problem is that the consulate requires you to nominate dates of entry and departure which can be difficult when you are driving. If your visas expire before you are ready to leave Russia you *may* be able to extend them at OVIR (Department of Visas and Registration) in regional centres. However, be wary of this – it is not as easy as it sounds and we have heard of people being made to pay for expensive non-existent tours before OVIR would give them an extension and then for only one month. Multiple-entry visas are valid for 12 months if you manage to get them.

Visas come in the form of a three-page pocket-size folder with your photo stuck in the top right hand corner. There is some confusion over whether the last page should be detached at your point of entry if it is a double-entry visa. Try to hang on to it if you can and it will then be removed at the time of your second entry – good luck!

Embassy and consulate addresses

Australia Russian Embassy, 78 Canberra Avenue, Griffith, ACT 2603; tel: (062) 95 9474; fax: 295 1847
Russian Consulate General, 7–9 Fullerton Street, Woollahra, NSW 2025; tel: (02) 9326 1188; fax: 9327 5065

Austria Russian Embassy, Reisnerstrasse 45–47, A-1030 Vienna;
tel: (0222) 712 1229; fax: 712 3388

Belarus Russian Embassy, vul Staravilenskaya 48, 220002 Minsk;
tel: (0172) 345 497; fax: 503 664

Belgium Russian Embassy, 66 Avenue de Fré, B-1180 Brussels;
tel: (02) 374 3406; fax: 374 2613
Russian Consulate, Della Faililaan 20, 2020 Antwerp; tel: (03) 829 1611

Canada Russian Embassy, 285 Charlotte Street, Ottawa, Ontario K1N 8L5;
tel: (613) 235 4341; fax: 236 6342
Russian Consulate, 2355 Avenue de Musée, Montreal, Quebec H3G 2E1;
tel: (514) 843 5901; fax: 842 2021

China Russian Embassy, 4 Baizhongjie, Beijing 100600;
tel: (10) 532 2051/1267
Russian Consulate, 20 Huangpu Lu, Shanghai 20080; tel: (21) 324 2682

Estonia Russian Embassy, Pikk 19, EE-0001 Tallin; tel: (2) 443 014;
fax: 443 773
Russian Consulate, Vilde 8, EE-2020 Narva; tel/fax: (235) 313 67

Finland Russian Embassy, Suurlahetysto, Tehtaankatu 1B, Fin-00140 Helsinki;
tel: (90) 661 449; fax: 661 006
Russian Consulate, Vartiovuorenkatu 2, 20700 Turku;
tel: (21) 223 6441/231 9779

France Russian Embassy, 40–50 Boulevard Lannes, 75116 Paris;
tel: (1) 4504 0550; fax: 4504 1765
Russian Consulate, 8 Ambroise-Pare, 13008 Marseille; tel: (91) 771 525;
fax: 773 454

Germany Russian Embassy, PO Box 200908, Waldstrasse 42, 53177 Bonn;
tel: (0228) 312 085; fax: 311 563
Russian Consulate, Unter den Linden 63–65, 10117 Berlin; tel: (030) 229 1420;
fax: 229 9397
Russian Consulate, Am Feenteich 20, 22085 Hamburg; tel: (040) 229 5201;
fax: 229 7727
Russian Consulate, Seidelstrasse 8, 80355 Munich; tel: (089) 592 503;
fax: 550 3828

Hungary Russian Embassy, Bajza utea 35, 1062 Budapest VI;
tel: (1) 132 0911; fax: 252 5077

Ireland Russian Embassy, 186 Orwell Road, Rathgar, Dublin;
tel: (01) 492 2084; fax: 492 3525

Latvia Russian Embassy, 2 Antonijas Iela, 1397 Riga; tel: (2) 733 2151;
fax: 721 2579

Lithuania Russian Embassy, Juozapaviciaus gatve 11, 2000 Vilnius;
tel: (2) 351 763; fax: 353 877

Mongolia Russian Embassy, Friendship St A-6, Ulaanbaatar;
tel: (1) 72 851/26 836/27 506

New Zealand Russian Embassy, 57 Messines Road, Karori, Wellington; tel: (04) 476 611; fax: 476 3846

Norway Russian Embassy, Drammensveen 74, 0271 Oslo; tel: 2255 3278; fax: 2255 0070

Poland Russian Embassy, ul Belwederska 49, 00-761 Warsaw; tel: (022) 213 453; fax: 625 3016

South Africa Russian Embassy, PO Box 6743, Pretoria 001, Butano Building, 316 Brooks Street, Menlo Park 0081; tel: (12) 432 731; fax: 432 842

Ukraine Russian Embassy, vul Kutuzova 8, Kiev; tel: (044) 294 7936; fax: 292 6631

United Kingdom Russian Embassy, 13 Kensington Palace Gardens, London W8 4QX; tel: (0171) 229 3628/229 8027; fax: 727 8624
Russian Consul General, 58 Melville Street, Edinburgh EH3 7HL; tel: (0131) 225 7098; fax: 225 9587

United States Russian Embassy, 1607 23rd Street NW, Washington DC 20036; tel: (202) 298 5700; fax: 298 5735
Russian Consulate, 9 East 91 Street, New York, NY 10128; tel: (212) 348 0926; fax: 831 9162
Russian Consulate, 2790 Green Street, San Francisco, CA 94123; tel: (415) 202 9800; fax: 929 0306
Russian Consulate, 2001 6th Avenue, Suite 2323, Westin Building, Seattle, WA 98121; tel: (206) 728 1910; fax: 728 1871; email: consul@consul.seanet.com; http//www.seanet.com/RussianPage/htm

Insurance
Comprehensive
Black Sea and Baltic General Insurance Company, 65 Fenchurch Street, London EC3M 4EY; tel: (0171) 709 9202; fax: 702 3557, seem to be the only firm who can arrange comprehensive motor vehicle insurance, including third party, in London for travel in Russia, republics formerly part of the USSR and former Eastern Bloc countries. However they do not cover western Europe or Mongolia so you will have to take out separate cover for other countries.

Campbell Irvine Ltd, 48 Earls Court Road, Kensington, London W8 6EJ; tel: (0171) 938 2250, will give insurance cover for fire, theft and damage in Europe, Russian Federation, Mongolia, China, Kazakstan, Kyrgyzstan, Uzbekistan and Turkmenistan but do not include third party.

Third party
Third party insurance for Russia only is available at a reasonable premium from **Ingosstrakh Insurance Company Ltd** (formerly the State insurance company), 113805, GSP, 12 Pyatnitskaya ul, Moscow M-35; tel: (095) 233 0327; fax: 230 2518/233 3405. The premium in 1996 for unlimited cover for a 1992 LandCruiser for five months was US$216. We were not able to obtain third party insurance for the 'Stans.

For Europe you should have a Green Card (International Motor Insurance Certificate) which provides cover to the minimum of the local compulsory insurance law. In theory (but not always in practice) it can be purchased at the border of all European countries which require it. On the Iran/Turkish border it was not available despite it being compulsory in Turkey, nor could we buy one in Venice when arriving by ferry from Alexandria on an earlier trip. However on the Turkish/Greek border we bought one quickly and easily on the Greek side. Remember to enter on the form all the countries you may wish to drive through in Europe. Cost varies according to duration, countries to be visited, your driving record and so on.

Marine insurance

This can be obtained through your shipping agent and costs will be a percentage of the value of the vehicle. In Russia it is available from **Dalrosso, Far Eastern Russian Insurance Company Ltd**, Leninskaya ul 7, Vladivostok; tel: (423 22) 261 425; fax: 229 891.

Medical insurance

This is obligatory – take the best you can afford. Hospitals, apart from the Mikof Eye Hospitals, are very basic and the means to fly home for medical treatment in an emergency are essential.

Vehicle documentation

You must fit a nationality plate to the rear of your vehicle – this indicates the country in which your car is registered, not necessarily your own nationality. You must take your registration papers with you as proof of ownership. An International Certificate for Motor Vehicles can be obtained from your local motoring organisation for a small fee although your registration papers should be enough. You must have an international driving permit which can be obtained from national motoring organisations for a small fee.

A Carnet de Passages en Douane (document which allows temporary import of vehicles into subscribing countries, without paying customs duty, and guarantees their export again) was not required for Russia, the CIS or Mongolia in 1996 but if you intend to drive through Iran you will be asked for one at the border (although we were allowed entry despite not having one). Carnets are available from your local automobile association but can be expensive. It is as well to check with the embassy before you leave.

If you intend to drive in the United Kingdom and you belong to an automobile club/association of a Commonwealth country then it is worth getting a Commonwealth Motoring Conference card (CMC) from your association before you leave. The card entitles you to the same benefits from the Automobile Association/Royal Automobile Club as it provides for its own members but remember to register with the organisation as soon as you reach Britain. The CMC is issued free of charge.

GETTING YOUR VEHICLE TO RUSSIA
From the United Kingdom
There are several routes to Russia, most, of course, involving ferries. If you have time, take the ferry from Newcastle-upon-Tyne to Bergen, Norway, and work your way up through the fjords and islands into the Arctic Circle and on another 1,000km to North Cape, the most northerly point in Europe and home of the midnight sun, before turning south through Finland and crossing the border into Russia a few kilometres from Lappeenranta at Vyborg.

There is a year-round ferry service between Stockholm and St Petersburg and a summer service between Helsinki and St Petersburg.

It is also possible to enter by car from Poland and Lithuania via Estonia, Latvia, Belarus and Ukraine; from the Czech Republic and Poland; from Hungary and Romania via Ukraine or variations on these European routes; from Turkey via Georgia, Azerbaijan and the Caspian Sea, Turkmenistan, Uzbekistan and Kazakstan; or Turkey, Iran, Turkmenistan, Uzbekistan and Kazakstan.

From the United States
Shipping from Seattle, WA, to Vladivostok is probably the cheapest direct way to freight your vehicle to Russia.

Shipping agents
Fesco Agencies NA, 614 Norton Building, 801 Second Avenue, Seattle, WA 98104; tel: (206) 583 0860; fax: 583 0889.

From Australia
As Australia is so far from Europe it doesn't matter much whether you go from east to west or vice versa. On our first trip, in 1994, we had shipped our LandCruiser across to Durban and zig-zagged up through Africa, gone by ferry from Alexandria to Venice and driven across Europe to England; so we drove west to east across Russia. In 1996 we shipped to Vladivostok and drove east to west.

In some ways it is easier to travel from west to east the first time as western Russia is accustomed to tourists, many people speak a little English and there are a number of fairly reliable guidebooks available. By the time you reach Siberia, you are accustomed to the Cyrillic alphabet and your few phrases of Russian flow freely from your tongue.

If you decide to go from east to west, FESCO, the Far East Shipping Company, has regular sailings from Australian ports to Vostochny, the port a few kilometres from Vladivostok, via Hong Kong. As you will have packed your vehicle full of spare parts, basic tinned and dried food, books, camping equipment etc, it is advisable to send it in a container. Costs, in 1996, port to port were A$2,900 plus port service and lift-on/lift-off charges of between A$70 and A$80 in Vladivostok. Smith Bros charged around A$350 for loading a 20ft container, tie-down and delivery to ship. You can save a few dollars by tying down yourself.

To Vladivostok
Shipping agents (FESCO agents)
Ausbridge, 1st flr, 595 Little Collins Street, Melbourne, Victoria 3000; tel: (03) 9614 6336

Ausbridge, 1/8 Bay Street, Botany, NSW 2019; tel: (02) 9666 4400

Freight agents
Smith Bros, 4 Bumborah Point Road, Botany, NSW 2019; tel: (02) 9666 3466,

There is a weekly flight to Vladivostok via Korea using Qantas/Aeroflot or Korean Airlines, or Korean all the way. Either way it means spending a night in Seoul. Neither Aeroflot nor Qantas has direct flights from Australia to Vladivostok.

To Europe
The Eastern and Australian Steamship Company, 160 Sussex Street, Sydney 2001; tel: (02) 9364 8600; fax: 9364 8582. Agents for P & O Containers Limited, they offer two services which take up to 12 passengers on regular container ship routes.

One route is from Fremantle, Adelaide, Melbourne and Sydney via New Zealand and Cape Horn to Lisbon, Zeebrugge, Tilbury, Hamburg and Rotterdam, taking approximately six weeks. It is not cheap – approximately A$5,000 per person, twin share, and A$1,650 per child under 16, plus vehicle freight.

The second route is from Australian ports via New Zealand to Japan which takes three weeks and costs A$2,100 per person. 'Ferries' run from Niigata and Fushiki to Vladivostok from June to September but they are not drive-on – vehicles have to be lifted on by crane. Check costs of unloading containers in Japan – this may be an expensive alternative.

CUSTOMS AND IMMIGRATION
Whenever you enter or leave Russia, other than through most CIS countries, you will have to fill in a Customs Declaration. The front is fairly self-explanatory but do not forget to complete the reverse declaring camera equipment, computers, video cameras and any other items, such as rugs from the CIS, you feel are valuable or likely to be queried on your way out. It speeds things up if you carry a list of the serial numbers of camera and computer equipment with your passport.

You will be asked to fill in a short form in triplicate at the Russian road border undertaking to export your vehicle again when you leave the country. As the form is in Russian, unless you read Russian or there is a helpful English-speaker there to translate for you, it will be a matter of guesswork. In 1994, on leaving Russia, we insisted that the shipping company, Silver Wind, wrote on our copy that the car had been exported but the Customs Officer at Vladivostok Airport was not at all interested. In fact we wondered if he understood what it was all about as it was very unusual to drive across the continent in a foreign vehicle. In 1996 we left Russia through Kazakstan and did not even have to fill in a form or go through Customs.

Customs agents

If you take your vehicle in by sea as unaccompanied freight, the forms are longer and the procedure more complicated – getting a good agent to act for you will save you time and probably money. We recommend:

Silver Wind, 15/2 Fontannaya Street, Vladivostok, 690001; tel/fax: (4232) 22 57 19, 26 92 23, 22 44 79, 22 47 81.

Gary Wescott, who drove across Siberia in winter, says: 'I can also recommend our customs guy in Magadan. He was magic!'

ISCON Ltd, Yuri E Koudliy, Director, 79 Proletarskaya ul, Apt 31, Magadan, Russia; tel hm: (41322) 5 66 04; tel wk: 2 34 75; fax: 5 66 04.

You will be given a certificate of temporary import permission (pink with green border) at most borders which you may be asked for by the GAI (traffic police). You must carry the vehicle registration papers with you and you may be asked to show them at GAI barriers when entering cities – mostly flourishing your international driving permit and saying 'Tourist!' with a big smile will get you through.

HEALTH

with Dr Jane Wilson-Howarth

Health is less of a problem than in tropical climes if you are reasonably careful, although travellers' diarrhoea is a risk in much of the region. You will be asked to supply proof of HIV negative status when applying for a visa.

Consult your travellers' medical health centre over immunisations: generally, polio, hepatitis A and typhoid are advisable; check where diphtheria is necessary.

Ask for advice about mosquito-borne diseases, such as Japanese encephalitis which occurs in areas where rice is grown. Also enquire about rabies.

Particular health risks in the region include several tick-borne diseases: Lyme disease, Crimean-Congo haemorrhagic fever, tick-borne typhus and tick-borne encephalitis. As a precaution against ticks, wear long-sleeved clothing and long trousers when walking in overgrown areas, and be sure to remove ticks immediately you notice them. Grasp the tick as close to your body as possible and pull steadily and firmly away at right angles to your skin. The whole tick will then come away as long as you do not jerk or twist. If possible douse the wound with alcohol (any spirit will do) or iodine. Spreading redness around the bite and/or fever and/or aching joints after a tick bite imply that you have an infection which requires antibiotic treatment, so seek advice.

In Moscow and St Petersburg there are several Western medical services – ask at your embassy for their addresses and telephone numbers.

Medical centres
United Kingdom
British Airways Travel Clinic and Vaccination Centre, 156 Regent Street, London W1R 7HG; tel: (0171) 439 9584; for other locations tel: (01276) 685040.

USA
Center for Disease Control and Prevention, Atlanta, Georgia; tel: (404) 332 4559

Australia
Travellers Medical & Vaccination Centre Pty Ltd, 7th Floor, 428 George Street, Sydney 2000; tel: (02) 9221 7133 or information line 1902 261 560. This group has centres in all capital cities.

Hospitals
Russian and CIS public hospitals are not as well equipped as in the West. Syringes are often re-used so take a few disposable syringes and needles and sterile dressings with you in case of emergency.

What to take
First aid
A well-equipped first aid kit, including a good supply of such basics as soluble aspirin or paracetamol, Elastoplast, antiseptics and eye drops, is essential.

Prescription drugs
Consult your medical centre about antibiotics and anti-diarrhoea drugs. It's always sensible to carry your prescriptions with you to prove the drugs were prescribed by a doctor. Replenish your supplies in capital cities as the need arises. Most large hotels in Central Asia have pharmaceutical counters in the foyer selling antibiotics as well as bandages, aspirin and so on.

Take your own supply of contraceptive pills, HRT, asthma medication or any other prescription drugs you take regularly as it is unlikely you will be able to get your brand there.

Miscellaneous
Although, according to official figures, AIDS is not a huge problem as yet in Russia, it is advisable to take condoms if you think you may need them.

Tampons are difficult to find in many places so take a supply if you use them.

Insect repellent, sunscreen, lip salve and contact lens solution may be hard to locate when you need them so take your own.

Water

It is a good idea to carry drinking and washing water separately. Tap water in the cities *may* be safe to drink, or at least to clean your teeth in, but communal taps and pumps in the villages must be treated as suspect. Bottled mineral water is available in many towns but some is very salty. There are excellent small filters on the market which are a good investment.

SAFETY

Don't believe all you read in the media. Russia is not nearly as dangerous as many other countries and the so-called 'mafia' are not interested in individual travellers. However, no matter what you wear, people will know you are a foreigner even before you speak. It may be your shoes or your glasses or that your hair is its natural colour or the fact that you don't look as careworn as many Russians – whatever the reason, they will know. Often this is a bonus and people will be willing to help you but equally they will equate being a foreigner with being rich – or at least considerably richer than they are – so take all the usual precautions.

Safety hints

- Register at your embassy or consular office and leave a rough idea of your route. Write the embassy phone number in your pocket diary.
- Carry the address and phone number of your hotel or homestay with you.
- Money belts, big enough to hold passport, visa, travellers cheques and other valuables, worn inside your clothing are good but remember to keep cash accessible for immediate needs.
- Don't wear jewellery or expensive watches.
- Cameras can be a problem – some people advise against carrying them but if you're an avid photographer that is not practical. I always use a cheap camera bag with a zip top and keep my camera and lenses out of sight until I need to take a shot. (Leave the camera on automatic for a quick pic and fiddle with exposures and f stops after your first shot.)
- If you are travelling with a companion be aware of their safety – if they are concentrating on photography, keep an eye out for pickpockets.
- In the metro and on other crowded public transport keep your day-pack in front of you.
- Avoid dimly lit streets at night.

• Taxis can be a problem. Russians still use private cars as taxis – taking passengers in the direction they are going helps pay the petrol bill. We did not hear of foreigners having problems but it would seem a dangerous practice – particularly if you do not know your way around the town. Companies with signs on their taxis are opening up but they charge more than private cars.

MONEY

Note: the $ sign indicates US dollars unless stated otherwise, eg: A$ for Australian dollars.

The demise of the USSR heralded roaring inflation but by March 1997 the rouble had steadied and the exchange rate was around 5,600 roubles to the US dollar.

Organising your money safely is more of a problem than in most other parts of the world although it is gradually getting easier. In 1994 we had to take all our money in US dollar bills – a great safety worry, especially as currency declaration forms must be completed at the border. Two years later we found we could get dollar cash advances on Visa and other credit cards and cash travellers cheques in most of the major cities in Russia and in capital cities of the CIS and Mongolia. A few banks in regional centres will give cash advances on Visa but don't rely on it – make sure you have enough US dollars in cash between cities. All cities and towns of any size have banks which will change dollars into roubles quickly and with little fuss. Only tourist-class hotels have licences to accept foreign currency and there are few tourist hotels in Siberia.

Make sure your dollar bills are in good condition – the banks will refuse any which are dirty, torn or defaced, for example ones that are scribbled on. Take only recent notes – pre-1990 ones may be refused – and watch what the banks give you when getting cash advances. There are forged $100 bills in circulation. Never accept bills dated before 1990 and if possible carry the new 1996 'forgery proof' issue (with the large portrait of Benjamin Franklin). Gone are the days when a dollar would buy you anything so you do not need huge quantities of small denominations. Also everyone wears jeans in Russia now so forget any ideas of trading jeans for anything.

Exchange rates in 1996 – values of US$1:

Russia (rouble)	R4,950 for traveller's cheques R5,000–5,200 for cash or credit card
Kazakstan (tenge)	T67 for credit card
Kyrgyzstan (som)	S9.6
Turkmenistan (manat)	M5,000
Uzbekistan (sum)	S41 (or S59 on very active black market)
Mongolia (tögrög)	T532 for credit card

Money and safety
The risks of changing money on the black market far outweigh the often small gains. Keep your money in a money belt. Have a wallet with ready money for day-to-day purchases handy but try to avoid keeping your credit cards in it. Replacing cards in the more remote areas of Russia, the CIS and Mongolia can be a problem.

Credit cards
Euro/MasterCard and American Express are often accepted in big cities but Visa is by far the most popular. As more shops and hotels accept credit cards so the risk of fraud increases. Try to avoid losing sight of your card – there's always the chance of it being run through old-fashioned machines twice – and always check your receipts against your statements as soon as you can. Ask the issuing company for information about which countries accept their card before you leave home.

Travellers cheques
Although travellers cheques are beginning to be used in Russia, the 'Stans and Mongolia, do not rely on their being accepted. Visa, Thomas Cook and American Express travellers cheques were the most easily cashed.

Fuel costs
Diesel fuel costs per litre in 1996:

Russia	$0.22–46
Kazakstan	$0.15–22
Kyrgyzstan	$0.20–25
Turkmenistan	$0.9
Uzbekistan	$0.17–20
Mongolia*	$0.20

*Fuel prices were fixed throughout Mongolia.

Petrol was up to 50% more expensive than diesel, according to octane rating.

In Iran fuel was $0.07 per litre. However, at the border a calculation was made estimating how much fuel we would need on our chosen route to Turkey. We were then asked to pay $150 which brought the cost of our diesel up to $0.56 per litre, making it the most expensive until we reached Europe.

ACCOMMODATION

Hotels
Although inflation in Russia and Central Asia has slowed considerably in the past year we do not usually include specific prices in this guide. Hotels are generally classed per double room as 'Inexpensive' (up to $50); 'Moderate' ($51–100); 'Expensive' ($101–180); 'Very expensive' ($181 plus). Prices in capital cities tend to be higher than in smaller cities and

country prices cheaper than in towns. These are cost classifications and quite often do not reflect the quality of the accommodation, plumbing and service except in the 'Very expensive' category.

Examples
Inexpensive
Sasha and Lena's B & B Molodyozhnaya 13, Bukhara; tel: 3 38 90, has three doubles and one three-bed room, clean, modern shared bathrooms but unreliable hot water pressure. Breakfast is included in the tariff and an excellent dinner with Uzbek wine can be served if you order at breakfast time. Sasha was due to open a new hotel close to Labi-hauz early in 1997 with even better facilities at the same price. $20 per person including good breakfast.

Russ Hotel Magdagache, Russian Far East; tel: (41653) 97 2 67. A suite on the third floor comprises two rooms and en-suite bathroom, with no way of getting the water from the tap to the bath and a loo needing a more efficient filling cistern. The bedroom has comfortable beds, the sitting room has two armchairs plus table and tea-making facilities – actually you take the teapot down to the concierge on the ground floor. $20 for a suite.

Moderate
Hotel Dostuk Frunze 429, Bishkek, Kyrgyzstan; tel: 28 42 78. Small but comfortable rooms with tiny bathroom and views of the mountains. Visa and MasterCard accepted. Satellite ISD (expensive) and local telephones, TV with nine stations including BBC & CNN, air-conditioning and bar fridges. Doubles $94 including breakfast.

Moderate to expensive
Iris Hotels in twelve cities from Moscow to Khabarovsk offer scrupulously clean suites – bedroom, sitting-room and bathroom. They have bedside lights, hot water, TV – Russian channels only – an electric samovar for tea-making in the corridor and medium-sized but thin towels. Helpful friendly service. $80–120 per suite.

Very expensive
Versailles Hotel ul Svetlanskaya 10, Vladivostok. The equivalent of a 5-star hotel. It has a casino, restaurant, café and bars. Rooms are well furnished, with satellite phones, bedside lamps, TV with English-language channels, large fluffy towels in the tiled bathroom and room service. The business centre with English-speaking staff will send faxes, book flights and help with translation. Double room $300.

Homestays (moderate)
Your room may be small but the shared bathroom will be clean and the family friendly and welcoming. It is a good idea to arrange your first Homestay before arriving in Russia but once you have stayed with one

family they often have friends in towns further down the track who also do Homestays. It's a great way to make friends and see how ordinary people live, and the food is much better than even the more expensive hotels. From $30 per person. Bed and breakfast, half board or full board, can be arranged.

Homestay organisations

Host Families Association (HOFA) 5-25 Tavricheskaya, 193015 St Petersburg, Russia; tel/fax: (812) 275 1992; email: alexei@hofak.hop.stu.neva.ru. This is the head office of a Homestay organisation with agents in a number of countries.

Australia Host Families Association 34 Main Street, Croydon, Vic 3136; tel: (03) 9725 8555; fax: 9723 9560; email: croydon@ozemail.com.au

United Kingdom Host Families Association; tel: (01295) 710 648

United States Host Families Association (HOFA); tel: (202) 333 9343 HOFA will arrange accommodation, in private homes with English-speaking hosts, in 13 Russian cities, as well as in the rest of the CIS and the Baltic states. Many of the hosts are families from the faculty or research staff of local universities. HOFA accommodation can provide basic Bed and Breakfast, Full Service which includes all meals and guided walking tours, or Deluxe Full Service which includes up to two hours a day of car tours.

In Moscow and St Petersburg they offer two grades of Homestay – within three miles of the city centre, or Metro locations (close to metro stations). HOFA insist on a minimum stay of two nights – any shorter stay defeats the purpose of Homestays. They can arrange business visa invitations, airport transfers, theatre and concert bookings.

Iris Tours PO Box 60, Hurstville, NSW 2200; tel: (02) 9580 6466; fax: 9580 7256; email: iristour@mpx.com.au. Iris Tours are the agents for Iris Hotels (adjoining Mikof microsurgery clinics) across Russia. The company is owned and run by Valentina and Brian Colyer who can also arrange Homestays in most major Russian cities, including Chita, Krasnoyarsk and Perm. Iris Tours has recently been authorised to issue visas for Ukraine and can arrange Homestays there too. Warning: most Iris Hotels, outside St Petersburg and Moscow, close in July and August when the Mikof Clinics close for maintenance.

Note: We have heard of tourists taking advantage of their Homestay hosts. We cannot stress too firmly that people in Russia and Central Asia are traditionally very hospitable. They are likely to produce far more food than you are paying for; for example you arrive back after a morning's sightseeing exhausted and immediately your hosts will make snacks and tea, regardless of the fact you are on B & B or half-board terms; or they will take you to dinner at their parents' flat; or they will take you to their *dacha*. PLEASE make sure you compensate them for all the extras, or make it clear you do not want them provided – and don't forget any phone calls you have made. If they refuse extra money, say it is for the children. Remember people are going through a very hard time and if you can afford to drive through their country you are much better off than they are.

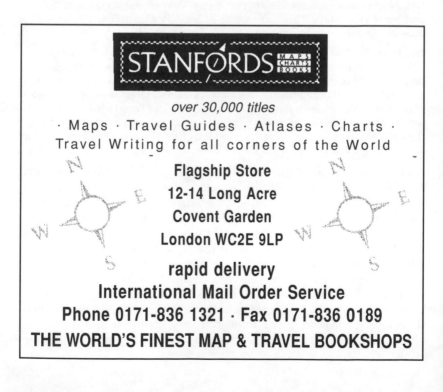

Part Two

RUSSIA AND MONGOLIA

Chapter Two

Russian Federation

The Russian Federation comprises 21 autonomous republics, 49 *oblasts* (regions), one autonomous oblast, 10 autonomous *okrugs* (districts) and six *krais* (territories). Besides these, the federal cities of Moscow and St Petersburg hold oblast-level status. Until the disintegration of the Soviet Union in 1991 the area now known as the Russian Federation was called the Russian Soviet Federated Socialist Republic and was the biggest and most influential of the 15 republics of the USSR.

Twelve of the former members of the USSR, Russia, Azerbaijan, Armenia, Belarus, Georgia, Kazakstan, Kyrgyzstan, Moldova, Tajikistan, Turkmenistan, Ukraine and Uzbekistan, are members of the CIS (Commonwealth of Independent States) – Estonia, Latvia and Lithuania opted out – and there is still some overlapping of authority, particularly in the area of defence. For instance Russian troops are deployed along the border between Tajikistan and Afghanistan.

FACTS AND FIGURES

Time

Moscow: GMT +3 hours; +4 hours during daylight-saving time which starts on the last Saturday in March and finishes on the last Saturday in September.

There are nine time zones across Russia and when driving it is easy to forget to adjust your watch.

The railway runs on Moscow Time.

Perm and Ekaterinburg are Moscow Time +2 hours, Novosibirsk +3 hours, Irkutsk +5 hours, Chita +6 hours, Khabarovsk and Vladivostok +7 hours, Sakhalin +8 hours, and Kamchatka +9 hours.

Population

Russia has a population of approximately 155,000,000 with a density of 8.7 per km² (22.6 per square mile). Population distribution is 74% urban, 26% rural; and approximately 80% live in the western part of the country.

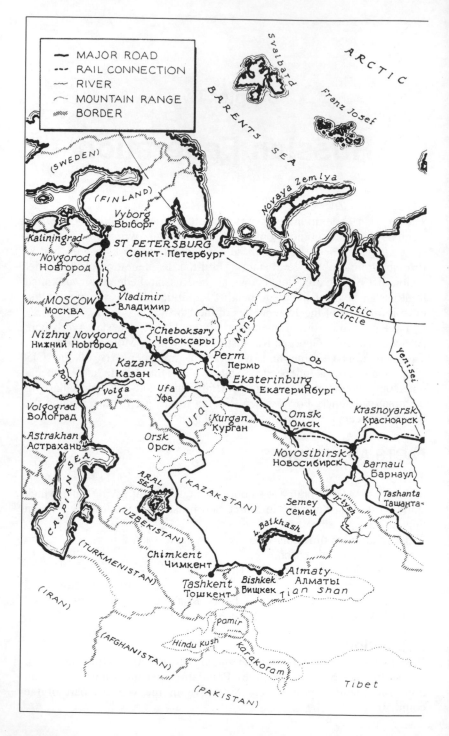

MAJOR ROAD
RAIL CONNECTION
RIVER
MOUNTAIN RANGE
BORDER

ARCTIC

Svalbard

Franz Josef

BARENTS SEA

(SWEDEN)

Novaya zemlya

(FINLAND)

Vyborg
Выборг

Kaliningrad

ST PETERSBURG
Санкт-Петербург

Novgorod
Новгород

Arctic circle

MOSCOW
Москва

Vladimir
Владимир

Mts.

Nizhny Novgorod
Нижний Новгород

Cheboksary
Чебоксары

Perm
Пермь

Ob

Yenisei

Kazan
Казан

Ufa
Уфа

Ekaterinburg
Екатеринбург

Don

Volga

Ural

Kurgan
Курган

Omsk
Омск

Krasnoyarsk
Красноярск

Volgograd
Волоград

Orsk
Орск

Novosibirsk
Новосибирск

Barnaul
Барнаул

Astrakhan
Астрахань

ARAL SEA

(KAZAKSTAN)

Tashanta
Ташанта

CASPIAN SEA

(UZBEKISTAN)

Semey
Семей

L. Balkhash

Altai

(TURKMENISTAN)

Chimkent
Чимкент

Almaty
Алматы

Tian shan

(IRAN)

Tashkent
Тошкент

Bishkek
Бишкек

pamir

(AFGHANISTAN)

Hindu Kush

karakoram

Tibet

(PAKISTAN)

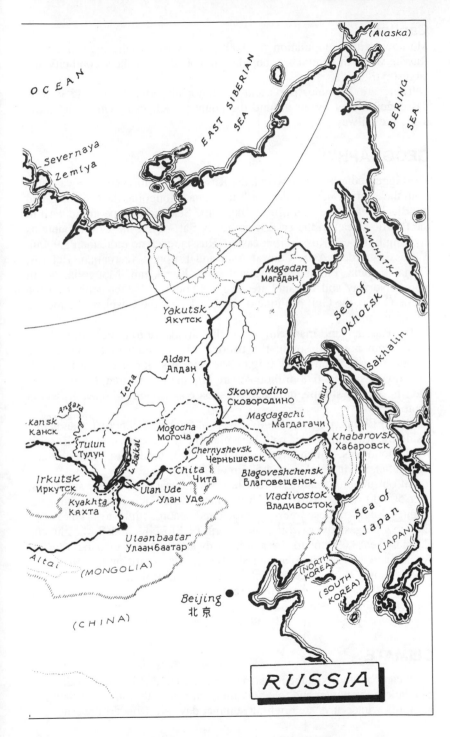

Capital

Moscow, with a population of 9,000,000, is by far the biggest city in Russia; while St Petersburg, population 5,000,000, is the second city and largest port.

There are 23 major ports and 19 major airports. About 145 million passengers travel by air around the country each year with many more using the railway.

GEOGRAPHY

The biggest country in the world, the Russian Federation covers a vast area from the Arctic Ocean in the north to China, Mongolia, the Caucasus and the Black Sea in the south; from the Baltic Sea and Europe in the west to the Pacific Ocean in the east. It is mostly flat – even the Ural Mountains dividing European Russia from eastern Russia reach no more than 1,900m.

Russia borders Asia, Central Asia and Europe. Azerbaijan, Belarus, China, Estonia, Finland, Georgia, Latvia, Kazakstan, Mongolia, North Korea, Norway and Ukraine are all neighbours. It has coastlines on the Arctic Ocean, the Gulf of Finland, the Black Sea, the Caspian Sea and the Sea of Japan.

The Russian land-mass can be roughly divided into three geographical zones from north to south: the **tundra** where much of the ground is permanently frozen; the **taiga**, the world's largest forest which encompasses about five million square kilometres of birch, larch, spruce and firs; and the **steppe**, thousands of square kilometres of open grassland plain.

Mount Elbrus, Europe's highest peak at 5,642m (18,506ft), stands just inside the Russian border with Georgia. The highest peak in the Russian Altai Mountains, which stretch south of Novosibirsk into Mongolia and Kazakstan, is Mt Belukha at 4,506m (14,780ft).

An outstanding feature of Russia is its thousands of rivers and lakes, over 50,000 rivers east of the Urals alone, which spread throughout the country. Many of these freeze in winter and become highways. The Volga, Europe's longest river, which rises north of Moscow and flows into the Caspian Sea 3,690km to the south, is dwarfed by the Ob, the Yenisei-Angara and the Lena in Siberia. Lake Baikal, a magnificent lake in central Siberia, holds almost one-fifth of the world's fresh water.

More than 200 volcanoes create a dramatic landscape on the Kamchatka Peninsula in the Far East. The highest peak, Mt Klyuchevskaya (4,750m or 15,580ft) is one of 30 active volcanoes.

CLIMATE

What can you say about the Russian climate except that it is universally cold and dark in the winter and tolerably mild but wet in the summer? Being so far north, winter days are brief but summer days are wonderfully long.

Temperatures vary over the vast country but Moscow and St Petersburg average around –6°C (20°F) in winter and an average maximum of between 21° and 23°C (71°F) in summer, with most rain in July and August. Irkutsk is even colder: –20°C (–5°F) in winter to 24°C (75°F) in summer, highest rainfall in August and September. Surprisingly, Vladivostok is colder than Moscow in winter but with less snow and a little warmer in summer – August and September are the wettest months. The Republic of Sakha (until recently Yakutia) has the coldest climate averaging in winter –40°C (–40°F) but sometimes dropping as low as –60°C (–76°F.) Summer average temperature is 13°C (55°F) but occasionally soaring to 37°C (100°F).

A town in northeastern Siberia, Olekminsk, recorded the greatest temperature range in the world with –66°C (–87°F) to +45°C (113°F).

The reason for Siberia's exceptionally low temperatures is that the area has no protection from the Arctic Ocean in the north and the Himalaya creates a barrier in the south preventing warm air from the Indian Ocean moving north.

Place	Elevation	Jan °C		Apr °C		Jul °C		Oct °C	
	m	max	min	max	min	max	min	max	min
Chita	676	–23	–33	5	–6	23	10	4	–7
Irkutsk	476	–15	–25	5	–7	21	10	4	–6
Khabarovsk	50	–19	–25	5	–3	23	17	8	2
Krasnoyarsk	152	–15	–23	2	–5	19	12	2	–4
Omsk	85	–18	–25	4	–6	23	12	4	–3
Ekaterinburg	273	–14	–20	5	–4	21	12	3	–3
Vladivostok	29	–10	–17	7	2	21	15	12	4
Yakutsk	163	–43	–48	–3	–14	22	12	–5	–12
Arkhangelsk	7	–12	–16	2	–5	18	10	2	–1
Astrakhan	14	–5	–9	14	4	29	20	12	4
Vyatka	181	–14	–18	5	–3	22	12	3	–1
St Petersburg	5	–5	–10	7	–1	21	13	7	3
Lviv	298	–1	–5	11	3	24	15	12	6
Minsk	225	–5	–10	8	–1	21	12	8	2
Moscow	154	–6	–12	8	0	23	12	7	2
Volgograd	42	–9	–15	10	2	29	18	11	3

NATURAL HISTORY AND CONSERVATION

Flora and fauna

The **tundra** is an inhospitable environment yet, even here, flora and fauna have adapted and survive. Grasses, lichens and mosses grow on the permafrost providing feed for lemmings, hares, arctic ground squirrels, voles and reindeer which, in turn, support arctic foxes, ermines and wolves. Along the coastline polar bears, sea lions, walruses and seals feed on fish. The crested auklet, rough legged buzzard, snowy owl, snow bunting, red-breasted goose and Siberian white crane are some of the spectacular birds which live in the north.

The **taiga** is the habitat for reindeer, elk, lynx, beavers, five-toed jerboas, common hamsters, Siberian chipmunks, ermines, sables, polecats, red squirrels, weasels, red foxes and brown bears. Bird life is prolific so watch for species such as the whooper swan, black woodpecker, merlin, red-throated loon, greylag goose, greater spotted eagle and other birds of prey.

A region of particular interest is the **Lake Baikal/Transbaikal** area. Nerpa (freshwater seals) and golomyanka, fish which live at depths of up to 1,500m, are but two of the unique species which live in and around the lake. Among other animals of interest are Siberian goats, steppe foxes, wolves, maral deer, ermines, sables, musk deer, Siberian flying squirrels, Siberian marmots and wild boars. As you might expect, waterbirds proliferate and include the great cormorant, horned grebe, ruddy shelduck, falcated teal, spotbill duck, white-fronted goose, grey heron, whooper swan and black-throated loon, so keep your binoculars handy.

The **Far East** has perhaps the most spectacular wildlife, much of it unfortunately threatened by poachers and hunters. Sea bears, Tibetan bears, elk, antelope, mountain wolves, Amur raccoons, Kamchatka beavers, Siberian bighorn sheep, Amur leopards, Siberian tigers, Mongolian gazelle, arctic ground squirrels, Asian wild asses, irbis (panther), lynx and otters are just some of the fascinating animals of the area, though you'd be very lucky to see many of these species. Tengmalm's owl, crested auklet, eagle owl, three-toed woodpecker, great grey and hawk owl, blackbilled capercaillie, hazel grouse and Mongolian lark are birds to watch out for.

In the **Altai-Sayan** area you may be very lucky and spot mountain rams, mountain wolves, ibex, maral deer, wild cats, goitred gazelle, Eurasian badgers, musk deer, wild boars, argali (wild sheep) and snow leopards. Keep an eye out for Altai snowcock, grey partridge, lammergeyer and black vulture.

In the **west** small herds of saiga (small antelope) still roam the dry plains north of the Caspian Sea while higher up in the alpine regions of the Caucasus the bezoar and the tur (mountain and wild goats), mouflon (endangered mountain sheep), chamois and brown bear survive. Magnificent birds of prey such as the lammergeyer, imperial eagle, peregrine falcon and griffon vulture soar over the Caucasus. The wonderful pink and white Caspian lotuses and brilliant wild flowers of the Volga delta and magnificent alpine plants and flowers will delight any botanist – amateur or professional.

Unfortunately hunting is still permitted and tourists are encouraged to indulge in shooting safaris.

A publication called *Krasnaya Kniga* (Red Book) lists all endangered species, alerting the world to the urgent need to conserve what is left.

Nature reserves

Throughout the Russian Federation there is a vast network of nature reserves – areas specifically set aside for the conservation of endangered species. Scientists and other enthusiasts have worked long and hard to document the flora and fauna of this vast country. Recently the crumbling economy has seen huge cuts in funding and it is only the dedication of these workers that is keeping the reserves functioning.

Many of the 160 state nature reserves are in European Russia. However, the first to be established, the Barguzinka Nature Reserve on the shores of Lake Baikal, was at the decree of Tsar Nicholas II in 1916 to preserve the shrinking sable population. Other Siberian and Far Eastern reserves include Olysky Zakaznik Nature Reserve where it is possible to see bear, elk and salmon; and the Kronotski Zapovednik Nature Reserve, on Kamchatka, where visitors traverse wooden walkways to protect the hundreds of endangered plant species.

In the northwest, near Monchegorsk, the Lapland Nature Reserve struggles, with the help of UNESCO, WWF and the American Association for the Support of Ecological Initiatives, to preserve its wilderness. Quite close to St Petersburg, on the southeastern shore of Lake Ladoga, the Nizhnezvirsky Nature Reserve is home to the ringed seal, a freshwater subspecies endemic to the area. It is also a great place to watch migratory birds at certain times of the year.

Besides these large reserves dedicated people struggle valiantly to preserve endangered species. Victor and Lena Yudin at Gaivoron in the Far East have devoted years to breeding Siberian tigers with minimal help from the government.

HISTORICAL OUTLINE

Excavations at the Dering Yuryakh site in Siberia suggest that human history goes back much farther than had been thought. Indeed artefacts believed to be over a million years old have been uncovered in the area.

The history of human settlement in European Russia is much more recent, going back to 20,000 BC when people lived in the Don River basin. In the 5th century BC, Herodotus, the Greek historian, describes the Scythians as being much admired for their horsemanship and feared for their fighting skills. The nomadic Scythians, who are thought to have originated in Central Asia, conquered an empire which spread from the Danube to the Don, across the Caucasus and into Asia Minor before the Samartians, in turn, conquered them. A number of different groups, including the Goths, the Huns, the Avars and the Khazars, dominated the area until the 9th century AD and the rise of the Kievan Rus state – the first Russian state.

There is ongoing controversy as to the origins of the Rus peoples – some historians claim they were Vikings, while others say they were Slavs from southern Russia. Whatever the truth may be, the first rulers of early Russia were Scandinavians: Rurik, who founded Novgorod, and Oleg who conquered Kiev and became the founder of Kievan Rus. In 988 Vladimir I declared Christianity the state religion and had himself baptised in Constantinople.

The first years of the 13th century saw the Mongols, led by Genghis Khan, sweeping across from the east. In 1223 they reached the Caucasus and defeated the Russians at the Kalka River. Despite the death of Genghis Khan in 1227, the push eastward did not falter; in 1236 they crossed the Urals and the following year conquered Vladimir-Suzdal. In 1242 Batu, a grandson of Genghis Khan, set up his headquarters at Old Sarai, which became the capital of the Golden Horde.

For 150 years from 1240 the Mongols had effective control over all of Russia, indeed in 1294 the vast Mongol Empire spread from the coast of China to the Black Sea and Ukraine. In 1380, when Prince Dimitry of Moscow defeated them at the battle of Kulikovo, the tide began to turn. However it was not until 1480 that Ivan III threw off the Mongol yoke, refusing to pay allegiance to the Khan.

Towards the end of the 13th century and beginning of the 14th, the power of Vladimir began to give way to Moscow; and around 1328 Ivan I persuaded the head of the Orthodox Church to move there. Despite a violent history Moscow remained the capital until Peter the Great, inspired by a tour of Europe, built his new capital of St Petersburg in 1712.

Ivan IV became the first Tsar of all the Russias in 1547, at the age of 16, after 13 years of court chaos brought about by two princely houses competing for the regency or even the throne. Later that year he married Anastasia, from the *boyar* (land owners) Romanov family, but had only thirteen years of happy married life before she died in 1560. During the first years of his reign, Ivan IV, with the help of a group of advisers, brought in a number of reforms including a new code of law, as well as changes to local government and laws relating to the Church. He established the first regular army regiments and formalised the proportion of soldiers and horses a landlord must supply according to the size of his estate. Ivan IV had some notable military victories against Kazan and Astrakhan in the 1550s and also established an English trade connection in return for specialist help in mining and medicine.

After the death of Anastasia, in 1560, a reign of terror began and Ivan IV became Ivan the Terrible. He formed a body of men, *oprichniki*, dressed in black and riding black horses, whose duty was to exterminate the Tsar's enemies (setting a precedent for Stalin).

In the last years of Ivan the Terrible's reign some 1650 Cossacks led by Ermak rode east across the Urals and into Siberia where they established the fortified towns of Tyumen and Tobolsk.

During the 14 years following the death of Ivan the Terrible in 1584, his son Theodore ruled comparatively peacefully with the help of advisers, the most powerful of whom was Boris Godunov. The death of Theodore in 1598 saw the end of the Muscovite dynasty and the beginning of the Time of Troubles. Boris Godunov's brief reign was marred by False Dimitry who claimed to be Theodore's son and heir. Backed by the Poles, Dimitry succeeded in reaching Moscow. Boris collapsed and died and his family were murdered, but within a year Prince Basil Shuisky and friends staged a coup, Dimitry was murdered and Prince Basil became Tsar.

However, the Time of Troubles was not yet over – a new False Dimitry, the Felon of Tushino, emerged in 1607 with a large band of Cossack, Polish and Lithuanian mercenaries and anyone else who cared to join in the fight to depose Prince Basil. The next three years saw Sweden and Poland fighting for control of Russia. In 1610 Tsar Basil was deposed and a boyar *duma*, led by Prince Theodore Mstislavsky, took over the government. The search for a new Tsar began and, in order to defeat the Felon of Tushino now ensconced near Moscow, the Muscovites invited King Sigismund of Poland to send his 15-year-old son, Wladyslaw, to be Tsar of Russia. Surprisingly Sigismund turned down the offer – partly because he refused to allow his son's conversion to Orthodoxy but also because he had ambitions to rule Russia himself.

In 1612 the Russian army evicted the Poles from Moscow with the help of one group of Cossacks. However it was not until 1613, when 16-year-old Mikhail Romanov was elected Tsar, that the Time of Troubles could be said to be over. The Romanovs were related to the last strong Tsar, Ivan the Terrible, through Ivan's marriage to Anastasia Romanov, and were popular with the people. The Romanov family ruled Russia for the next 300 years. The rest of the 17th century was a time of consolidation and stability for Russia as well as massive expansion of Russian lands. The Cossacks pushed deeper into Siberia, founding Yakutsk in 1632 and Chita in 1653.

It was again the Cossacks – this time in Ukraine – who were the catalyst for Russian expansion when they asked for help against the Poles. By 1667 Russia was in control of Kiev, Smolensk and lands east of the Dnepr River.

However, all was not peaceful and in 1670 the Cossacks led a revolt by the serfs who had lost their freedom of movement in 1646. In 1675 the serfs became slaves of the boyars when a law was passed allowing them to be sold separately from the estates.

In 1696 Peter the Great became sole ruler after the death of his mother and half-brother Ivan. Having suffered from plots and intrigue among his family he established a group of advisers, including a number of Europeans, chosen for ability rather than birth. After defeating the Turks at Azov and establishing a Russian port on the Black Sea, he turned his attention to Sweden and in 1709 destroyed the Swedish army at Poltava; but it was not until 1721 that the Treaty of Nystadt gave Russia control of the Gulf of Finland.

Despite these wars Peter, with the help of European experts, built St Petersburg and moved the capital there in 1712. He was also a great reformer and moderniser. Although he failed to abolish serfdom, which was virtual slavery, he did establish a system of service to the state by the gentry and advancement according to merit.

In the years following the death of Peter the Great in 1725 Westernisation continued; but in the 37 years before the accession of Catherine II (the Great) Russia had a series of ineffectual rulers.

Catherine, a German princess, went to Moscow to marry Peter III when she was 15. It was not a happy marriage but the intelligent young woman was politically shrewd, learned Russian, converted to the Orthodox Church and read widely in the area of political philosophy – this was, of course, the Age of Enlightenment when intellectuals began to embrace the idea of human rights and the separation of powers.

Within six months of Peter III's accession to the throne, Catherine was crowned Empress Catherine II, having deposed and subsequently killed Peter. She continued Peter the Great's building programme in St Petersburg and also shared his eagerness for reform. She secularised Church lands, despite angry protests by the clergy whose position declined.

Catherine encouraged free trade, founded a medical college and revolutionised medical procedures. She set up the Legislative Commission, consisting of elected and appointed deputies, including peasants (but not serfs), to codify laws which modernised Russian law following an *Instruction* which she wrote herself. Considering Catherine's despotic rule of over 30 years, it was a remarkably liberal document. Unfortunately, despite 203 sessions over 18 months, the Commission failed to agree on reforms – mainly because it divided along class lines.

In spite of her professed progressive views Catherine made no effort to eliminate serfdom and, indeed, endorsed the power and privileges of the gentry; so it was not surprising that yet another Cossack-led uprising occurred in 1773, starting in the Urals and spreading along the Don River and into the Don valley. Many enemies of the Establishment, serfs, miners, Old Believers, Tartars and other minorities, banded together in a mass rebellion. However, once more, the revolt was put down and its leader executed in Moscow. When confronted with the French Revolution in the latter years of her reign, she, not unnaturally, reacted with bitterness and hostility, despite her long association with French philosophers such as Voltaire and Montesquieu, who challenged the divine right of kings.

After the brief reign of Catherine's son Paul I (he was killed in a coup), Alexander I came to the throne in 1801. The first half of his reign was marked by an increase in educational spending, and a law which provided for the voluntary freeing of the serfs by the landlords and ensured they be given land and the status of peasants. Few landlords took up the offer.

The Treaty of Tilsit in 1807 saw Russia allied with Napoleon against England but by 1810 the alliance lapsed and Russian/English trade resumed, provoking an angry Napoleon into invading Russia. After a bloody but inconclusive battle at Borodino, which resulted in 42,000 Russian and 58,000 French casualties, Napoleon swept on to Moscow to find it deserted. As the Grande Armée arrived fire broke out and Moscow, still mainly a city of wooden buildings, burned down. With the onset of winter Napoleon retreated. Eventually only around 50,000 out of 600,000 men limped out of Russia. The Holy Alliance, a vague but optimistic fellowship between Christian European monarchs, was one of Alexander's stranger ideas after the defeat of Napoleon.

As so often happened in Russia, Alexander died suddenly in 1825 leaving no clear heir. His oldest brother, Constantine, had given up his right to the throne when he married a Polish aristocrat. He was living in Poland and not interested in returning to Moscow, even as Tsar. In a rather secretive manifesto written in 1822, Alexander made it clear that Nicholas, the younger brother, should succeed him. However each brother swore allegiance to the other on their father's death – a pleasant, if confusing, change from the usual fight for the throne. In the subsequent confusion, army officers, who had absorbed liberal ideas in Paris after the defeat of Napoleon, rallied in St Petersburg in support of Constantine on 26 December 1825 when the guard regiments were due to swear allegiance to Nicholas. The mutiny was put down and five of the Decembrists, as the rebels were called, were executed and nearly 300 sent to Siberia.

During Nicholas' reign the serfs on state lands in Western Russia were given their freedom and title to the land in the hope that they would help in the struggle against the Polish-influenced landlords. In 1854 he sent the Russian army into the Ottoman provinces of Wallacia and Moldavia resulting in the Crimean War against Anglo-French-Turkish forces. Nicholas died in 1855 and Alexander II signed the Treaty of Paris in 1856.

Alexander II carried through a number of long-overdue reforms during his reign. Historians estimate that there had been between 550 and 1,500 peasant uprisings in the first half of the 19th century. In 1858 Alexander persuaded the gentry to abolish serfdom. The democratisation of local government and the reform of the judiciary, the reorganisation of military service and changes in the administration of the treasury were reforms which led to Alexander's nickname 'Tsar-liberator' and, ultimately, to his assassination in 1881.

The Russian gains in the Far East and Asia continued apace during Alexander's reign. Khabarovsk was founded in 1858, shortly after the Treaty of Aigun, which ceded all lands north of the Amur River to Russia, was signed with China. The Treaty of Peking, which recognised Russia's claim to all lands east of the Ussuri River, followed; and the port of Vladivostok was founded in 1860. Rather short-sightedly Alexander sold Alaska to the USA in 1867.

The reigns of Alexander III and Nicholas II until the Revolution of 1905 were a reactionary period when the aim seems to have been to put the clock back 50 years. The defeat of the Russian forces by the greatly outnumbered Japanese was a blow to national pride and the desire for representative government gathered momentum in the west. Tsar Nicholas' refusal, like that of his predecessor Alexander III, to allow further reforms resulted in the Revolution of 1905. The events of 'Bloody Sunday' when police opened fire on a peaceful demonstration in St Petersburg had far-reaching effects. By the end of 1905 the Tsar had issued the October Manifesto which gave the appearance of a constitutional monarchy without allowing the Duma (parliament) much real power.

Real reform came too slowly, unrest spread and the terrible losses during World War I led to the disintegration of the monarchy. In 1917, Tsar Nicholas II was forced to abdicate. He was arrested and, with the rest of the Royal Family, was sent to Ekaterinburg where they were murdered in 1918.

Lenin and the Bolsheviks took control in the west and, although there were five years of civil war before Vladivostok and the Far East capitulated, the Bolshevik victory was never seriously in doubt.

In 1920 the capital was moved back to Moscow from St Petersburg.

The Union of Soviet Socialist Republics was created in 1922, incorporating Russia, Ukraine, White Russia and Transcaucasia. Two years later, in 1924, the division of Central Asia began and by 1936 Uzbekistan, Turkmenistan, Kazakstan and Kyrgyzstan had been created and had become states within the USSR.

Lenin died in 1924, after suffering a series of strokes, and his embalmed remains were placed in a tomb in Red Square which became a place of pilgrimage for decades.

Stalin took over leadership after a struggle within the Party – Lenin had failed to appoint a successor – and began the collectivisation of industry and agriculture in a series of five-year plans. Resistance was met with imprisonment or death and soon *gulags* (concentration camps), which provided cheap labour, were set up across Russia. By the mid 1930s the infamous purges were in full swing and some eight million Bolsheviks, Party members, intellectuals and other 'enemies of the people' were either sent to the *gulags* or executed.

The 1939 peace pact between Germany and the USSR came to an abrupt end with Hitler's invasion of the Soviet Union in 1941. The USSR expansion in eastern Europe in the immediate post-war years was possibly as much a response to the massive losses sustained against a brutal enemy as a conscious empire-building strategy.

After a brief period of co-operation the 'iron curtain' descended and remained in place until the mid 1980s. Stalin, like Lenin, left no obvious successor but within three years Khrushchev had removed all possible rivals and was to rule unchallenged until 1964. Apart from Beria, Stalin's police chief, who was murdered very soon after Stalin's death, these rivals were allowed to enjoy a peaceful if powerless retirement. In 1956, to the amazement of the world, Khrushchev denounced Stalin and his purges. One of Khrushchev's greatest achievements was beating the USA into space in 1957 by launching the world's first satellite, and again in 1961 when Yuri Gagarin became the first person in space, thus proving to his satisfaction that communism could defeat capitalism.

In 1961 Khrushchev managed to have Stalin's remains removed from the mausoleum in Red Square but already his power was declining. Conflict with China, dating back to the 1920s, re-erupted in 1960 and by 1963 it seemed unlikely that it would ever be healed. In 1964 Khrushchev was 'released due to advanced age and deterioration of his health'.

During the rule of Brezhnev, 1964–82, a change could be seen and a form of capitalism crept on to the scene. By the late 1970s Party officials and government elite began to enjoy a high standard of living – Brezhnev's collection of cars was a symbol of the changes taking place. Brezhnev died in 1982 and Andropov and Chernenko died in quick succession after only a year each as General Secretary.

When, in 1985, the comparatively young Mikhail Gorbachev was elected to the general secretaryship of the Party change gathered momentum. The economy was in a bad way and it was essential to try to revitalise it. *Glasnost* (openness) and *perestroika* (restructuring) became the buzz words and suddenly the US and the USSR were agreeing to discuss bi-lateral disarmament. Russian troops were pulled out of Mongolia, Afghanistan and Eastern Europe, political prisoners were freed, the practice of religion was accepted and even censorship of the press was relaxed.

In 1988, at Gorbachev's instigation, elections were held for two-thirds of the Congress of People's Deputies – a huge step forward in the democratisation of the USSR. From then on the USSR began to disintegrate, with the Eastern Bloc states gaining independence one after the other, and in 1989 the Berlin Wall came down.

In 1990 Boris Yeltsin became chairman of the parliament of the Russian Republic and the power struggle between him and Gorbachev increased in intensity. Gorbachev, then President of the USSR, was awarded the Nobel Peace Prize at a time when the Russian people were suffering rather than benefiting from the changes. Inflation was rampant and shortages created long food queues.

On August 18 1991 Gorbachev, holidaying at a Crimean dacha, was put under house arrest in an attempt by the old guard of the Communist Party to restore the fortunes of the USSR. Yeltsin rallied the opposition in Moscow and won the day – huge crowds gathered in front of the White House, troops refused an order to storm it, Ukraine and Kazakstan rejected the coup and by August 21 the attempted coup was over.

The signing of the Belovezhskaya agreement on December 8 1991 by Russia, Ukraine and Belarus brought about the dissolution of the USSR. On December 21 the heads of state of 12 former Soviet republics met in Almaty and formed the CIS. It was the end of an era – the USSR no longer existed, the Communist Party was banned, Gorbachev, president without a country, resigned and Boris Yeltsin became president of the Russia Federation.

Yeltsin's reforms, introducing a free-market economy and the privatisation of business, land, housing and agriculture, were pushed through too fast for the parliament which was still dominated by communists and nationalists who opposed the changes. Despite Yeltsin winning a big vote of confidence in the referendum of April 1993, the parliament, led by Yeltsin's vice-president, Alexander Rutskoi, continued to make government almost impossible.

Once more, in October 1993, the power struggle was played out in front of the White House; but this time it was Yeltsin who set up a blockade, dissolving parliament and ordering all members to leave by October 4. The National Salvation Front overran the troops and attacked the Ostankino TV station – 62 people were killed in the affray. Yeltsin managed to summon sufficient loyal troops next morning to storm the White House, and retained power; but another 70 people were killed.

Elections in December 1993 created a mixed parliament with even the neo-fascist Zhirinovsky winning a number of seats; and a national referendum endorsed a new constitution which gave the president ultimate power over parliament.

The presidential election of 1996 resulted in the return to power of an ailing Boris Yeltsin. In November he had a quadruple heart by-pass operation but despite rumours of plots he managed to retain power.

Historical chronology

860–1240	Kievan Rus – founding of Novgorod and birth of Russian state
980–1015	Vladimir I ruled Russia from Kiev
988	Vladimir I baptised and ordered the mass conversion of the Russian people
1024	Founding of Suzdal, later to become capital of Rostov-Suzdal principality around 1158
1108	Founding of fort at Vladimir, by Vladimir I
1113–1125	Vladimir Monomakh, Prince of Kiev
1147	Founding of Moscow
1223	Genghis Khan invaded and defeated Russia through the Caucasus
1227	Death of Genghis Khan
1240–1480	Mongol domination of Russia
1462–1505	Ivan III – 'the Great', first ruler to call himself Tsar of all Russia
1533–84	Ivan IV – 'the Terrible'
1613–45	Mikhail – first of the long line of Romanovs to rule Russia
1682–1725	Peter I – 'the Great' – founder of St Petersburg (1703)
1712	Peter moved the capital from Moscow to St Petersburg
1762–96	Catherine II – 'the Great'
1812	Napoleon invaded Russia and reached Moscow before retreating as winter set in, losing over 90% of his men
Dec 1825	A rally, in St Petersburg, of Constantine's supporters ended in the execution of the leaders and exile to Siberia for the rest of the Decembrists
1825–55	Nicholas I
1861	Emancipation of the serfs
1867	Alaska sold to the USA
1905	An attempted revolution began on 'Bloody Sunday' but petered out towards the end of the year as Jews, liberals and intellectuals were beaten and even killed
1914	World War I – by 1915 about 2 million Russians had been killed defending first the Balkans and then Russia
1917	The Great October Revolution and abdication of the last Tsar, Nicholas II
1918	The Tsar and his family murdered at Ekaterinburg
1924	Death of Lenin

1941–45	Great Patriotic War (WWII)
1953	Death of Stalin
1953–64	Khrushchev rules. USSR beats the West into space
1968	USSR invades Czechoslovakia
1979–89	War in Afghanistan
1964–82	Brezhnev rules USSR
1982–84	Yury Andropov rules
1984–5	Konstantin Chernenko rules
1986	Chernobyl nuclear power station disaster
1985–90	Mikhail Gorbachev embraces glasnost (openness) and perestroika (restructuring)
1991–	Boris Yeltsin takes over as president
1993	First democratic elections and referendum support Yeltsin and his new constitution
1994–	Chechnya war starts
1996	Presidential election – Yeltsin re-elected despite heart surgery and doubts about his health

POLITICS AND GOVERNMENT

After more than 70 years of communism Russia found it easier to destroy the old system than to create a new one. In 1993 a new constitution was adopted, establishing a bicameral Federal Assembly, the supreme governing body. The upper house, the Federation Council, consists of 178 deputies; and the lower house, the State Duma, has 450 members.

Under the new constitution the head of state is also the executive president and holds wide-ranging powers. He nominates the prime minister, senior judges and the governor of the central bank although they must be approved by the State Duma. The rights to dissolve the duma, call elections, declare states of emergency and even to suspend civil rights are all the president's. He can be impeached only by the constitutional and supreme courts acting with a two-thirds vote of both chambers of the Federal Assembly.

The abolition of the position of vice-president under the new constitution caused some confusion as to who should take control when President Yeltsin was incapacitated by major heart surgery in 1996.

ECONOMY

In the early 1990s inflation was rampant but by 1996 it had slowed considerably although it is difficult to judge the exact rate. In 1992 President Boris Yeltsin introduced a programme aimed at reforming the economy. Privatisation of banks, factories, farms and housing was encouraged and restrictions on foreign investment and trade eased. Unfortunately much capital has left Russia in recent years, going to banks in Europe and the United States.

Attempts to convert huge factories, which manufactured military and space exploration equipment under the communist regime, to production of consumer goods has been only partially successful. Plant and equipment are out of date but there is a lack of capital to replace it.

Despite its vast natural and human resources it will be some years before Russia can compete with Asia and the West.

PEOPLE

Of the population of approximately 155 million, around 80% are Russian. The other 20% is made up of numerous minority groups the major one being the Tatars, descendants of the Mongols who swept through the country with Genghis Khan and his successors. Several other groups in western Russia include the Chuvash, the Bashkirs and the Finno-Ugric peoples. In the north, the Kerlians, also Finno-Ugric, live on both sides of the Finnish border and, in the far northwest, a tiny group of Saami (Laplanders).

In the south, Stalin's shocking treatment of the people in the Caucasus – he deported four groups, including the Muslim Chechens, to Central Asia during the Great Patriotic War – created ethnic tensions over the years. The Avars, a group of some 600,000 people descended from the Huns who invaded the area about 1,500 years ago, are another of the many small groups in the south.

It is hard to decide whether to include Cossacks as a specific racial minority; but since their history goes back to the 15th century when they became recognised as an elite body of fighting men, although from different areas, and as they claim to be a separate ethnic group, they cannot be ignored. As a result of fighting on the White Russian side during the Civil War they suffered greatly under the Communist government and have only recently felt free to reclaim their ethnicity.

Of the 33 million people in Siberia and the Far East 4% are from 30 indigenous groups. The rest are a mixture of Russians, Tatars, Germans, Ukrainians, Kazaks and other nationalities, many of whom were sent east as political prisoners or came of their own free will as pioneers seeking a better way of life. The Altay, Buryat, Tuvan, Khakass and Yakut are the largest indigenous ethnic groups. Until comparatively recently they had their own culture, languages and shamanist religion – now many have adopted Tibetan Buddhism or Russian Orthodox Christianity.

It is difficult to estimate the number of Jews still living in the Russian Federation. Many have migrated to Israel and other countries in recent years. In 1928 an attempt was made to solve the so-called 'Jewish problem' and a Jewish Autonomous Oblast was established in Khabarovski Krai. Over the following ten years some 35,000 Jews migrated from as far afield as Ukraine. With the recurrence of Jewish persecution after World War II many Jews in the JAO dropped their Jewish background but, since 1991, those remaining have begun to re-establish their cultural roots.

LANGUAGE

Russian is the official and predominant language throughout the Federation with many other languages and dialects used by minority groups. The new republics in the CIS, such as Kazakstan, have reverted to their own languages as the official ones but still use Russian to communicate with other ethnic groups.

It is essential to learn the Cyrillic alphabet (see *Appendix One*) before you go because almost all road signs are in Russian and so is your bible, the *Automobile Road Atlas*.

Language books and tapes

You will feel more comfortable if you have done at least a short 'Russian for travellers' course which will teach you basic pronunciation, greetings, how to ask the way and how to count to twenty. If you enrol in classes ask your teachers what books and tapes they recommend. If you don't have time for lessons the following audio courses are helpful:

Russian language and people: a course for beginners learning Russian, BBC Worldwide Ltd. ISBN 0-563-40013-7

Breakthrough Russian: introductory course, Macmillan. ISBN 0-333-55726-3

Don't despair if you feel you are not learning much – the fact that you can read the phrase-book and have some idea of pronunciation will give you confidence when you reach Russia.

Few people outside the major cities speak any English although some have a few words of German. It may be worth writing a few basic notes on cards, asking the way to the hotel, the fuel station or the road to...? Often people in smaller towns are so surprised to see foreigners they seem to be too busy looking to listen. If they don't understand your pronunciation or your writing don't panic – mime is a useful means of communication. Most Russians are very friendly and will often go out of their way to lead you to where you want to go.

If you are in a smallish town and have problems being understood, it is a good idea to approach the local institute of further education. If the town is too small to have one ask for the secondary school teacher.

RELIGION
Buddhism

The Kalmyks, in the area north of the Caspian Sea, and the Buryats and Tuvans in Siberia follow the Gelugpa or 'Yellow Hat' sect of Tibetan Buddhism. Stalin was not biased in his attempt to wipe out religion – Buddhists suffered similar persecution to Jews, Christians and Muslims.

Christianity

Founded in 988 by Prince Vladimir, the Russian Orthodox Church came via Byzantium rather than Rome. From that date it was closely linked to the imperial regime so the Marxist view that religion was the opiate of the masses is not surprising, and from the October Revolution until 1990 religion was banned or, at the very least, discouraged.

Churches were closed and the clergy executed or exiled during the twenty-year period following the revolution but this did not extinguish Christianity. The patriotism of the Orthodox Church during the Great Patriotic War created a lull in the opposition of Stalin and the Politburo and the Church was allowed to elect a patriarch in 1943. Khrushchev returned to the attack in the 1950s, closing thousands of churches and turning them into museums.

Since 1990 the Orthodox Church has enjoyed a revival but it is doubtful whether it will ever achieve the power it had during the centuries of the imperial regime.

Other Christian groups such as Baptists, Lutherans, Roman Catholics, Seventh Day Adventists and the Salvation Army have a small following.

Islam

The majority of Muslims live in the Caucasus and southeast of the country – the Chechens, Tatars and Bashkirs. Islam, like Christianity, was discouraged after the October Revolution and many mosques were destroyed or closed. There was great persecution of Muslims, including deportation and execution between 1917 and World War II. A revival of the practice of Islam has occurred in recent years.

Judaism

There are still possibly 700,000 Jews living in Russia although there has been an exodus in the 1990s since emigration laws were relaxed.

Shamanism

Shamanism was the religion of the early inhabitants of Russia. It is a form of animism with shamans acting as intermediary between the spirits and the people. The Udmurts and Mari people of the northwest and some Buryats and Khakass still practise Shamanism.

CULTURE AND THE ARTS

Literature

Russians are remarkably well read and are surprisingly impressed if you are familiar with the Russian classics. Alexander Pushkin (1799–1837) is probably the most respected poet and you will find many monuments and memorials to him as you travel through Russia.

A contemporary of Pushkin, Mikhail Lermontov (1814–41), wrote *A Hero of Our Time*, considered to be the first important Russian novel.

Pushkin and Lermontov started the tradition of criticising the State and both died young, possibly in duels contrived by the authorities.

The novels of Ivan Turgenev (1818–83), Fyodor Dostoyevsky (1821–81) and Leo Tolstoy (1828–1910) have been read for pleasure and widely studied in schools and universities in the West for many years. All their books give a wonderful view of life in Russia in the 19th century.

An enjoyable way to get an idea of Russia during the Revolution and farm collectivisation period is to read *And Quiet Flows the Don*, *The Don Flows Home to the Sea* and *Virgin Soil Upturned* by Mikhail Sholokov (b.1905).

Boris Pasternak (1890–1960), best known in the West for *Dr Zhivago*, was also a poet of note and, like many other writers, was persecuted for his efforts.

Contemporary novelist Alexander Solzhenitsyn (b.1918) went into exile in the USA in 1974. His most famous book *The Gulag Archipelago* recounts the terrible stories of hundreds of people sent to the gulags. Solzhenitsyn returned to Russia to a hero's welcome in 1994.

Tatyana Tolstaya's short stories published in 1989 as *On the Golden Porch* give us a glimpse of what living in tiny Moscow flats is like.

The plays of Anton Chekhov (1860–1904) are familiar to theatregoers all over the world, describing the ennui of middle class people relegated to life in the provinces in the 19th century. The colourful autobiography *My Childhood* by Maxim Gorky (1868–1936) describes life in poverty in the city as anything but romantic.

See *Further Reading, Appendix Two*.

Music

Classical music in Russia owes much to its folk heritage. Operas by Mikhail Glinka (1804–57), Modeste Mussorgsky (1839–81) and Rimsky-Korsakov (1844–1908) are familiar to lovers of classical music the world over. The opera *Prince Igor* and symphonic sketch *On the Steppes of Central Asia* by Alexander Borodin (1833–87) are also much loved around the world. Borodin, incidentally, was a professor of chemistry and opened a School of Medicine for Women in St Petersburg.

The music of Peter Ilich Tchaikovsky (1840–93) was, perhaps, a little less nationalistic and quickly became popular in Britain and America as it is still.

Igor Stravinsky (1882–1971) and Serge Prokofiev (1891–1953) were the first Russian modernists and their music quickly became familiar in the West. Stravinsky became a French citizen in 1936 but fled to the USA during World War II. After travelling the world on a League of Nations passport in the 1920s and early 30s, Prokofiev returned to Russia in 1934 and lived in Moscow with his family until he died aged 61 on the same day as Stalin.

Russian musicians, like artists and intellectuals, had a difficult time during the Soviet period – some sought exile in the West but many stayed.

In the 1940s Shostakovich, Prokofiev, Khachaturian and other composers were, according to the 10th edition of *The Oxford Companion to Music*, accused of 'formalistic perversion' and 'failure to express Soviet reality'. Apparently they were writing music which was neither optimistic nor easily accessible to the proletariat – both were considered essential ingredients by the Party.

Dance

The ballet tradition goes back to the 18th century in St Petersburg and Moscow. Surprisingly it thrived through the turbulent times of the Revolution and even during the 'cold war' the Bolshoy and Kirov ballets toured the West with huge success. Despite a number of their brightest stars being seduced by the freedom and lifestyle of the West, Soviet ballet companies managed to maintain their standards.

Most of the big cities have their own ballet companies of varying quality.

Circus

Almost all the big cities have a resident circus with its own large 'theatre'. Unlike the opera, ballet and orchestras which take their holidays and also go on international tours in the summer, the circus plays all through the year. Be warned that these are the old-fashioned circuses with performing animals as well as high-wire acts and wonderful clowns. The performing bears are very popular with adult Russians but distressing for animal lovers from the West.

Film

You do not have to be a film buff to appreciate Russian films. Who can ever forget the scene of the pram bumping down the steps in Odessa during Sergey Eisenstein's *Battleship Potemkin* or the battle scenes in his *Alexander Nevsky*? And now we have Nikita Mikalkov's *Burnt by the Sun* or the very funny satire *Window to Paris* directed by Yuri Mamin.

Folk culture

There are a number of big folk dance and music groups such as the Igor Moiseev Folk Dance Ensemble and the Pyatnitsky Russian Folk Chorus whose programmes give a wonderful overview of folk art from Russia and the CIS. Small companies which perform in provincial theatres and even smaller groups which play in hotels and restaurants are very entertaining.

Applied and decorative art is often brightly coloured and fun. *Matryoshka* dolls, lacquered wooden spoons and bowls and enamelled metal trays and samovars all make good souvenirs but are also to be seen in people's homes.

RUSSIA
Above: *Assumption Cathedral, Moscow Kremlin*
Below left: *Vitoslavlitsy Museum of Wooden Architecture, Novgorod*
Below left: *Amur tiger at Victor Yudin's reserve, Gaivoron*

RUSSIA

Above: *Novosibirsk carwash, supervised by* babushka (below left)

Below right: *Kazan: Where to now?*

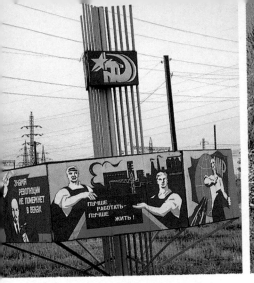

Above left: *Work better, live better!*
Above right: *A roadside grave, Siberia*
Below: *Lenin's great-grandchildren, Ulan Ude*

WORK AND PLAY

Above: *Weaving a wall-bag in a* ger, *Mongolia*

Below: *East meets West: Uzbekistan children, Samarkand*

Chapter Three

In Russia

COMMUNICATIONS

Country telephone code for Russia and the CIS: 7

Mail

Post offices are generally in the town centre and well signed. The postal system is slow, compared with most developed countries. Airmail items take from two to six weeks to reach their destination. We have been warned, many times, not to send articles of any value by mail as they are not likely to arrive; but we have no first-hand experience of this. Letters, cards and small packets sent by us into and out of Russia have, with one exception, eventually reached their destination.

Telephone

Local calls only can be made from call boxes in the street – use *zhetons* (tokens) bought at post offices and metro stations or from your hotel. **Inter-city calls**: dial 8 – wait for dial tone – dial area code and number. **International calls**: dial 8 – wait for dial tone – dial 10 followed by country and area codes and number.

The telephone system varies from good to bad to virtually non-existent. Most tourist-class hotels have satellite phones which send all calls through the USA and are very expensive – US$6–12 per minute.

The cheapest way to make international and inter-city phone calls is at telephone offices which are often attached to the post office but sometimes in a separate building. The counter staff who take your booking usually speak enough English to understand your request. You will have to either fill in a form or, more often, write the number you wish to call on a piece of paper, state how long you want to speak for and pay the cashier. You will then wait for up to an hour or longer for your call, getting increasingly anxious as you try to understand the shouted announcements which come over the loudspeaker telling callers which phone booth to go to. In a few telephone offices there are dial-yourself phones in the booths and you pay after the call – very civilised.

It is possible to call America collect from the CIS by ringing AT&T in Moscow (095) 155 50 42. The same number accepts AT&T phone cards.

Emergency numbers
01   Fire
02   Police
03   Ambulance
04   Gas leaks

Useful numbers
08   Long distance telephone connections
088   Time
09   Directory assistance

Fax
Fax offices are often in the post office but sometimes in the telephone office building. Faxes are expensive mainly because of the poor quality of the phone system. This results in the operator phoning the recipient to ask if the message has been received and is legible and, if necessary, sending it again and again until satisfactory transmission is achieved.

Email
This is probably the cheapest and fastest way to communicate internationally, provided the telephone connection is viable. You will need a special five-point plug to connect to many of the older telephones (difficult to buy outside Russia and the CIS but ask at your local computer software shop) as well as the standard RJ connection for more modern ones. However it can be frustrating if you have problems connecting or the line drops out again and again after you have at last managed to connect. Email is available at many post offices.

There are many service providers across Russia and your home provider will be able to tell you which they recommend. The baud rate changes between cities even if using the same provider. We found Sprintnet satisfactory.

Air connections
There are international flights to USA, Europe, Asia and the rest of the CIS. Internal flights serve most large cities in the Russia Federation.

Roads
In 1994 there were 934,000km of roads, 725,000 sealed, but many of these are impassable in winter. The inclement climate and the great distances between major cities mean that there is comparatively little travel by road outside the towns and cities. However we noticed a great increase in traffic between 1994 and 1996 as more and more Russians drive second-hand Japanese cars from Vladivostok to sell in western

Russia and European cars from the west to sell in Siberia. There is also a big increase in heavy long-haul trucks.

Surprisingly, major road-building programmes are continuing and conditions are improving. For instance between 1994 and 1996 almost every bridge and culvert on the road from Vladivostok to Khabarovsk had been, or was being, renewed or repaired and a major realignment had been completed.

The worst roads, apart from those in northern Siberia, are still those in the cities where potholes and uncovered raised man-holes make driving hazardous. Unmarked lanes on multi-lane highways in the cities are also unnerving.

Railways
These consist of 87,000 route kilometres (49,000km diesel and 38,000 electrified) plus a further 67,000km serving specific industries.

ELECTRICITY

220 volt, standard European two-pin plug.

DRIVING IN RUSSIA
Rules of the road
Drive on the right.

Speed limits are 60km/h (37mph) in town and 90km/h (56mph) in the country which most people ignore unless they can see a GAI (transport police) car. Watch for variations, especially approaching GAI posts: 40km/h then 20km/h, which everyone obeys.

Road signs, when there are any, use international symbols. If in doubt check the back of the *Automobile Road Atlas*, which you bought before you left home (if you were lucky) or in your first CIS city.

It is a criminal offence to drink alcohol and drive.

Once out in the country you will find lay-bys with long ramps which you can use to check under your vehicle and carry out oil changes and minor repairs. Some town security carparks have small ramps.

You must have an international driving permit (see *Chapter One*, page 22). As these permits have a few words of Russian and your photograph, the GAI find them reassuring and will often not bother asking for any other documents.

Road conditions
Driving in Russia and Central Asia is quite an experience. In the bigger cities many of the main roads are wide but the six or eight lanes are unmarked so driving becomes a slalom as people career all over the surface trying to avoid huge uncovered manholes and deep potholes. However, outside the cities the main roads are usually sealed and devoid

of potholes because, until recently, all heavy freight was sent by rail. Regrettably, more and more heavy trucks are doing long-haul runs and the road surfaces are suffering as a result. Once off the main roads between cities the country roads deteriorate and driving conditions can be difficult especially in Siberia.

Railway crossings usually have gates and warning bells but should be taken with care as they can be bone-shakingly rough.

The main Moscow-to-Vladivostok road detours towns. The city centre is usually signposted at the turn-off but then you are on your own. To head for the high-rise buildings seems logical but, more often than not, these are the nine-storey blocks of flats some way out of town – the centre of town is older low-rise architecture. Fortunately people are very friendly and helpful once they have got over their astonishment at seeing a foreign vehicle, often with the steering wheel on the wrong side, and will give you directions – another reason why it's a great idea to have learned a few simple phrases of Russian. Ignore the detailed directions and listen for left, right, go straight, traffic lights, bridge and so on; and you will be surprised how easy it is to follow directions.

Police

Militsiya are the civilian police. They wear grey uniforms and drive around in small jeeps. As usual so much depends on your attitude. We found them generally very helpful in giving directions and allowing us to park in their enclosed yard overnight if there was not a GAI station close by.

GAI are traffic police whose main function is the same as traffic police the world over. Like the Militsiya they have grey uniforms and use small jeeps. Although some GAI posts have closed you will still find them on the outskirts of most towns. Avoid eye contact and you are less likely to be stopped. However, if they wave their lollipop batons at you, pull over. Stay in your car and one of the officers will greet you politely and ask for your *documenti*. Hand over your international driving permit with a smile and what few Russian pleasantries you have learned and they will almost certainly wave you on with the Russian equivalent of 'Have a nice day!'

We heard of fines and demands for bribes by the GAI but never experienced any problems when stopped. It seems they only fine their fellow countrymen. They were also very helpful in giving directions, sometimes even leading us to the hotel and locking up our car for the night. At major GAI posts you may have to enter the office to register.

Transportnaya militsiya are the railway police. They may or may not wear uniform but they usually have an official badge. If you are taking your vehicle by train they are likely to visit you once you have loaded. They will check how much fuel you are carrying and will probably say you are carrying too much. Cover up your jerry-cans, show them your half-empty main tank gauge and then claim you don't understand the problem. Fortunately they don't know about sub-tanks so don't point it out.

They may also insist that you disconnect your battery. This is all for fire safety. It is no good protesting that you use diesel which is not a fire hazard; although it can confuse the issue and they may give up. Generally speaking treat them the way you would any person you suspect may be about to fine you: smile a lot, shrug your shoulders and play dumb, maybe offer them a badge or souvenir from your country or some cigarettes, and you will usually not have to pay anything.

On the train

Until recently there was no road between Chernyshevsk and Svobodny so the trip involved putting your vehicle on to the train and spending several days on a *platforma* (flat-topped wagon). However, a road is being constructed and now only the stretch between Skovorodino and Mogocha is unmade. The road from Skovorodino to Svobodny varies from new tarmac to quagmires to good gravel surface. In 1996 a group of Australians, driving east to west, reached a river beyond Skovorodino, quite close to the Chinese border, but were turned back by Russian border guards. It seems likely that by the end of 1997 it may be possible to drive all the way provided the weather is good. In wet weather you may still need to travel by train for a few hundred kilometres. This is expensive – particularly if you have to have a whole wagon to yourselves. You load first and pay later so make sure you know how much it will cost and have this in roubles. Charges from Skovorodino to Chernyshevsk are around $1,200 per platforma which will hold two 4WD vehicles.

Fuel

The fuel pump symbol shown in the *Automobile Road Atlas* is fairly reliable. Generally there is no shortage of diesel or leaded petrol of various octane ratings but unleaded petrol was not on sale in 1996. Some fuel stations stock only petrol but don't panic; there will be another in the area which has diesel. Keep a logbook so you know how much fuel you need to fill the tank as you have to pay the cashier before filling up – if you over-estimate you can claim the change from the cashier. The diesel pump usually has a Д (D) on it and is also the dirtiest. After paying at the kiosk you will be told which pump to use and the power will be turned on. There is usually a button or lever on the pump which you must press to start the flow – make sure the nozzle is in the tank before pressing the button as there is rarely a working safety release on the nozzle.

Fuel stations were just that – no water, no air, no mechanic – until recently, but now service stations are springing up and some even have cafés and toilets.

Workshops and vehicle agencies

Try to get the addresses of agents for your vehicle before entering Russia. (see *Appendix Two*). Moscow has agents for most makes; and from Irkutsk eastward, Japanese vehicle agencies are appearing. Otherwise you may see signs saying *Remont* Ремонт (repair) over small workshops. Do not scorn these – Russian mechanics are wizards at fixing things.

Security parking

All **Iris Hotels** have safe parking but otherwise it is rarely available at hotels outside the Moscow and St Petersburg areas and the Golden Ring. In larger towns 24-hour security carparks have been set up – these are fenced-off areas in the centre of town, guarded from an office at the entrance. For between $2 and $10 a night your car will be safe. In smaller towns you may be able to leave your car at the GAI compound – it's definitely worth asking their advice.

Often small boys will offer to wash your car – they do a good job for around $4 but may 'souvenir' stickers, so take spares.

CYCLING IN RUSSIA

Two young Australians, Rohan Pigott and Marc Llewellyn, cycled 4,500km from Sevastopol, on the Black Sea in the Crimea, to the Arctic Circle, via Odessa, the Ukrainian steppe to Belarus, and through Lithuania, Latvia and Estonia to St Petersburg ending their adventure in Murmansk in 1996. One of their crazier ideas was to visit all the nuclear power stations along the way – Marc is close to finishing a book about the trip.

Rohan describes some of their adventures in Russia and gives some suggestions on how to avoid trouble:

I heard the rasping engine long before the pale green Lada pulled up beside us and spluttered into a lower gear. Two men in dark wind jackets stared through the grimy windscreen. A third angled his head out of a half-opened passenger window.

'*Skolka stoit, velosipyet!*' he demanded. Marc and I smiled, hoping he would just drive on.

'*Velosipyet, skolka?*' jabbing his finger at my bicycle, still with traces of the packing tape which we used in transporting them from Germany. We were warned before we left that cycling in cities of the former Soviet Union was strictly forbidden and we'd be stopped at the first opportunity.

'Dollar, dollar. One hundred, two hundred?' the man prompted to the sniggers of his mates.

How much for the bikes? I flicked through my phrasebook, '*Sto dollari*'. The men appeared to argue between them and I wondered whether one hundred dollars sounded too much or too little. Above the bickering in the car, the man, who had spoken to us, smiled, mumbled a farewell, and the car sped off, dragging clouds of black smoke in its path.

This conversation became very familiar over the next two months and, though we always understated their value, it was obvious to us that we were seen as immensely wealthy. Western bicycles are rarely seen in the former Soviet Union; the only examples are likely to have been stolen from Germany and sold on the black market. Russians don't cycle for fun. It's the way to get somewhere when the bus or the train doesn't go there. So when Marc and I said we were spending our holiday cycling from Sevastopol in the Ukraine to Murmansk in arctic Russia, a distance of some 4,500km, they generally thought us one nip short of a bottle. The fact that we camped at night and didn't eat meat only confirmed our insanity to all who met us.

A cyclist in this part of the world is somewhat of a novelty and is met with a mixture of intense interest, disbelief and indifference. It is by far the quickest way to get through interminably long queues at border crossings and guaranteed to send your hotel floor-lady into a flap over where to put the bike overnight. You'll also get to see parts of the region most travellers don't, where you can experience the friendliness of a people renowned for their welcoming hospitality.

And there's more good news – much of it is flat. The Russian steppe, spreading over the Ukraine, Western Russia, Belarus and the Baltic States, is a vast tableland of open farmland, golden rape fields, forests and arid plains. North of St Petersburg are the icy lakes and tundra plains of the Kola Peninsula with a few hills to stretch the quadriceps.

Whether you're thinking about a few days' jaunt between towns or a whole cycling odyssey, here are a few tips for making things easier on yourself.

Finding a map any smaller than one which embraces the entire Soviet Union is near impossible. Russian maps are notoriously unreliable because they include streets with different names and roads that aren't there. It was a defensive measure in case they were invaded by the West. We bought several maps in Germany, but they were useful only as a rough guide. The most essential tool, failing fluency in Russian, is a reliable phrase-book. People in villages and towns fell over each other trying to help point us in the right direction. Cycling into the northern Belarusian town of Hrodna (Grodno), we asked a group of men returning from their Club the directions to a hotel. Before long an argument had broken out, maps were drawn and redrawn on old shopping receipts, and fingers pointed in all directions, until eventually one man jumped into his car and instructed us to follow behind.

Start working on your visas early – it may take some time, especially if you plan to visit several countries in the region. This part of the world is only beginning to come to terms with non-package-tour travel, where each day is planned and hotels are booked ahead; and the level of freedom a trans-Russian cyclist requires is not well understood. Though you will be told otherwise by officials and tour operators hoping to make a sale, it is possible to get flexible visas which don't tie you down to any particular arrangements. Lonely Planet's Russian internet site is a useful source of up-to-date information on getting visas.

Take all the gear you need with you, because you can bet it's not available even in the Baltic States or big cities like St Petersburg. We took 'travelling light' a bit too far. We thought we'd make do with one bike pump, a spare inner tube each and a small repair kit. By the end of the first day in the Crimean Mountains I had had two punctures and had discovered our one and only pump didn't work. By the end of the first month all our inner tubes leaked as though they'd been taken with the measles and we had no repair patches left. Fortunately the valves on our tyres were the same as those on Russian cars; so we pushed on by regularly flagging down drivers, who inevitably kept a foot pump in the trunk. Not even in Vilnius, capital of Lithuania and supposed cycling centre of the Baltics, could we find inner tubes to fit.

You will hear a lot about the shocking state of the roads throughout the region. These stories tend to emanate from car drivers who find the regular tyre-changes and axle repairs inconvenient. For the cyclist, however, the potholes, humps and soft edges pose no greater danger than roads at home. After all, you only need a bit of the road and, because car ownership is fairly uncommon, there are fewer cars on the road, though beware the oil-smoke-puffing trucks which prowl the highways and cough at you as they shift down a gear. Travelling at bike-pace, you will have taken the opportunity to inspect the roadside photo-encrusted tombstones of drivers killed in that stretch of the road – a good reminder of why you chose to cycle.

You will also hear monstrous tales, how a friend of a friend had everything stolen, or how a traveller got caught in Mafia cross-fire and another woke up in a Moscow car-park, minus one kidney. Doubtless some of the stories are true but we never came close to being threatened. All the commonsense rules apply here, as in any part of the world where there are obvious inequities of wealth. Don't go around in the latest sporting designs, leave your jewellery at home and dress your bike down – we gave ours a roll in some gravel before we left home.

You'll also need to acquire a taste for vodka or invent a good excuse early on (I began to say I was pregnant, though that didn't wash with some). Hand in hand with warm hospitality is the expectation that you will join your hosts in drinking themselves into a stupor. The fact you have to cycle 80km tomorrow doesn't register as a reason to stay sober tonight – the economies of many former Soviet countries seem to be based upon this principle. May Day in Krasnoarmijs'ke in southern Ukraine was as good a reason as any for the entire village to get plastered. Kola, a young man who was a farmer on his good days, stumbled into us when we stopped to ask directions and demanded we stay the night at his house. Inside his tiny kitchen, chewing on dark bread and cheese, he waved aside our protestations as he pulled the cap off another bottle with his teeth and poured a fourth teacup of vodka. 'You drink tonight and tomorrow I arrive you Murmansk!'

He never did get the point of our trip!

PUBLIC HOLIDAYS
National holidays

January 1–2	New Year
January 7	Russian Orthodox Christmas
January 13	New Year's Day (old Julian calendar)
February 15	Defenders of the Motherland
1st week March	Maslenitsa Day (Blini Day)
March 8	International Women's Day
April 7	World Health Day
1st Sun in April	Geologists' Day
April 22	Lenin Memorial Day (unofficial)
Last Sun in April	World Sister Cities' Day
April/early May	Pashka (Easter)
Week after Easter	Memorial Day
May 1	Holiday of Spring and Labour
May 9	Great Patriotic War Victory Day
May 28	Border Guard Day
Late May	End of school year
June 1	International Children's Day
June 6	Pushkin's birthday
June 12	Russian Independence Day
Last Sun in June	Russian Youth Day
July 20	International Chess Day
2nd Sun in July	Fishermen's Day
Last Sun in July	Navy Day
1st Sun in August	Rail Workers' Day
2nd Sun in August	Builders' Day
Aug 22	Holiday in honour of defeat of 1993 coup
Last Sun in August	Miners' Day
September 1	Knowledge Day – first day of school or next weekday
3rd Sun in September	Forestry Workers' Day
November 7	Anniversary of the October Revolution (unofficial)
November 10	World Youth Day and Militia Day
November 17	International Students' Day
November 19	Rocket and Artillery Forces' Day
December 12	Constitution Day (the 4th constitution)
December 25	Non-Orthodox Christmas Day (not much celebrated)

Regional festivals and holidays

Late February/March	Goodbye Winter Festival, St Petersburg, Petrozavodsk, Murmansk
Last week March	Festival of the North, Murmansk region
April/May	St Petersburg Classical Music Spring Festival
May 5–13	Festival of Moscow States
June 21–July 11	St Petersburg White Nights Festival
June 21–29	St Petersburg Festival of the Arts
Autumn	Moscow International Film Festival
Mid November	St Petersburg Autumn Jazz Festival
December 25–January 5	Russian Winter Festival – most big cities

SHOPPING

Shopping for food is fun now that the days of lengthy bread queues are over. Although shops are much better stocked than they used to be supplies can be erratic. It's a good idea to take batteries, film, video cassettes and other 'luxury' items with you. We take some tinned food, powdered milk, sliced processed cheese (keeps without refrigeration), home-made marmalade and other goodies for when we need a change of diet but mostly shop at markets and local shops along the way.

Street kiosks sell fruit juices, instant coffee, biscuits and cakes besides the inevitable vodka, imported beer, Mars and Snickers bars and bottled soft drinks. In summer there is a plentiful supply of fresh fruit and vegetables – though you would never guess this from the meals supplied in local hotels and restaurants. You can buy fresh vegetables, locally grown fruit, kiwi fruit and bananas from street stalls, as well as from markets, in the towns.

Moscow, St Petersburg and some other big cities have modern Western-style supermarkets where you can buy almost anything – at a price. In smaller cities it's often necessary to visit a number of shops – the butcher, the baker and the grocer. In small towns and villages it is different again. There are often a number of shops but each will have only a selection of goods – a small pile of tinned food, some bottles of vodka and wine, maybe some imported or local cheese, a few Mars bars (the real thing), some shirts and blouses hanging from the ceiling and so on. Eventually you may be lucky and track down what you are looking for. Watch out for 'truck shops' parked on the roadside in small towns and villages – they often have a better selection than conventional shops. The quality of the food is quite good but the variety is very limited.

Throughout Siberia, roadside stalls sell buckets of raspberries, blueberries, mushrooms and other fresh fruit and vegetables very cheaply in season – you have to buy the whole bucketful so keep plastic bags or buckets ready to put your purchases in. Don't worry that you only wanted a kilo, as you can always give some away.

Souvenirs

Museum shops are some of the best places to buy gifts to take home. Although obviously for the tourist market, they are of good quality and not excessively expensive.

It is against the law to take antiques, ancient icons and old medals out of Russia.

FOOD AND DRINK

Food

Russian bread is generally very good and varies from region to region. In summer there is plenty of fresh fruit and vegetables for sale. Fish is usually frozen or dried. Meat is often poor quality but chicken is a fairly safe bet.

Outside the main cities most restaurants serve poorly cooked basic meals – beefsteak (бифштекс), entrecôte (антрекот) and escalope (шницель) which often turn out to be flattened hamburger steak, served with greasy fried potatoes and cucumber and tomato salad. For good quality, well cooked food, you need to eat at home with Russians.

In the Russian Far East, Chinese, Japanese and Korean restaurants make a pleasant change. In Siberia, around Lake Baikal, you can sometimes get fresh *omul* (similar to salmon) and fish soup is a speciality along the rivers. At Iris Hotels you may be served 'red caviar', large red balls of salmon or omul roe, for breakfast and/or dinner.

Look out for local specialities such as pelmeni (пелмени), somewhere between ravioli and small dumplings, and small pies with meat, mushroom and other fillings (пирожок).

Drinks
Beverages
Tea is made very strong in a small teapot and is never served with milk. A little tea is poured into a cup and topped up with boiling water. After you have been given a cup of tea a pot of homemade jam may be thrust at you. As there is no bread in sight this can throw the unsuspecting foreigner. Hopefully you enjoy sweet tea, for you are being invited to stir two or three teaspoonfuls of jam into your cup. Actually it's delicious.

Instant coffee of varying quality is served in many restaurants and tins can be bought in shops and at street stalls and kiosks.

Cartons of fruit juice are on sale in kiosks and street stalls. The inevitable Coca Cola and other bottled soft drinks are available in most places.

Alcohol
Vodka is the favourite spirit and Russians are eager to share theirs with you. They believe that if you follow a slug of vodka with a piece of cucumber, tomato or bread it will take longer to get drunk. Don't believe them – although it does alleviate the hit of the vodka and gives you time to catch your breath before you have to continue the conversation. Vodka comes in various flavours such as pepper, cherry and lemon, as well as straight.

Wine
Russian sparkling wine, known as Russian champagne, is cheap and drinkable, if often rather sweet. In Khabarovsk we bought an Italian Lambrushka to take to our friends' *dacha,* much to their delight. In western Russia and parts of the 'Stans it is possible to buy very pleasant Moldavian and Georgian wine.

Kvas (Квас) is a very slightly alcoholic drink made from fermented rye bread and water. You will see tanks on wheels parked in the street selling glasses of kvas – it's not unpleasant and quite refreshing on a hot day.

Restaurants and cafés

St Petersburg, Moscow, Ekaterinburg, Novosibirsk, Khabarovsk and Vladivostok have many restaurants of varying standards and prices. All the tourist-class hotels have restaurants but it is more fun, and cheaper, to ferret out the places the locals frequent. If you are having a Homestay your hosts will steer you in the right direction.

Small cafés and bakeries on the main streets sell coffee, tea and cakes. They run on a cafeteria system – you queue up to order and pay before taking your purchases over to a shelf around the walls where you stand up to eat. This isn't much help if your need to sit down is greater than your urge for coffee and cake.

In smaller towns there is often only one restaurant and maybe a *stolovaya* (workers' self-service canteen, open to the public). The former is usually in the same building as, or close to, the only hotel while the latter is often near the station or industrial area. Stolovayas are very cheap although the quality of the food is variable – but then the same could be said for restaurants.

Menus are a source of frustration and irritation in restaurants. Usually pale blue carbon copies on flimsy paper, they appear to be quite extensive. After spending what seems like hours deciphering them you find something you understand and try to attract the waiter's attention. Eventually she comes to your table and triumphantly you ask, in your very best Russian, for your choice. *'Nyet!'* she says. Nonplussed, you make a second choice. *'Nyet!'* again. Maybe she then takes pity on you and tells you everything, except one dish, is off and you end up with tomato and cucumber salad, 'hamburger' steak and greasy fried potatoes, grateful not to go hungry!

TIPS AND TIPPING

Russians are very proud people and tips are rarely accepted outside the tourist cities. We took packets of cigarettes (many people smoke), as 'thank you' presents for people who made a special effort to show us the way or to help; but often they were refused with a cheery smile and a wave. In tourist-class hotels tipping is becoming normal practice but service is rarely increasing at the same rate as expectation. Try not to tip unless service is acceptable. Some expensive hotels include a service charge on their bills.

ACCOMMODATION AND CAMPING

Hotels

In Moscow, St Petersburg and other large cities there is a wide range of accommodation varying in price and facilities. In the smaller towns in Siberia there is often only one hotel which will take foreigners – remember you must pay in roubles. They rarely have in-house restaurants but usually there is one close by.

Homestays

These are often the best accommodation at a reasonable price. See *Chapter One*, page 30.

Camping

Generally speaking, campsites, where there are any, are best avoided. They are usually a long way out of town and it may not be safe to leave your gear whilst you go into the city centre. Worst of all, the toilet blocks are often filthy. Russia is full of rivers and streams and, in the country, 'free' camping can be delightful. As long as you are away from villages and main roads you are unlikely to be disturbed. Mosquitoes can be a problem around still water but some lakes are too beautiful to miss. Most of the main roads have wide grassy verges and then belts of trees sheltering crops. Follow a tractor track through the trees and you will often find a pleasant place to camp. For safety reasons do not camp where you can be seen from the road.

If you intend to enter or leave Russia or the CIS through Europe it is a good idea to buy a **Camping Card International** (CCI) from your local automobile club/association before you go. Remember that the card becomes invalid if your club/association membership expires. The CCI is evidence that you have paid a premium for insurance against accidents involving third parties not caused by a motor vehicle. In Europe a CCI can often be used at campsites for registration purposes instead of a passport.

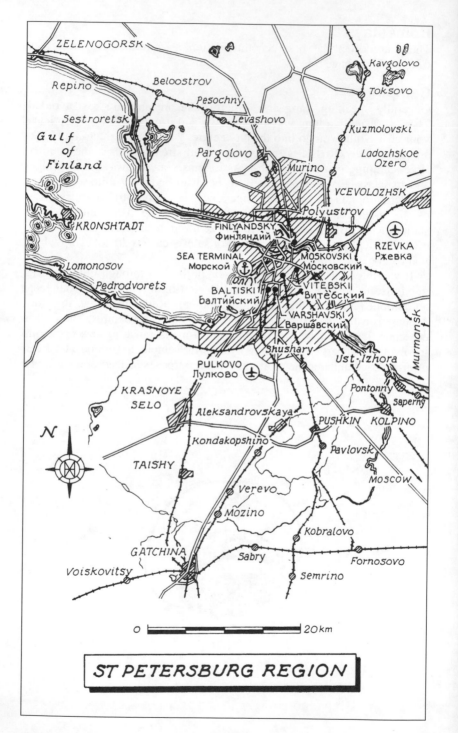

ST PETERSBURG REGION

Chapter Four

Russian Routes

The distances we recorded in our logbook do not always agree with those in the *Automobile Road Atlas*. We have chosen to use the atlas distances here but you should be aware that they are not always accurate.

VYBORG Выборг
Time as Moscow
Population 100,000
Vyborg is the first Russian town reached after crossing the border from Finland. Set on the Gulf of Finland it has mixed antecedents. Dating back to the 13th century, it has been claimed variously by Sweden, Russia and Finland.

Where to stay
Hotel Druzhba, ul Zheleznodorozhnaya 5; tel: (278) 2 47 60

What to see
Vyborg Castle, built on a rock in the bay by the Swedes 700 years ago. Its small museum is worth a visit too. Eighteenth-century Anniskaya Krepost (Anna Fortress), built as a defence against the Swedes and named after Empress Anna Ivanovna, is also of interest.

VYBORG TO ST PETERSBURG

Route M10; distance 141km
Good sealed road

ST PETERSBURG Санкт–Петербург
Time as Moscow
Population 5,000,000
A comparatively young city, St Petersburg has had three name changes in its 300-year history – St Petersburg, Petrograd and Leningrad. Designed by Domenico Trezzini and built by Peter the Great, St

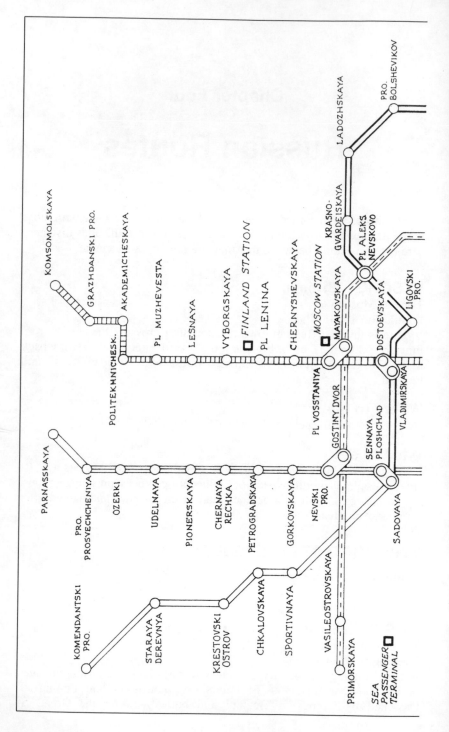

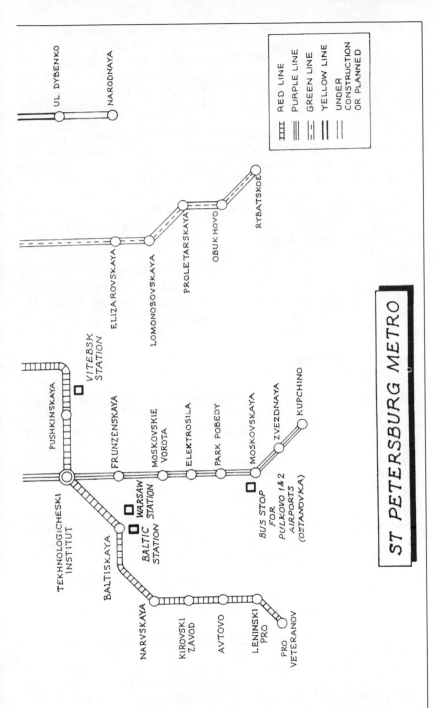

ST PETERSBURG METRO

Petersburg became the capital of Russia in 1712. It was the setting for both the 'Bloody Sunday' uprising in 1905 and the Great October Socialist Revolution of 1917. The German form of the name, St Petersburg, was changed to the Russian, Petrograd, in 1914 at the outbreak of World War I. After Lenin's death in 1924 the name was changed again to Leningrad, reverting to St Petersburg in 1991 by popular vote.

In 1918 the seat of government was returned to Moscow.

Between 500,000 and a million people died from starvation, disease and bombing in what was then Leningrad during the horrific World War II Nazi Blockade which lasted for almost two and a half years.

An attractive mixture of Russian and European architecture, much of which had to be rebuilt after the devastation of the German siege, the city is divided by rivers and canals and spreads across the delta of the River Neva to the Gulf of Finland.

Money

Travellers cheques can be cashed at many banks and tourist hotels. Cash advances on Visa and MasterCard are offered at many banks. The American Express Travel Service is at the Grand Hotel Europe, ul Mikhailovskaya 1/7; tel: 119 6009.

Communications

City telephone code: 812

Mail and fax The main post and telegraph office is at ul Pochtamskaya 9 and there are hundreds of branches around the city. Some of the bigger tourist hotels have their own small post offices some of which will accept parcels and register items.

If you have an American Express card or traveller's cheques you can use the American Express Travel Service office for mail collection – mail is held for 30 days.

Telephone The telephone system is slowly improving. If you are unable to get through any other way, work out what you want to say before you ring and then make a short call on a satellite phone in one of the big tourist hotels – but be warned, the cost is exorbitant!

Air connections There are direct international air services to most European capitals by Aeroflot, Air France, British Airways, KLM and many other airlines. Internal flights serve most large Russian and CIS cities.

Foreign embassy and consulate addresses

Canada pro Malodetskoselski 32; tel: 119 8448; fax: 119 8393
Czech Republic ul Tverskaya 5; tel: 271 0459, 271 6101; fax: 271 4615
Denmark alleya Bolshaya 13, Kameny Ostrov; tel: 234 3755
Estonia ul Bolshaya Monetnaya 14; tel: 233 5548
Finland ul Chaykovskovo 71; tel: 273 7321

France nab Reki Moyki 15; tel: 312 1130, 314 1443; fax: 312 7283
Germany ul Furshtadskaya 39; tel: 273 5598, 279 3207
Latvia ul Galernaya 69; tel: 315 1774
Netherlands pro Morisa Toreza; tel: 554 4890, 554 4900
Norway 21 Vasilevski ostrov 8A; tel: 213 9295
Pakistan ul Sadova Kudrinskaya 17; tel: 250 3991, 254 9791, 230 20143,
254 6877; fax: 254 3965
Poland ul 5th Sovetskaya 12; tel: 274 4318, 274 4170
United Kingdom pl Proletarsky Diktatury 5; tel: 119 6036
United States ul Furshtadskaya 15; tel: 274 8689, 274 8568

Health
A number of sources suggest that tap water in St Petersburg is infected
with giardia lamblia, a very unpleasant infection. Drink only bottled water
and avoid salads and unpeeled fresh fruit.

Where to stay
Inexpensive
Hotel Sputnik, pro Morisa Toreza 34; tel: 552 5632

Expensive
Iris Hotel, ul Ya Gasheka 21, tel: 178 593, fax: 101 3551, is a long way
out of town but not far from the main road to Moscow. It is the usual clean,
comfortable Iris Hotel with pleasant staff. Your car will be safe here and
it's close to the metro so easy to get into the city centre.

Very expensive
Nevski Palace Hotel, Nevski Prospekt 57; tel: 275 2001; fax: 133 1470

Homestays
See *Chapter One*, page 30.

Security parking
Many security carparks and the bigger tourist hotels have their own
parking.

Where to eat
Restaurants and cafés abound in St Petersburg so, if you're spending more
than a day or two on your way through, buy a good guide to the city and
environs. See *Further Reading, Appendix Three*.

What to see
There are so many places of interest it's hard to get back on the road again.
If time is limited, whet your appetite by spending a morning at the
Hermitage, (enter from the river side on Dvortsovaya Naberezhnaya) in
Peter the Great's Winter Palace, which has one of the best collections of
Impressionist art as well as works by Rembrandt, Botticelli, Fra Angelico,
Titian and Leonardo da Vinci and much, much more. Try to find the

magnificent ancient carpet rescued from an icy grave in the Altai Mountains where it had been preserved for 2,000 years. Open: Tue–Sat, 10.30–17.30, Sun 10.30–17.00, closed Mon.

A walk along the Universitetskaya Naberezhnaya at sunset gives a wonderful view of the Winter Palace across the Bolshaya Neva (big Neva river).

Choose a fine summer's day to take a picnic and go by hydrofoil from Ploshchad Dekabristov landing, in front of the Winter Palace, to **Petrodvorets** (Peter's Palace) on the Gulf of Finland. Badly damaged by the German forces in World War II, it has been reconstructed from photographs and drawings and is a fun place to visit. The stroll from the wharf beside the Grand Cascade and Water Avenue, where golden fountains line the canal leading to the Grand Palace, now a museum, is a great introduction to Petrodvorets. Throughout the grounds paths lead to more waterworks, many designed by Peter the Great himself – a huge chess-board cascade fed by colourful dragons, elegant fountains and trick ones to amuse young visitors. Grounds are open during daylight, the museum buildings open 10.00–20.00 in summer but vary as to closing days. The fountains are turned off from October to April.

Theatres and concert halls
There are over 40 so, again, use your guide to St Petersburg to choose which appeals to you most. Tickets may be difficult to get in the summer as tourist companies buy in bulk but it's worth trying at the theatre or a *kassa* (kiosk) on Nevsky Prospekt. Failing that, you may find a scalper (tout) outside the theatre, though check the validity of the tickets offered (especially as they will be printed in Russian).

ST PETERSBURG TO MOSCOW

Route M10; distance 679km
Good sealed road

NOVGOROD   Новгород
Time as Moscow
Population 240,000
On the main road 173km south of St Petersburg and 506km northwest of Moscow, the walled city of Novgorod (New Town) belies its name, being one of Russia's oldest cities and dating back to the 9th century and the Varangians or Vikings. Divided by the Volkhov River, Novgorod was the provincial capital of the area until St Petersburg was built in the early 18th century. Street names in the city have been changed in recent years. For a list of old and new names see page 270.

Money
The Novobank, Beresta Palace and Intourist hotels will change money.

Communications
Area telephone code: 816 00

Mail The post office is on ul B St Petersburgskaya on the west side of the river, not far from the kremlin.

Telephone The telegraph office, ul Rogalitsa, is on the east side of the river.

Air connections Internal and CIS only, to Moscow, St Petersburg and Kiev.

Where to stay
Inexpensive
Hotel Volkov, ul Zabavskaya 24, tel: 9 24 98/ 7 59 39, is on the left bank. On the right bank are the **Hotel Sadko**, Prospekt Fyodorovsky Ruchey 16; tel: 7 53 66, and the **Hotel Rossiya**, on the river bank with a view of the kremlin.

Moderate
Intourist Hotel, 16 ul Velikaya; tel: 7 30 87/ 7 46 44; fax: 7 41 57, email: root@intour.nov.su; parking under the hotel. It is clean and quite comfortable once you have found your way through the cavernous foyer. Rooms with en suite facilities, telephone and TV. Exchange bureau, left-luggage room, souvenir kiosk, post kiosk, hairdresser, conference hall and restaurant. Tariff includes breakfast.

Expensive
Beresta Palace Hotel, ul Studencheskaya; tel: 3 47 07. It has a swimming pool, tennis court and health club and better service than most.

Campsite
One of the few reasonably clean and well-run campsites in Russia, the **Novgorodsky**, can be found in Savino, a pretty village 10km (6 miles) from the city centre (tel: 7 24 48). It also has motel-type units and a café but is only open in the summer.

Security parking
Available for guests at the Intourist Hotel and the Beresta Palace.

Where to eat
Don't miss the **Detinets Restaurant**, if only for the ambience. Set in the 14th-century Pokrovsky Tower in the kremlin, it is a bit touristy with prices to match but it's certainly unique.

What to see
In the kremlin
The Byzantine **Cathedral of St Sophia**, completed in 1050, is one of the oldest stone buildings in Russia. Open 10.00–18.00, closed Wednesdays and last Monday of the month. The bronze west doors captured from the

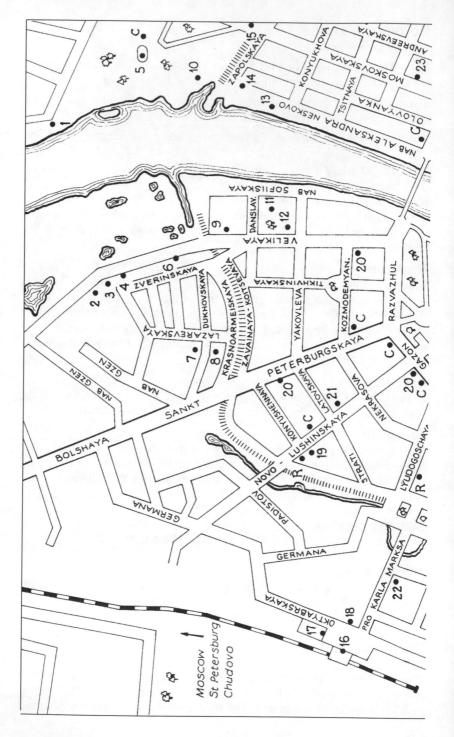

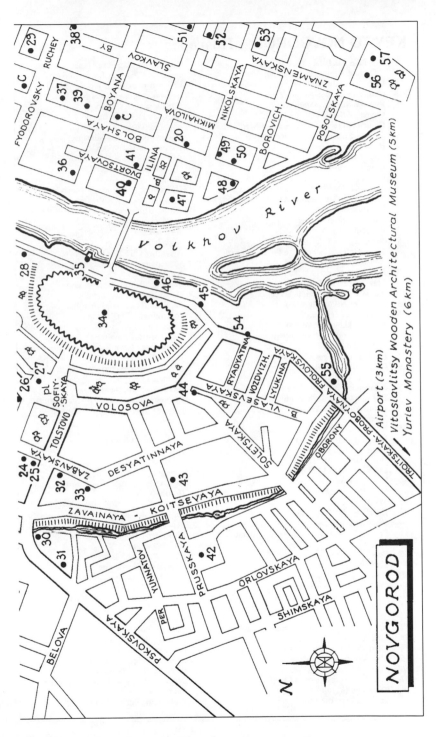

NOVGOROD

KEY TO NOVGOROD   Новгород

1	Hotel Beresta Palace (*Gostinitsa*)	гостиница «Береста Паласе»
2	Church of Simeon Bogopriimets	церковь Симеона Богоприимца
3	Cathedral and Church of Intercession Monastery	собор и церковь Покрова Зверина
4	Church of St Nicholas the White	церковь Николы Белого
5	Elektron Stadium (*Stadion*)	Стадион «Электрон»
6	Church of Saints Peter and Paul	церковь Петра и Павла
7	Church of the Trinity (*Troitsy*) of Spirits Monastery	церковь Троицы
8	Cathedral of Holy Spirit Monastery	Собор Духова монастыря
9	Hotel Intourist (*Gostinitsa*)	гостиница Интурист
10	Church of John the Divine	церковь Иоанна Богослова
11	Drama Theatre (*Teatr*)	Драматический театр
12	Casino	Казино
13	Aleksandr Nevski monument	Памятник Александру Невскому
14	Church of Saints Boris and Gleb	церковь Бориса и Глеба
15	Polytechnic (*Institut*)	Политехнический институт
16	Railway station (*Vokzal*)	Ж-Д вокзал
17	Bus station (*Avtovokzal*)	Автовокзал
18	Aeroflot	Аэрофлот
19	Youth hostel (*Gostinitsa*) at the Institute of Advanced Studies (*Institut*)	гостиница ПУУ в Институте усовершенствования учителей
20	Book shop (*Knigi*)	Книги
21	Church of Fedor Statilat	церковь Федора Стратилата
22	Advance purchase rail ticket office	Предварительная ж-д касса
23	Church of Nikita Muchenik	церковь Никиты Мученика
24	Hotel AZOT (*Gostinitsa*)	гостиница АЗОТ
25	Hotel Volkhov (*Gostinitsa*)	гостиница Волхов
26	Telephone office (*Peregovorny punkt*)	Переговорный пункт
27	Lenin monument	Памятник Ленина
28	Playing area of *gorodki* game	Парк «Городки»
29	Church of Fedor Statilat in Ruche	церковь Федора Стратилата на Ручье
30	Palace of Culture (*Dvorets*)	Дворец культуры
31	Agricultural Institute (*Institut*)	Сельскохозяйственный институт
32	Bus stop to Vitoslavlitsy Museum	Остановка за музей «Витославлицы»
33	Church of the 12 Apostles	церковь Двенадцати Апостолов
34	Kremlin	Кремль
35	Kremlin river pier (*Prichal Kremlya*)	Причал Кремля
36	Hotel Ilmen (*Gostinitsa*)	гостиница Ильмень
37	Church of Kliment	церковь Климента
38	Hotel Sadko (*Gostinitsa*)	гостиница Сакдо
39	Church of Dmitri Solunski	церковь Дмитрия Солунского
40	Vasilev's Palace of Culture (*Dvorets*)	Дом культуры им. Васильева
41	Post office (*Pochtamt*)	Почтамт
42	Market (*Rynok*)	Рынок
43	Hotel Rynok (*Gostinitsa*)	гостиница Рынок
44	Vlasiya Church	церковь Власия
45	Freedom from Fascist Germany monument	Монумент Победы в честь освобождения
46	Beach (*Plyazh*)	Пляж
47	Yaroslav's court	Ярославово дворище
48	Hotel Rossiya (*Gostinitsa*)	гостиница Россия
49	Church of the Archangel Michael	церковь Микаила Архангела
50	Church of Annunciation on the Market	церковь Влаговещения на Торгу
51	Church of the Saviour and Transfiguration on Ilin	церковь Спаса Преображения на Ильине
52	Apparition of the Virgin Monastery (*Znamenski*)	Знаменской монастырь
53	Church of Apostle Phillip	церковь Филиппа Апостола
54	Church of the Trinity (*Troitsy*)	церковь Троицы
55	Church in Bronnits village	церковь в Бронницах
56	Church of Ilya Prorok	церковь Ильи Пророка
57	Church of Saints Peter and Paul	церковь Петра и Павла на Славне
R	Restaurant (*Restoran*)	Ресторан
C	Café (*Kafé*) or Bar (*Bar*)	Кафе или Бар

Swedes in the 12th century, with their tiny biblical scenes, are fascinating. The 15th-century belfry has an interesting selection of bells on the ground as well as in the tower.

The 15th-century **Valdichny Dvor** (Archbishop's palace) is notable for two reasons. It was here that Ivan the Terrible murdered many nobles who refused to obey his orders; the Gothic **Chamber of Facets** houses a magnificent collection of religious icons from the region.

The **Millennium of Russia Monument** is a huge bronze sculpture erected in 1862 to commemorate the 1,000th anniversary of the arrival of the Varangian Prince, Rurik.

Around Novgorod

The **Museum of Wooden Architecture**, 5km (3 miles) south of town near Yuriev, has a selection of beautiful wooden churches and houses from the region. Unfortunately you can only enter one or two but it's still worth a visit and is a pretty place to picnic. Open 10.00–18.00, closed Wednesdays.

NOVGOROD TO MOSCOW

Route M10; distance 506km
Good sealed road

MOSCOW Москва
Time GMT +3 hours
Population 9,000,000

Founded in 1147 by Yuri Dolgoruky, Prince of Suzdal, Moscow has a long and often violent history. Dominated by the Tatars from the 13th century, when Ghengis Khan's grandson, Batu, sacked the city, it was not until the 16th century and the reign of Ivan the Great that Moscow stopped paying tribute to the Golden Horde. Over the centuries the city was invaded by Tatars, Poles, Cossacks, French and Germans but it was the horrific fires, which burnt much of Moscow to the ground on numerous occasions, that inflicted the worst damage. Despite this a number of beautiful 15th- and 16th-century buildings survive.

The capital city for centuries, Moscow was displaced in 1712 when Peter the Great moved the court and seat of government to St Petersburg where it remained until Lenin reinstated it after the revolution of 1917.

Money

Major credit cards are accepted at most tourist hotels and stores. ATMs are on the increase and some will give you US dollars if you have Visa, MasterCard or Cirrus Maestro cards. Travellers cheques can be cashed at many banks and tourist hotels. Inkombank Headquarters, ul Mytnaya 16, tel: 230 7335, 230 7124, 230 7353 will tell you which of their branches will give cash advances on credit cards. American Express, ul Sadovaya-

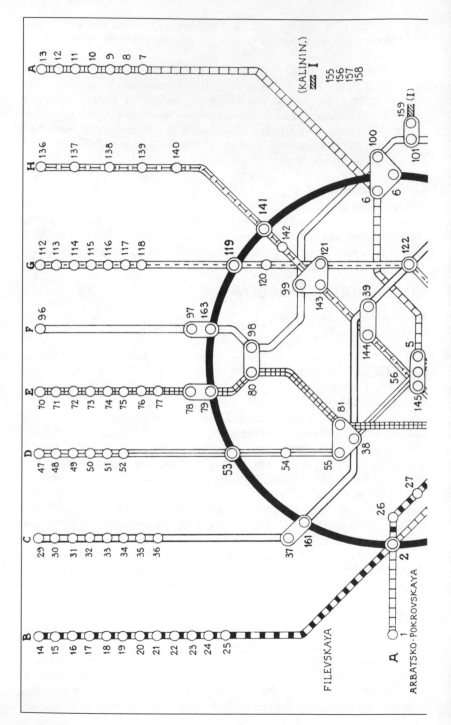

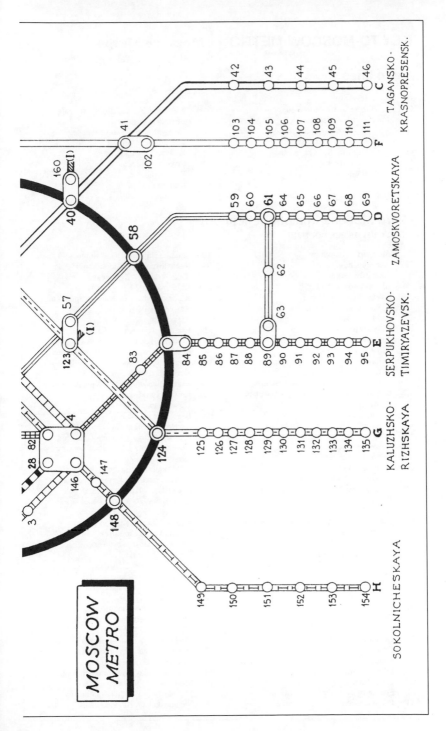

MOSCOW METRO

KEY TO MOSCOW METRO   Москвое Метро

Metro lines

A	Arbatsko-Pokrovskaya	Арбатско-Покровская
B	Filevskaya	Филевская
C	Tagansko-Krasnopresenskaya	Таганско-Краснопресненская
D	Zamoskvoretskaya	Замоскворецкая
E	Serpukhovsko-Timryazevskaya Line	Серпуховско-Тимирязевская
F	Line under construction	Строящиеся линии
G	Kaluzhsko-Rizhskaya Line	Калужско-Рижская
H	Sokolnicheskaya	Сокольническая
I	Kalininskaya	Калининская
J	Circular	Кольцевая

Metro stations in alphabetical order
Note: (nb) means not built

51	Aeroport	Аэропорт
127	Akademicheskaya	Академическая
28	Aleksandrovski Sad	Александровский сад
117	Alekseevskaya	Алексеевская
70	Altufevo	Алтуфьево
94	Anino (nb)	Анино
4	Arbatskaya	Арбатская
27	Arbatskaya	Арбатская
158	Aviamotornaya	Авиамоторная
59	Avtozavodskaya	Автозаводская
113	Babushkinskaya	Бабушкинская
22	Bagrationovskaya	Багратионовская
37	Barrikadnaya	Баррикадная
7	Baumanskaya	Бауманская
35	Begovaya	Беговая
53	Belorusskaya	Белорусская
131	Belyaevo	Беляево
71	Bibirevo	Бибирево
146	Biblioteka Lenina	Библиотека им. Ленина
135	Bitsevski Park	Битцевский Парк
111	Borisovo (nb)	Борисово
82	Borovitskaya	Боровицкая
115	Botanicheski Sad	Ботанический сад
110	Brateevo (nb)	Братеево
81	Chekovskaya	Чеховская
137	Cherkizovskaya	Черкизовская
90	Chertanovskaya	Чертановская
143	Chistye prudy	Чистые пруды
100	Chkalovskaya (nb)	Чкаловская
52	Dinamo	Динамо
76	Dmitrovskaya	Дмитровская
162	Dobryninskaya	Добрынинская
67	Domodedovskaya	Домодедовская
97	Dostoevskaya (nb)	Достоевская
103	Dubrovka (nb)	Дубровка
8	Elektrozavodskaya	Электрозаводская
21	Filevski Park	Филевский парк
23	Fili	Фили
149	Frunzenskaya	Фрунзенская
11	Izmailovskaya	Измайловская
10	Izmailovski Park	Измайловский парк
95	Kachalovo (nb)	Качалово
63	Kakhovskaya	Каховская
130	Kaluzhskaya	Калужская
64	Kantemirovskaya	Кантемировская
61	Kashirskaya	Каширская
2	Kievskaya	Киевская
122	Kitai-Gorod	Китай-Город
60	Kolomenskaya	Коломенская
141	Komsomolskaya	Комсомольская
132	Konkovo	Коньково
104	Kozhukhovskaya (nb)	Кожуховская
108	Krasnodonskaya (nb)	Краснодонская
68	Krasnogvardeiskaya	Красногвардейская
161	Krasnoprosnenskaya	Краснопресненская
140	Krasnoselskaya	Красносельская
142	Krasnye vorota	Красные ворота
102	Krestyanskaya Zastava (nb)	Крестьянская Застава
147	Kropotkinskaya	Кропоткинская
17	Krylatskoe	Крылатское
19	Kuntsevskaya	Кунцевская
6	Kurskaya	Курская
24	Kutuzovskaya	Кутузовская
44	Kuzminki	Кузьминки
39	Kuznetski Most	Кузнецкий мост
126	Leninski prospekt	Ленинский проспект
151	Leninskie gory (closed)	Ленинские горы (закрыт)
144	Lubyanka	Лубянка
107	Lyublino (nb)	Люблино
96	Marina Roshcha (nb)	Марьина Роща
109	Marino (nb)	Марьино
160	Marksistskaya	Марксистская
54	Mayakovskaya	Маяковская
112	Medvedkovo	Медведково
78	Mendeleevskaya	Менделеевская
14	Mitino (nb)	Митино
18	Molodezhnaya	Молодежная
86	Nagatinskaya	Нагатинская

87	Nagornaya Нагорная		125	Shabolovskaya Шаболовская
88	Nakhimovski prospekt		13	Shchelkovskaya Щелковская
	Нахимовский проспект		32	Shchukinskaya Щикинская
155	Novogireevo Новогиреево		157	Shosse Entuziastov
57	Novokuznetskaya Новокузнецкая			шоссе Энтузиастов
79	Novoslobodskaya Новослободская		30	Skhodnenskaya Сходненская
129	Novye Chermushki		3	Smolenskaya Смоленская
	Новые Черемушки		26	Smolenskaya Смоленская
145	Okhotny Ryad Охотный ряд		50	Sokol Сокол
124	Oktyabrskaya Октябрьская		139	Sokolniki Сокольники
33	Oktyabrskoe Pole Октябрьское поле		150	Sportivnaya Спортивная
66	Orekhovo Орехово		99	Sretenski bulvar (nb)
72	Otradnoe Отрадное			Сретенский бульвар
148	Park Kultury Парк Культуры		16	Strogino (nb) Строгино
1	Park Pobedy (nb) Парк Победы		25	Studencheskaya Студенческая
58	Paveletskaya Павелецкая		120	Sukharevskaya Сухаревская
105	Pechatniki (nb) Печатники		89	Svestopolskaya Севостопельская
156	Perovo Перово		114	Sviblovo Свиблово
12	Pervomaiskaya Первомайская		40	Taganskaya Таганская
74	Petrovsko-Razumovskaya		56	Teatralnaya Театральная
	Петровско-Разумовская		43	Tekstilshchiki Текстильщики
20	Pionerskaya Пионерская		133	Teply Stan Тёплый Стан
29	Planernaya Планерная		75	Timiryazevskaya Тимирязевская
158	Ploshchad Ilicha площадь Ильичи		123	Tretyakovskaya Третьяковская
5	Ploshchad Revolyutsi		98	Trubnaya (nb) Трубная
	площадь Революции		65	Tsaritsyno Царицыно
163	Ploshchad Suvorova		80	Tsvetnoi bulvar Цветной бульвар
	площадь Суворова		85	Tulskaya Тульская
34	Polezhaevskaya Полежаевская		121	Turgenevskaya Тургеневская
83	Polyanka Полянка		31	Tushinskaya Тушинская
92	Prazhskaya Пражская		55	Tverskaya Тверская
138	Preobrazhenskaya ploshchad		36	ulitsa 1905 улица 1905 года
	Преображенская площадь		136	ulitsa Podbelskogo
128	Profsoyuznaya Профсоюзная			улица Подбельского
41	Proletarskaya Пролетарская		152	Universitet Университет
69	Promzona (nb) Промзона		62	Varshavskaya Варшавская
119	Prospekt Mira Проспект Мира		116	VDNKh ВДНХ
153	Prospekt Verdadskovo		73	Vladykino Владыкино
	Проспект Вернадского		48	Vodny Stadion Водный стадион
38	Pushkinskaya Пушкинская		49	Voikovskaya Войковская
47	Rechnoi Vokzal Речной вокзал		42	Volgogradski prospekt
101	Rimskaya (nb) Римская			Волгоградский проспект
118	Rizhskaya Рижская		15	Volokolamskaya (nb) Волоколамская
93	Rossoshanskaya (nb) Россошанская		106	Volzhskaya (nb) Волжская
45	Ryazanski prospekt		46	Vykhino Выхино
	Рязанский проспект		134	Yasenevo Ясенево
77	Savelovskaya Савеловская		154	Yugo-Zapadnaya Юго-западная
9	Semenovskaya Семеновская		91	Yuzhnaya Южная
84	Serpukhovskaya Серпуховская			

Stations which have changed their names

No.	New Name	Новое название	Old name	Старое название
28	Aleksandrovski Sad	Александровский сад	Kalininskaya	Калининская
55	Tverskaya	Тверская	Gorkovskaya	Горьковская
56	Teatralnaya	Театральная	Ploshchad Sverdlova	площадь Свердлова
65	Tsaritsyno	Царицыно	Lenino	Ленино
117	Alekseevskaya	Алексеевская	Shchervakovskaya	Щербаковская
120	Sukharevskaya	Сухаревская	Kolkhoznaya	Колхозная
122	Kitai-Gorod	Китай-Город	Ploshchad Nogina	площадь Ногина
143	Chistye prudy	Чистые пруды	Kirovskaya	Кировская
144	Lubyanka	Лубянка	Dzerzhinskaya	Дзержинская
145	Okhotny Ryad	Охотный ряд	Prospekt Marksa	проспект Маркса

Kudrinskaya 21A, 103001 Moscow; tel: 956 9000/9004, offers all the usual services; open: 09.00–17.00.

Communications
City telephone code: 095

Mail The main international post office is at Varshavskoe shosse 37A and the main domestic post office is at ul Kirova 26. There are branch offices in most suburbs as well as in the big tourist hotels. If you have an American Express card or travellers cheques you can use the American Express Travel Service office for mail collection – mail is held for 30 days.

Telephone Many hotels have direct dial phones and also satellite phones but beware, calls from the latter cost from US$6 to US$10 per minute so it's easy to run up a huge bill. Phone cards are convenient but also cost more than phoning from a post office. The larger post offices have international lines but often you must wait a long time for your turn.

Fax These can be sent from most big post offices, hotels and business centres.

Air connections There are international flights to and from many countries by Aeroflot, Transaero and major national airlines. Internal flights serve most large cities. Some foreign embassies and companies discourage their employees from using Aeroflot and send them to the Far East and Siberia via Japan or Korea, using Japanese or Korean airlines.

Foreign embassy and consulate addresses
Australia per Kropotinski 13; tel: 956 6070
Austria per Kropotinski 1; tel: 201 7317
Canada per Strokonyushenni 23; tel: 956 6666; fax: 241 9034
China ul Druzhby 6; tel: 143 1540, 143 1543
Finland per Kropotinski 15/17; tel: 246 4027
France ul Bolshaya Yakimanka 45; tel: 236 0003, 237 9034; fax: 237 1956
Germany Embassy: ul Mosfilmovskaya 56, 119285 Moscow; tel: 956 1080; fax: 938 2354. Consulate: Leninski prospekt 95A; tel: 938 2401, 938 24190, 936 2456; fax: 938 2143
Hungary ul Mosfilmovskaya 62; tel: 146 8611
Italy Denezhny per 5; tel: 241 1533
Kazakstan bul Chistoprudny 3A; tel: 208 9852, 927 1836
Latvia ul Chaplygina 3; tel: 925 2707
Lithuania per Borisoglebski 19; tel: 291 2643
Mongolia Embassy: per Borisoglebski 11; tel: 290 6792. Consulate: per Spasopeskovski 7; tel: 244 7867
Netherlands per Kalashny 6; tel: 291 2999
New Zealand ul Povarskaya 44; tel: 956 3579
Norway ul Povarskaya 7; tel: 290 3872/74; fax: 200 1221
Poland ul Klimashkina 4; tel: 255 0017, 254 3621
Turkey Rostovsky per 12; tel: 246 0009/10, 246 1989; fax: 245 6348, 245 6502

United Kingdom nab Sofiyskaya 18; tel: 956 7400
Ukraine ul Stanislavsky 18; tel: 229 3422, 229 1079, 229 3442; fax: 229 3542
United States bul Novinski 19/23; tel: 252 2451

Where to stay

Inexpensive

Hotel Rossia, ul Varvarka 6; tel: 298 54 00; fax: 298 55 41, is very central, close to the Kremlin.

Moderate

Hotel Izmaylova is a huge complex originally built as accommodation for the 1980 Moscow Olympic Games. It is split into six blocks which vary in price. An Australian group recommend it as somewhere safe to leave vehicles while exploring Moscow via the metro. Close to the Izmaylovsky Park metro station.

Expensive

As usual, the **Iris Hotel,** Beskudnikovsky Boulevard 59A; tel: 483 92 15/485 75 81; fax: 485 59 54, is a long way out of town and public transport involves both bus and metro or an expensive private bus ($15 return) from the Hotel Pullman Iris next door.

Very expensive

The plush **Hotel Pullman Iris**, Korovinskoye shosse 10, Moscow 127486; tel: 488 8000; fax 906 0105, is a 5-star hotel with swimming pool, sauna and gym. A courtesy bus for guests runs several times a day into the city centre. Hotel Metropol, Teatralni proezd 1; tel: 927 60 00; fax: 927 60 10 is a short walk from the Kremlin.

Security parking

This is available at the Iris Hotels, Hotel Izmaylova and security carparks throughout the city and suburbs.

Where to eat

If you are travelling east to west you may be desperate enough to visit one of the McDonald's which are springing up all over Moscow. Alas, you will also find Kombis, Taco Bells and Pizza Huts.

There are many restaurants and cafés of varying quality around central Moscow. John Lee recommends the **Bozgulaya Restaurant**, near the Baumanskaya Metro Station on the Arbatsko–Pokrovskaya Line, as having 'the best food we have eaten in Russia (Russian cuisine) at about R130,000 (US$25) per person, including drinks, band and Russian singers – no microphones or amplifiers'.

Kiosks are the cheapest way to eat in Moscow and can be very good – they can also be awful, so look before you order. Look out for *shashlik* and *khachipuri* (a kind of doughnut with cheese filling).

Stolovayas (cafeterias), where most Russian workers eat, are very cheap and the food is variable.

What to see

Even if you have only a limited time in Moscow you must spend a day wandering around Red Square, Lenin's tomb and the Kremlin. The entrance to the Kremlin is past the eternal flame on the far side from Red Square but admission tickets are sold at a cashier's kiosk in the Alexandrovsky Garden on the way. Scalpers hang around the entrance for those who failed to see the ticket kiosk and are too tired or short of time to walk back.

The Kremlin boasts five magnificent cathedrals, the Armoury, now a museum, the Palace of Deputies and the Palace of Congresses and much, much more, all set in attractive and well maintained gardens, so plan to spend at least a day exploring here. A huge statue of Lenin gazes pensively across at the Grand Palace while American, British, German, Japanese and other tourists pose beside the Tsar's majestic cannon or clamber over the broken Tsar Bell. Opening times differ for various buildings and many are closed on Thursday; check before you go.

To bring you down to earth visit the GUM department store, Red Square 3, on your way back from the Kremlin. Here you will find all the big Western names in cosmetics, perfumery and fashion – but the open-air markets in ul Arbat are much more fun.

There are numerous excellent art galleries in Moscow. The Pushkin Museum of Fine Arts, 12 ul Volkhonka, has a great collection of Egyptology as well as an extensive collection of French Impressionists. Open 09.00–17.00, closed Mondays and last Tuesday in the month.

THE GOLDEN RING

A circle of some of the most interesting historic towns in northwest Russia has been nicknamed the Golden Ring and includes Pereslavl-Zalessky, Rostov-Veliky, Yaroslavl, Vladimir and Suzdal, all of which are well worth visiting. Suzdal is, perhaps, the most enchanting.

MOSCOW TO SUZDAL

Route M7 and A113; distance 194km
Take the M7 west out of Moscow to the Vladimir bypass, 165km. The M7 will, one day, be a four-lane highway but is now in varying stages of construction with a few rough bypasses where bridges have yet to be built. Turn north on to the A113 to Suzdal, 29km. Good sealed road.

SUZDAL   Суздаль

Time as Moscow
Population 12,000
A medieval walled city founded in the 11th century, Suzdal is perhaps the most beautiful and least spoilt town in the Golden Ring and well worth diverting from the main road. (It's only 35km north of Vladimir.) In recent years much sympathetic restoration has been undertaken after the neglect of

the previous half century and, if you are lucky enough to be in Suzdal on a fine day when the numerous golden onion cupolas sparkle against the deep blue sky, you will find it hard to keep your finger off your camera button.

Communications
Area telephone code: 09231

Mail The post office is on ul Engelsa, Krasnaya ploshad.

Where to stay
Inexpensive
Likhoninsky Dom, ul Slobodskaya 34; tel: 2 19 01, 2 04 44; a bed and breakfast guesthouse and a pleasant place to stay.

Moderate
For once you must book ahead if you are to stand a chance of staying in one of the delightful *izbas* (wooden cottages) of the **Pokrovsky Sobor** (Intercession Convent); tel: 2 1137, 2 08 89, 2 09 08. Enclosed by a high wall the convent is set in a sweet-smelling herb garden and nuns in black habits wander between the old church and their living quarters. There are rumours that it will close and be returned to the church in the near future. The huge **Main Tourist Complex**; tel: 2 0131, 2 15 30; fax: 2 06 66, has little to recommend it.

Security parking
Your vehicle will be safe at both the Pokrovsky Monastery, parked beside your cottage, and the Tourist Complex in a guarded carpark.

Where to eat
Even if you are not staying at the **Pokrovsky** you can eat there in a delightful restaurant located upstairs in the old chapel. Ask for the local specialities – mushrooms and meat pies baked in clay pots – washed down with Moldavian and Georgian wine or, better still, the local brew, *medovukha*, made from honey.

What to see
The best way to explore Suzdal is on foot with a map. It's not large but there is much to see so you will need at least a day here. The deep blue domes, decorated with golden stars, of the Cathedral of the Nativity of the Virgin will stay in your mind long after you return home, as will the magnificent Golden Gates.

SUZDAL TO EKATERINBURG

Route M7; distance 1,779km
Via Nizhny Novgorod (Gorky), Cheboksary, Kazan and Perm. There is a more direct route from Kazan to Ufa but it is a pity to miss Ekaterinburg (Sverdlovsk).

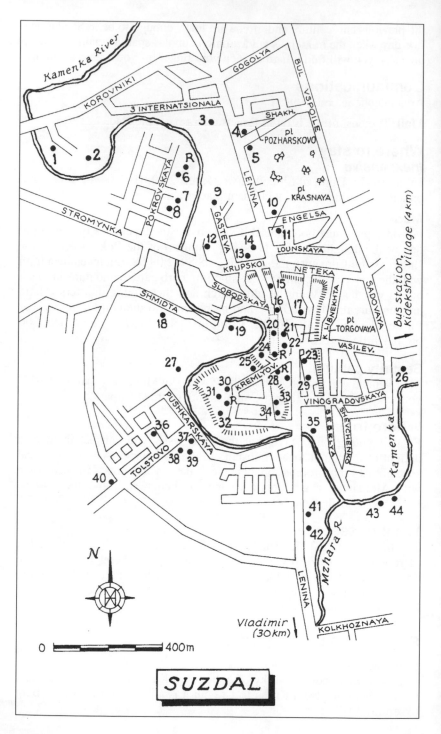

SUZDAL

KEY TO SUZDAL Суздаль

1	MTK Motel	Мотель
2	Main Tourist Hotel (*MTK*)	Главный туристский комплекс
3	Monastery of the Savior and St Euthimius (*Evfimievski*) and five museums (*Muzei*)	Спасо-Евфимиевский монастырь и 5 музеея
4	Our Lady of Smolensk (*Smolenskaya*) Church	Смоленская церковь
5	Posad House of the 18th century	Посадский дом
6	Intercession (*Pokrovski*) Monastery	Покровский монастырь
7	Church of Sts Peter and Paul (*Petropavlovskaya*)	Петропавловская церковь
8	Church of St Nicholas (*Nikolskaya*)	Никольская церковь
9	St Alexander Nevsky (*Aleksandrovski*) Monastery	Александровский монастырь
10	Bank	Банк
11	Post office (*pochtamt*)	почтамт
12	Likhoninsky Dom	Лихонинский Дом
13	Hotel Rizopolozhenskaya (*Gostinitsa*)	гостиница Ризоположенская
14	Monastery of the Deposition of the Robe (*Rizopolozhenski*)	Ризоположенский монастырь
15	Churches of St Lazarus and St Antipius (*Lazarevskaya i Antipevskaya*)	Церкви Лазаре и Антипия
16	Holy Cross Church (*Krestovskaya*)	Крестовская церковь
17	Churches of Emperor Constantine (*Tsarekonstantinovskaya*) and Virgin of All Sorrows (*Skorbyachshenskaya*)	Цареконстантиновская и Скорбященская церкви
18	Church of the Virgin of Tikhvin (*Tikhvinskaya*)	Тихвинская церковь
19	Churches of Epiphany (*Bogoyavlenskaya*) and Nativity (*Rozhdestvenskaya*)	Богоявленская и Рождественская церкви
20	Trading arcade (*Gostiny dvor*)	Гостиный двор
21	Kazan Church	Казанская церковь
22	Resurrection (*Voskresenskaya*) Church and museum (*Muzei*)	Воскресенская церковь и музей
23	Market (*Rynok*)	Рынок
24	Churches of the Entry into Jerusalem (*Vkhodoierusalimskaya*) and St Paraskeva Pyatnitsa (*Paraskeva Pyatnitskaya*)	Входоиерусалимская и Параскева Пятницкая церкви
25	Ascension (*Uspenskaya*) Church	Успенская церковь
26	Monastery of St Basil (*Vasilevski*)	Васильевский монастырь
27	Church of Elijah the Prophet (*Ilinskaya*)	Ильинская церковь
28	Church of St John the Baptist (*Ioanna Predtechi*)	Церковь Иоанна Предтечи
29	Hotel Sokol	гостиница Сокол
30	Cathedral of the Birth of the Mother of God (*Rozhdestva*)	Собор Рождества Богородицы
31	Archbishop's (*Arkhiereiskie*) Chambers and History Museum (*Muzei*)	Архиерейские палаты и Историко-художественный музей
32	Church of St Nicholas (*Nikoly*) from village of Glotovo	Церковь Николы из села Глотово
33	Church of St Nikolas (*Nikolskaya*)	Никольская церковь
34	Nativity (*Khristorozhdestbenskaya*) Church	Христорождестбенская церковь
35	Church of Sts Kosma and Damian (*Kosmodemyanskaya*)	Козьмодемьянская церковь
36	Church of Sts Boris and Gleb (*Borisoglevskaya*)	Борисоглебская церковь
37	Church of the Transfiguration (*Preobrazhenskaya*)	Преображенская церковь
38	Resurrection (*Voskresenskaya*) Church	Воскресенская церковь
39	Museum of Wooden Architecture and Peasant Life of the 18th to the start of the 20th century (*Muzei*)	Музеи деревянного зодчества и крестьянского быта 18-начала 20вв
40	Ivanovskoe village church	Церковь в Ивановское
41	Church of the Deposition of the Robe (*Rizopolozhenskaya*)	Ризоположенская церковь
42	Church of the Sign (*Znamenskaya*)	Знаменская церковь
43	Church of St Michael the Archangel (*Mikhailo-Arkhangelovo*)	Церковь Михайло-Архангелого
44	Church of Flora and Laura	Церковь Флора и Лавра
R	Restaurant (*Restoran*)	Ресторан

Be warned that the routes from and into both Cheboksary and Kazan are confusing. The M7 was not complete in 1996 and truck drivers seemed to be the only people who knew the route. From Suzdal retrace your route until you rejoin the M7. Turn east towards Cheboksary. At Cheboksary cross the Volga River and head for Novocheboksarsk, Krasnogorskii and Zelenodolsk where you meet the M7 again. There are some good camping spots along the Volga.

CHEBOKSARY   Чебоксары
Between the industrial cities of Nizhny Novgorod and Kazan, this is a good place to take a break. Set on the banks of the mighty Volga, Cheboksary has an attractive holiday air about it.

Communications
Area telephone code: 835 0

Where to stay
Moderate
Iris Hotel, pr Traktorostroiteley 10; tel: 26 18 73; fax: 26 52 13, is, as usual, some way out of the town centre. The staff are very friendly and Sergei, the assistant manager, speaks good English.

The **Volzhanka Hotel** is even further out – 17 km from the centre – but it is set in the pine forests of the Taiga with views of the Cheboksary reservoir and islands. It offers swimming, boating and horse riding as well as hunting and fishing trips and shashlik picnics.

Security parking
In the Iris Hotel compound.

What to see
Ask at your hotel about visiting a Chuvash village where you can see traditional arts and crafts. It is also possible to go horse riding in the pine forests and picnic on islands in the Volga.

KAZAN   Казань
Time as Moscow
Population 1,100,000
One of the oldest Tatar cities, Kazan was established in the 13th century and became the capital of the area in the 15th century. It has a long history of invasion and revolt. In more recent times it has other claims to fame; Leo Tolstoy was educated here and Lenin was expelled from Kazan University for his Bolshevik ideas. After the Revolution it became the capital of the Tatar Autonomous Oblast and proudly flies the green, white and red Tatar flag.

Money
There is an exchange bureau in the Hotel Tatarstan.

Communications
City telephone code: 8432

Embassy and consulate addresses
Turkey Consulate General; tel: 643 090

Where to stay
Moderate
Hotel **Tatarstan**, ul Kuybysheva 2; tel: 32 69 79, is the usual unprepossessing concrete monolith so favoured by Intourist; but the rooms are clean, the plumbing works and it has a change bureau.

Security parking
The Tatarstan has parking available after the manager goes home at about 21.00.

Where to eat
The best bet here is the Hotel Tatarstan restaurant and the Vostok restaurant opposite – ask for Tatar dishes.

What to see
The 18th-century twin-towered cathedral of St Peter and St Paul with its highly decorated facade was built in honour of Peter I after his 1722 visit to Kazan. The two museums, the Tatar Regional History Museum, ul Baumana, and the Tatar Folk Art Museum, ul Lenina 2, are worth a visit.

KAZAN TO PERM

From the *Atlas* it would appear that the direct route is northeast from Kazan via Malmizh; but we ran out of road here and a truck driver gave us directions via Vyatskie Polyani and Kizner to Mozhga which were difficult to follow and meant a ferry crossing of the Vyamka River: approx 700km. An Australian group say there is a direct route between Malmizh and Igra but it is 'under construction', very slow and rough – the last 45km before Igra all first and second gear driving: approx 635km.

The better route seems to be to take the Ufa road east out of Kazan. After 215km turn north (left) at Elabuga, continue 98km to Mozhga and then turn northeast for 82km to Izhevsk, then north for 88km to Igra, and then turn east again for 249km to Perm: 732km

PERM   Пермь
Time Moscow +2 hours
Population 1,100,000
Although Perm was not established until 1723, thousands of Bronze Age artefacts testify to much earlier settlement. It is a large industrial city set

in an area rich in minerals on the Trans-Siberian railway close to the Ural Mountains. The Kama River flows along the northern boundary of the city. Professor Alexander Popov, inventor of the wireless, went to Perm University, which was the first university in the Urals.

Money
Permkombank, bulvar Gagarina 65, will cash Thomas Cook and American Express travellers cheques and also give cash advances on Visa and MasterCard.

Communications
City telephone code: 3422

Mail, telephone and fax The main post office and telegraph office is at the corner of ul Lenina and Komsomolsky prospekt.

Where to stay
Inexpensive
Hotel The Urals, ul Lenina 58; tel: 34 44 17, has an unfinished air about it and is the usual monumental grey high-rise. However it is reasonably clean and comfortable.

Security parking
The Urals' staff tell you that the market area beside the hotel is a guarded carpark at night but it is not fenced. A short distance east of The Urals, in ul Kommunisticheskaya, is a high fenced security park.

What to see
The **Ethnographic Museum**, corner of ul Ordzhonikidze and Komsomolsky prospekt, houses the Bronze-Age artefacts excavated on the Turbinski site close to Perm. Open: Tues–Sun: 10.00–18.00.

PERM TO EKATERINBURG

Route no road number; distance 390km
Take the road running southeast via Kungur (Кунгур), 90km, to Ekaterinburg, 300km. About 5km from Kungur is the magical Kungur Ice Cave (Ледная пещера).

EKATERINBURG   Екатеринбург
Time Moscow +2 hours
Population 1,400,000
Ekaterinburg is a large industrial city, best known as the place where the last Tsar and his family were exiled in 1917 and murdered the following year. It was established by Peter the Great in 1721 around the first ironworks which were of great importance as Russia was at war with

Sweden. The following year Peter built a fortress and named the town after his wife, Catherine.

After the revolution, in 1924, Ekaterinburg was renamed Sverdlovsk in honour of the official responsible for the murder of the Romanov family. In 1991 it reverted to its original name.

In May 1960 Sverdlovsk hit the headlines in the West when the American U2 pilot, Gary Powers, was shot down close by.

Ekaterinburg claims to be President Boris Yeltsin's home town, although he was actually born in a village some distance away. It was at his decree that the Romanov house was destroyed in 1976.

Money
Both the Zoloto-Platina Bank, ul Galgarina 14, and the UTA Bank, ul Dekabristov 14, will give cash advances on Visa and MasterCard. The Hotel Tsentralnaya and the Svak-Bank, both in Pokrovsky prospekt, will change money.

Communications
Area telephone code 3432

Mail and fax Main post office, Glavny prospekt, open Mon–Fri 08.00–13.00, 14.00–18.00, Sat 10.00–13.00.

Telephone Office at ul Tolmachyova 24

Air connections International flights go to Italy, Germany, Greece, Kazakstan and Uzbekistan; internal flights serve Moscow, Irkutsk, Novosibirsk, Omsk, Perm, St Petersburg, and Vladivostok.

Consulate addresses
Mongolia ul Fermanova 45; tel: 44 54 53
United States ul Gogolya 15A; tel: 56 46 19, 56 41 91; fax: 56 45 15, 60 11 81

Where to stay
Inexpensive
Hotel Iset, Glavny prospekt 69; tel: 55 69 43, double rooms with private bath. Seen from the distance its quirky architecture shows it is built in the shape of the hammer and sickle.

Moderate
Iris Hotel, ul Bardina 4; tel: 28 91 45/28 44 78; fax: 28 62 92, is some way out of town but is clean, comfortable and welcoming with safe parking and helpful staff. Offers suites of two rooms and bath – tea-making facilities in the corridor.

Hotel Sverdlovsk, ul Chelyuskintsev 106, opposite the railway station; tel: 53 62 61, has quite comfortable rooms with private bath and includes breakfast.

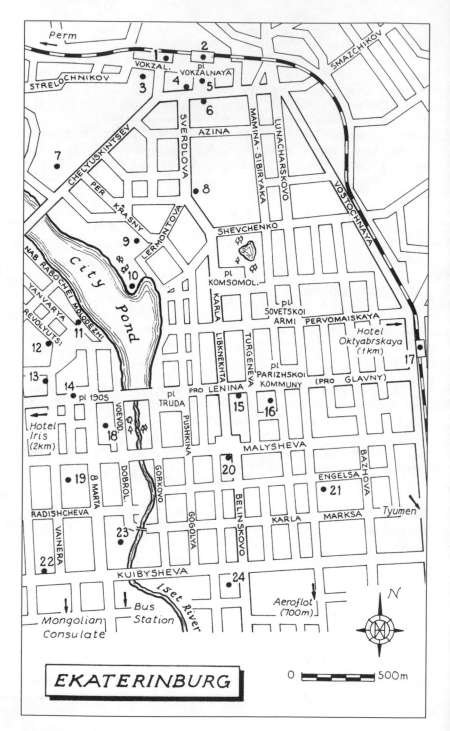

EKATERINBURG

KEY TO EKATERINBURG   Екатеринбург

1	Former railway station built in 1878	Старый железнодорожный вокзал
2	Ekaterinburg railway station (*Vokzal*)	Вокзал
3	Uralskaya metro station	Метро станция «Уральская»
4	Book shop (*Knigi*)	Книги
5	Monument to Ural Tank Corps	Памятник Уральского добровольческого Танкового Корпуса
6	Hotel Sverdlovsk (*Gostinitsa*)	гостиница Свердловск
7	Building of Sverdlovsk region railway (1928)	Управление Свердловской железной дороги
8	Advance purchase rail ticket office	Предварительная ж-д касса
9	Dinamo metro station	Метро станция «Динамо»
10	Stadium Dinamo (*Stadion*)	Стадион «Динамо»
11	Drama Theatre (*Teatr*)	Драматический театр
12	Residence built in the late 1800s	Особняк 19 века
13	Theatrical Institute (*Institut*)	Театральный институт
14	Lenin monument	Памятник Ленину
15	Hotel Yubileynaya (*Gostinitsa*)	гостиница Юбилейная
16	Hotel Bolshoi Ural (*Gostinitsa*)	гостиница Большой Урал
17	Pervomaiskaya suburban railway station	Первомайская ж-д станция
18	Ploshchad 1905 metro station	Метро станция «Площадь 1905г»
19	Museum of Decorative Arts (*Muzei*)	Музей изобразительных искусств
20	Hotel Tsentralnaya (*Gostinitsa*)	гостиница Центральная
21	Former House of the architect Malakhov	Быв. дом Малахова
22	Ural Geological Museum (*Muzei*)	Уральский реологический музей
23	Chapel (*Chasoviya*)	Часовня
24	Former Saint-Trinity Church (*Tserkov*)	Быв. Свято-Троицкая старообрядческая церковь
R	Restaurant (*Restoran*)	Ресторан
C	Café (*Kafe*) or Bar (*Bar*)	Кафе или Бар

Expensive
Probably the best hotel is the **Hotel Oktyabrskaya**, Sofy Kovalevskoi 17; tel: 44 51 46; fax: 44 50 16, in a quiet pleasant neighbourhood about 3.5km from the city centre.

Homestays
Svetlana and Alexander (Sasha) **Voloboyev**; tel: home 51 84 50, are wonderful hosts, who will welcome you as family friends, take you sightseeing, help with repairs, introduce you to family and friends and feed you magnificently in their spacious apartment in downtown Ekaterinburg. Svetlana speaks good English – she's been to Australia several times – and Alexander's English is getting more fluent as more foreigners visit their home. Their two boys, Ulyar, a law student and Nikita, still at primary school, also speak some English. Tariff includes meals and is great value.

Security parking
There are security carparks within easy reach of all hotels.

Where to eat
There are a number of cafés and restaurants in Ekaterinburg – these are just a few suggestions:

Inexpensive
The **Ural Chiken** and the **Cosmos** are good value at around US$8 a head.

Moderate
The **Harbin**, Sibersky prospekt 38, has good Chinese food. The **Hot Chocolate** is very European and serves good food with a Russian flavour.

What to see
A small wooden church was erected on the site of the house where the Romanovs were murdered after the house itself was demolished by the then mayor, Boris Yeltsin, in 1976 when he feared a royalist revival. Today you will often find bunches of flowers placed beside simple crosses on the site, and on July 16 and 17 for the anniversary of the deaths colourful religious memorial services are held there.

You may be able to find a guide who will take you to the well in the forest where the bodies of the Romanovs were first disposed of and then on to their current resting place. These are not tourist sites but if you are genuinely interested contact Svetlana and Alexander Voloboyev.

The remains of the U2 spy plane and equipment are on display in the Dom Officerov.

Set on the bank of the Iset River, the **Museum of Fine Arts** main claim to fame is that it houses the iron pavilion which won first prize in the Paris Exposition of 1900 – very appropriate when you realise that Ekaterinburg's *raison d'être* was its iron industry. The portraits of P A Stroganov, who gave the world Beef Stroganov, and the Polenov portrait of Christ are interesting. Open daily 09.00–17.00.

Don't miss the little **Post Office Museum**, home of writer F M Reshetnikov, ul Proletarskaya 6, which includes a living-room set up as it would have been in the 19th century and a small display of artefacts in the stables. If you are lucky enough to have the vivacious 50-something curator take your tour, she will do a wonderful *Lettice and Lovage* impersonation as she regales you with stories of the past. So exuberant was her body language we felt we understood every word and gesture without the help of our interpreter. Open Sun–Fri 11.00–18.00, closed Saturday.

The 'Europe meets Asia' monument 40km away on the Moscow road has been covered in graffiti and is often strewn with broken glass; but here you can stand with one foot in Europe and the other in Asia if you really want to.

EKATERINBURG TO OMSK

Distance 1,819km
Avoid the very polluted town of Chelyabinsk and take the direct road via Kataisk to Kurgan, 375km, then the M51 to Omsk, 533km. The road passes through Kazakstan briefly between Kurgan and Omsk. Petropavl (Petropavlovsk in *Automobile Atlas*) is in Kazakstan. There were no border formalities here in 1996.

KURGAN
This is a convenient place to break the journey to Omsk. However, the Hotel Moskva was overpriced for small town accommodation, at US$90 for a double room, and there was no secure parking.

PETROPAVL (KAZAKSTAN)
Population 240,000
More Russian than Kazakstani, with Russians making up around 80–90% of the population and showing a strong desire for this small area to become part of Siberia, Petropavl offers an alternative to Kurgan for breaking the journey.

OMSK   Омск
Time Moscow +3 hours
Population 1,300,000
An attractive city, established around 1716 on the west bank of the River Om, Omsk soon became the centre of an extensive agricultural region. By the beginning of the 19th century it was given city status as the regional administrative centre and is now the second largest city in Siberia. Russia's biggest tank manufacturer, Transmash, has its industrial complex here and changed to making tractors in the mid 1990s. Omsk is also the home of a large petrochemical industry.

It was here, in 1849, that Dostoevsky was imprisoned for four years for political crimes and later wrote *Memoirs from the House of the Dead*, or, *Prison Life in Siberia* which tells of his horrific experiences in the prison.

Omsk held out as the White Russian capital during the Civil War until 1919 when the Red Army captured the city.

Communications
Area telephone code: 3812

Where to stay
Moderate
Hotel Marx, beside the Om River, is reasonably comfortable with helpful staff. No parking but the large security lady allows cars to park on the pavement outside the main doors and, for about R17,500 ($3.50), guards them overnight.

Security parking
See above. There are also security parks around the town.

Where to eat
The cellar restaurant near the hotel serves good food and a 'gipsy band' serenades diners.

What to see
Pleasure ferries ply up and down the river. There are two 18th-century forts, the Stary (Old) Krepost and the Novy (New) Krepost, a 19th-century cathedral, and the usual huge war memorial.

OMSK TO NOVOSIBIRSK

Route M51; distance 716km
The M51 is the main road from Omsk to Novosibirsk, via Kuibishev. Until recently the M51 between Omsk and Kuibishev was the worst stretch of road between Moscow and Vladivostok and it paid to take the longer route via Kachiri. However a massive road-improvement programme over the past two years has made the diversion unnecessary. Appearances suggest that two desk-bound bureaucrats planned the Omsk to Novosibirsk M51 route – one from the west, the other from the east. The result was, perhaps, inevitable: the roads failed to meet and there is a gap at Kargat, where they run parallel for a few kilometres.

Alternative route, 809km
A longer route, 809km, is via the M38. Take the M38 for approximately 243km to Kachiri, then turn northeast (left) for another 150km to Karasuk. Continue on this road, now signposted to Novosibirsk, to a T-junction close to the southern reaches of the Ob Sea. Turn north (left) and after 119km the road meets the M51 just west of Novosibirsk. Apart from about 20km of unsealed, potholed road, the condition of this route is good.

KUIBISHEV
An overnight stop in the small town of Kuibishev breaks the journey if you choose the M51 route.

Where to stay
Inexpensive
There is one small hotel in the centre of town. The beds are clean but the en suite bathrooms are dirty and in a state of disrepair – no toilet seats and leaking cisterns. However, the people who run it are friendly and helpful and it's interesting to be completely off the tourist track.

Security parking
None, but the GAI are very helpful and will lock your vehicle in their garage a short walk from the hotel.

Where to eat
The hotel does not have a restaurant but there is one at the back of the building, near a cemented-down aeroplane, which serves the usual tomato salad, 'entrecote' steak, soggy chips and tea or coffee – the waitress was very kind despite being astounded to see us.

What to see
Nothing very exciting but the old wood-and-stone architecture in the main street is worth a photo.

NOVOSIBIRSK Новосибирск
Time Moscow +3 hours
Population 1,500,000
Novosibirsk is the biggest city in Siberia, and the third or fourth largest in Russia, Nizhny Novgorod being the other contender for this honour. It is the link city between the Trans-Siberian and the Turksib railways. Like so many Russian cities Novosibirsk has had several name changes. Originally it was called Novaya Derevnia (New Village) but this only lasted a year before it was renamed Aleksandrovsk after Tsar Alexander III. When he died the following year the new tsar, Nicholas II, changed it to Novonikolaevsk, meaning New Nicholas. Finally, in 1925, it became known as Novosibirsk or New Siberia.

Novosibirsk has a large busy port on the River Ob although it functions only for six months of the year – the rest of the year it is frozen over. Set in an area rich in natural resources, it has become the centre for engineering and metallurgy factories as well as military establishments now converted into manufacturers of electronic consumer goods. All this has been achieved in the 100 years since it began as a settlement for the workers building the railway bridge over the river in 1893.

Money
A number of hotels and banks will change money. Sibirsky Bank, ul Lenina 4, will give Visa cash advances and change Visa travellers cheques. The Mosbusinessbank, on Sovetskaya 18, will give Visa cash advances and cash American Express and Visa travellers cheques. The exchange bureau in the Hotel Sibir will give US$ cash advances on Visa Card and charges 3% commission.

Communications
Area telephone code: 3832

Mail, telephone and fax All are at the main post office on the corner of ul Lenina and Sovetskaya.

Where to stay
Moderate
Iris Hotel, ul Kolkhidskaya 10, tel: 41 01 55, fax: 40 37 37, is closed for some weeks in July/August but the rest of the year has the usual good standard of accommodation – it is some distance out of the city centre.

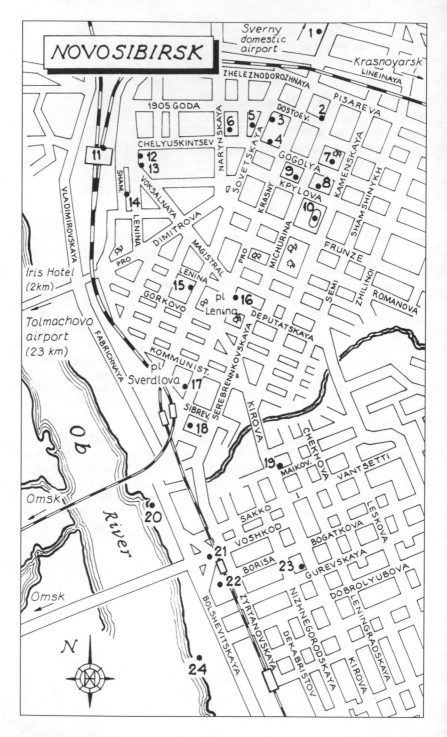

KEY TO NOVOSIBIRSK   Новосибирск

1	Gagarinskaya metro station	«пл Гагаринская» станции метро
2	Café (*Kafé*)	Кафе
3	Advance purchase rail ticket office for Russians	Предварительная ж-д касса
4	Aeroflot	Аэрофлот
5	Cathedral of the Ascension (*Voztsesenski*)	Возцесенский собор
6	Circus (*Tsirk*)	Цирк
7	Zoo (*Zoopark*)	Зоопарк
8	Market (*Rynok*)	Рынок
9	Krasny Prospekt metro station	«Красный проспект» станции метро
10	Stadium Spartak (*Stadion*)	Стадион «Спартак»
11	Railway station (*Vokzal*)	Ж-Д вокзал
12	Ploshchad Mikhailovskovo metro station	«пл Михайловсково» станции метро
13	Hotel Novosibirsk	гостиница Новосибирск
14	Railway ticket office for foreigners travelling within ex-USSR	ж-д касса для иностранецев
15	Central post office (*Pochtamt*)	Почтамт
16	Ploshchad Lenina metro station	«пл Ленина» станции метро
17	Picture gallery (*Galereya*)	Картинная галерея
18	Bus station (*Avtovokzal*)	Автовокзал
19	Ploshchad Oktyabrskaya metro station	«Октябрьская» станции метро
20	Oktyabrski commercial port	Октябрьский порт
21	Rechnoi Vokzal metro station	«Речной вокзал» станции метро
22	Stary Dom Drama Theatre (*Teatr*)	Драматический театр «Старый дом
23	Institute of Communications (*Teatr*)	Электротехнический институт связи
24	River station (*Rechnoi Vokzal*)	Речной вокзал

Expensive

Hotel Sibir, on the corner of ul Lenina and Dimitrova prospekt, tel: 23 12 15, fax: 23 87 66, is centrally located and is the usual big Intourist hotel but with reasonable restaurant and service. Room prices include breakfast.

Otel Tsentr Rossii, Krasny prospect 28, tel: 23 02 22, fax: 23 49 52, is a pleasant small hotel catering mainly for foreign business people.

Homestays

Right in the centre of town on ul Lenina, a young couple, **Tanya and Sergei Chekov**; tel: 22 41 80, give the warmest welcome, the best food and the most comfortable accommodation in their large apartment – they even have a washing machine you can use. Tanya speaks very good English and Sergei's vocabulary is increasing as more foreign visitors discover this home from home. They will help you with visas, car repairs, sight-seeing and even take you out to their dacha, where you can feast on raspberries, red- and blackcurrants in season and freshly dug new potatoes. Tariff includes two meals and is great value.

Security parking

There are many security carparks in and around the city. There's one just around the corner from the Chekovs' flat and another in front of the Hotel Sibir. The Iris has the usual parking arrangements.

Where to eat

There are so many restaurants and cafés in central Novosibirsk that it is best to try whichever takes your fancy.

Inexpensive

Restaurant Druzhba, ul Lenina 5, is open for lunch and dinner and serves good Russian food. There's a great bakery, the **Zolotoy Kolos**, at the top end of ul Lenina which also serves coffee.

Expensive

The restaurant on the ground floor of the **Hotel Sibir** has a selection of dishes and you are welcome whether you want a cup of coffee or a full meal.

What to see

The **Museum of Natural History**, Dimitrova prospekt, is well worth a visit and gives a good overview of Siberian flora, fauna and mineral wealth. A branch museum on Krasny prospekt is devoted to applied art and also worth visiting. The **Picture Gallery**, Krasny prospekt 5; tel: 22 22 67, 23 35 16, has temporary exhibitions often of interest – it's worth checking to see what's on. Open 11.00–19.00, closed Tuesdays.

The Novosibirsk ballet company has a fine reputation and performs at the **Opera and Ballet Theatre**, Krasny prospekt 36; tel: 22 38 66, 29 83 94 – unfortunately the ballet, opera and theatre companies are away touring for most of the summer.

The **Circus**, ul Narynskaya; tel: 23 75 84, performs all year round and is very popular with the local people. (We found the performing bears distressing.)

Around Novosibirsk

Akademgorodok, 35km south of Novosibirsk, was established in the 1950s as a centre of scientific learning. It grew into a self-contained city for academically gifted people and their families. There are several museums – one of the most interesting is the **Geological Museum** which has a world famous mineral collection. Try to arrange a guided tour by the director who has a vast knowledge of mineralogy. On the way to Akademgorodok you will drive past the Ob Sea, the huge reservoir created by damming the Ob River.

NOVOSIBIRSK TO SEMEY (SEMIPALANTINSK) AND KAZAKSTAN

Route M52/A349; distance 666km

Take the M52 south, then turn right on to the A349 after approximately 217km and follow the signs to Barnaul, which is about 12km to the east of the M52. There is a circuitous by-pass around Barnaul and it might be shorter to go through the city centre but unless your Russian is fluent it's probably quicker to follow the signs, such as they are, for Semey. Continue for approximately 437km to Semey. The M52 has a good sealed surface. The A349 is bumpy and corrugated in patches but has only a few potholes. See also *Chapter Six*, Barnaul to Semey, page 188.

BARNAUL   Барнаул
Time Moscow +4 hours
The capital of the Altaysky Krai, Barnaul is a medium-sized city on the Ob River founded in 1739. It is the crossroads between Novosibirsk, the Altai Mountains, Tashanta on the Mongolian border, and Semey. Depending on your planned route it is worth spending a few days exploring the rugged Altai region.

Communications
Area telephone code: 3852

Where to stay
Moderate
Hotel Barnaul, ul Pobedy 9, tel: 25 25 81, has rooms with or without en suite bathroom.

Security parking
Ask at the hotel.

Where to eat
The **Hotel Barnaul** has a restaurant and a buffet.

NOVOSIBIRSK TO IRKUTSK

Route M53; distance 1,860km
Take the M53 to Kemerovo (274km), continue via Mariinsk (170km), to Krasnoyarsk (352km). The M53 continues through Kansk (225km) Nizhneudinsk (325km) and Tulun (123km) to Irkutsk (391km).

KEMEROVO   Кемерово
Where to stay
Inexpensive
Mercury Sanatorium, up in the pine forest away from the city.

What to see
There has been a church-building boom since the demise of communism here in Kemerovo. The small wooden church on the M53 road to Mariinsk is worth stopping to look at.

KRASNOYARSK   Краснояск

Time Moscow +4 hours
Population 1,000,000

Krasnoyarsk, set on the banks of the Yenisei River which rises in Mongolia and flows into the Arctic Ocean, was established as a Cossack fort in the 17th century and is now the centre of a region rich in mineral and forest products.

In the late 19th century Lenin was banished to Siberia and spent some time studying in the library of a merchant called Yudin. In 1906 Yudin sold his magnificent book collection to the American Library of Congress in an attempt to foster a stronger friendship between the two countries.

Until the early 1990s Krasnoyarsk was a closed city – the home of the huge nuclear weapons industry at two satellite cities, Krasnoyarsk-26 and Krasnoyarsk-45. Recently these factories have diversified and the city now produces aluminium, electrical and other manufactured goods, and has a ship-building industry.

Money
Avtovazbank, prospekt Mira, will give cash advances on Visa and MasterCard.

Communications
Area telephone code: 3912

Mail, telephone, fax The main post office and telecommunications office is at ul Lenina 49.

Where to stay
Moderate
Moored at the River Station, the **Mikhail Godenko** hotel-ship, a hotel with a difference, offers accommodation varying from de luxe cabins with en suite shower and toilet to berths in cabins with shared bathrooms.

Expensive
Hotel Krasnoyarsk, tel: 27 37 54, 27 37 69, has rooms with phone, fridge and TV. Overlooking the Yenisei Bridge, it is reasonably comfortable with views over the river. It is being renovated in stages.

Security parking
In front of the Hotel Krasnoyarsk, between the Opera and Ballet Theatre and the river. There are many others around town.

Where to eat
Hotel Krasnoyarsk has a big restaurant as well as several smaller ones which stay open until late. The **Mikhail Godenko** also has a restaurant. The **Kafé Shakhmatnoe** serves sandwiches, salads and coffee and is open

until 20.00. The **Kafé Meteor** on a boat moored beside the ferry stop below the **Hotel Krasnoyarsk** has great views of the fountains in the river.

What to see
There are several museums worth a visit. If renovation is complete, you may be able to go on board the *SV Nikolai*, the paddle steamer which carried its most famous passenger, Lenin, south to exile in Shushenskoe in 1897.

NIZHNEUDINSK Нижнеудинск
About 18km south along the Ude River are the lovely Ukovskiy Falls and a wonderful place to camp. Continue upstream for another 75km and you will find the Nizhneudinskiye Caves, famous for their rock art. A small ethnic group, the Tofalars, live in the Nizhneudinsk area but their village is remote and inaccessible. There is an inexpensive hotel, with a pleasant restaurant next door, in the town, but no security parking anywhere.

IRKUTSK Иркутск
Time Moscow +5 hours
Population 640,000
The city is built on the banks of the Angara River, the only river to flow out of mighty Lake Baikal although 330 or so rivers flow in. Established as another Cossack stronghold in the mid 17th century, Irkutsk has a colourful history. Set close to the Chinese and Mongolian borders, and with its own Buryat tribes in the area, it was a great trading centre where furs and mammoth tusks from Siberia were exchanged for tea and silk from China.

In the 19th century it filled another role as a great place to exile troublemakers such as the Decembrists from Western Russia. The discovery of gold in the 1880s created a wealthy merchant class who were reluctant to embrace the Bolshevik Revolution and, in fact, held out until 1920.

Money
There are many exchange bureaux. The Hotel Intourist bureau, bulvar Gagarina 44, will not give cash advances on credit cards but will cash travellers cheques at a commission of 4%. Be warned: Intourist exchanged dollars at R5,000 to the dollar but converted bills, written in dollars in the restaurant, at the rate of R5,500 and refused to take dollars in payment – a nice little earner for someone. The Russio-Asiatic Bank, ul Lenina 3, will cash American Express and Citycorp travellers cheques.

Communications
Area telephone code 3952

Mail and fax The main post office is on ul Stepana Rozina; it also has a fax office

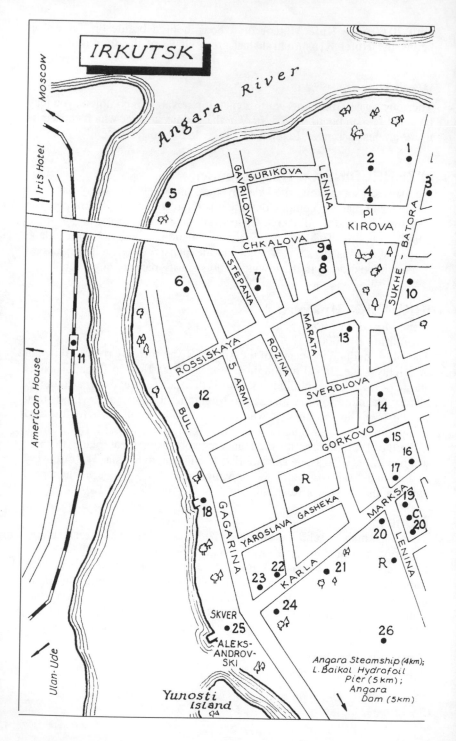

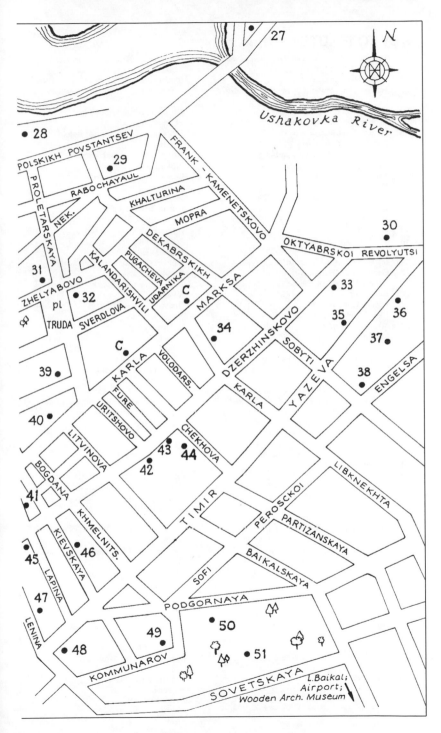

KEY TO IRKUTSK   Иркутск

1	Museum of Local Studies (*Muzei*) in Saviour Church	Краведческий музей-Спасская церковь
2	World War II memorial	Мемориальный комплекс 1941-1945
3	Hall of Organ Music (*Organy Zal*) in Polish Catholic Cathedral	Органный зал-Польский костёл
4	Government headquarters	Правительственный дом
5	River station (*Rechnoi Vokzal*)	Речной вокзал
6	Planetarium (*Planetari*) in the Trinity Church	Планетарий Троицкый церкови
7	Post office (*Pochtamt*)	Почтамт
8	Teaching Institute of Foreign Languages (*Institut*)	Педагогический институт иностранных языков
9	Kirov Square bus stop	Остановка «пл Кирова»
10	Hotel Angara	гостинца Ангара
11	Railway station (*Vokzal*)	Ж-Д вокзал
12	Hotel Intourist	гостиница Интурист
13	Hotel Sibir	гостиница Сибирь
14	Art Museum (*Muzei*)	Художественный музей
15	Youth Theatre (*Teatr*)	Театр юного зрителя
16	Museum of Local Studies (*Muzei*)	Краведческий музей
17	Institute of Economics (*Institute*)	Институт народного хозяйства
18	Gagarin Pier (*Prichal Gagarina*)	Причал Гагарина
19	Former Russia-Asia Bank	Быв. Русско-Азиатский банк
20	Book shop (*Knigi*)	Книги
21	Drama Theatre (*Teatr*)	Драматический театр
22	Irkutsk University (*Universitet*)	Университет
23	White House (*Bely Dom*)	Белый дом
24	Museum of Regional History	Музей Руссково Географического общества
25	Trans-Siberian Builders' Monument (*Obelisk*)	Обелиск строителям Транссибирской магистрали
26	Stadium Trud	Стадион
27	The Apparition of the Virgin (*Znamenski*) Monastery	Знаменский монастырь
28	Icon Museum (*Muzei*) in Epiphany Cathedral	Музей икон-Бороявленский собор
29	Church of Vladimir (*Vladimirskaya*)	Владимирская церковь
30	Bus station (*Avtovokzal*)	Автовокзал
31	Palace of the Pioneers (*Dvorets*)	Дворец пионеров
32	Circus (*Tsirk*)	Цирк
33	Museum – Estate of Trubetskoi (*Muzei*)	Музей-усадьба Трубецкого
34	Synagogue	Синагога
35	Agricultural Institute (*Institut*)	Сельскохозяйственный институт
36	Church of the Transfiguration (*Preobrazhenskaya*)	Преображенская церковь
37	Museum House of Volkonski (*Muzei*)	Музей-усадьба Волконского
38	Former house of Shastin	Быв. дом Шастина
39	Aeroflot	Аэрофлот
40	Exhibition Hall of Art Museum (*Muzei*)	Выставочный зал Художественного музея
41	Mongolian Consulate (*Kulsulstvo*)	Кулсульство Монголии
42	Trade Centre (*Torgovy kompleks*)	Торговый комплекс
43	Former residence of Kuznetsov	Быв. особняк Кузнецова
44	Market (*Rynok*)	Рынок
45	Philharmonic Hall (*Filarmoniya*)	Филармония
46	Former residence of Shubin	Быв. особняк Шубина
47	Musical Comedy Theatre (*Teatr*)	Театр музыкальной комедии
48	Church of the Elevation of the Cross (*Krestovozdvezhenskaya*)	Крестовоздвеженская церковь
49	1917 Revolutionary Monument	Памятник борцам революции
50	Churches of the Entry into Jerusalem (*Vkhodoierusalimskaya*)	Входоиерусалимская церковь
51	Central Park	Центральный парк
R	Restaurant (*Restoran*)	Ресторан
C	Café (*Kafé*) or Bar (*Bar*)	Кафе или Бар

Telephone and fax The telecommunications office is on ul Sverdlova, open 24 hours; but the fax office is only open 08.00–17.00. Hotel Intourist has a small post office on the 2nd floor and an efficient Business Centre on the 3rd where you can make direct dial international phone calls (expensive but convenient) and send faxes.

Email The Hotel Intourist Business Centre on the 3rd floor has very helpful staff. You can collect and send your email here for $3 per connection (if you're staying at the hotel you can use the phone connection in your room if you have a white telephone – if it's red you'll need a Russian plug), use a computer, rent an electronic mail box, and do photocopying.

Consulate addresses
Mongolia ul Lapina 11; tel: 24 23 70, 34 21 45; open Mon–Fri 09.00–18.00

Where to stay
Expensive
Iris Hotel, ul Lermontova 337; tel: 46 25 69; fax: 46 17 62, in the Mikof Eye Hospital compound, is some way out of town on the west side of the river but has the comfort, cleanliness and pleasant staff of all Iris Hotels.

Hotel Intourist, bulvar Gagarina 44; tel: 29 63 35 fax: 27 78 72, is the usual bleak monumental high-rise but is centrally situated with fine views over the Angara River. The service, however, leaves much to be desired.

Security parking
In the compound of the Iris Hotel and public security carparks. Hotel Intourist charges $15 in an open-to-the-street but well-lit carpark in front of the hotel.

Where to eat
Inexpensive
Dragon, ul Pyatoy Armii, serves good Asian food at very reasonable prices. There are a number of cheap cafés – **Niva** serves good coffee but it's a 'stand up' place. For somewhere to relax after sightseeing you can sit and watch Irkutsk go by from the big picture windows of the **Theatre Kafe**, corner of Lenina and Karla Marksa ulitsas.

Expensive
The **Sibirsky Traktir**, in Hotel Intourist, serves indifferent Russian cuisine – if you can persuade the staff to serve you. There is also a Chinese restaurant in the hotel but when we were there it was serving a banquet for a tourist group only.

What to see
Museum of Regional History, ul Karla Marksa 2, has an interesting collection of exhibits and a good souvenir shop. Opening hours Tues–Sun

10.00–18.00. The **Decembrists' Museum**, ul Dzerzhinskovo 64, would be fascinating if information were in English as well as Russian. As one American wrote in the Visitors' Book: 'If you charge tourist prices for foreigners perhaps you should have labels in other languages!' Try to make time to stroll along the river bank, through avenues of trees and planted flowerbeds, in the evening – Irkutsk has some of the best landscaping in Siberia.

EXCURSIONS FROM IRKUTSK

Shishkino   Шишкино

The reason for venturing 200km north of Irkutsk is the Neolithic to Bronze-Age petroglyphs. For more detailed information refer to the second edition of the *Siberian BAM Railway Guide* by Athol Yates. See *Further Reading, Appendix Three.*

Lake Baikal   Оэеро Байкал

This is one of the most beautiful areas of all Russia. The lake holds approximately 20% of the world's freshwater and is 644km (400 miles) long by up to 64km (40 miles) wide. The incredibly clear water is 1,637m (over a mile) deep and is home to hundreds of unique species, including the *nerpa* (freshwater seal) and the strange *golomyanka* fish.

There is concern about pollution from new industrial cities established along the BAM railway in the north, the wood-pulp mill at Baikalsk and industrial waste carried down the Selenga River from Ulan Ude. Conservationists are hoping the lake will be adopted by UNESCO as a World Heritage Site.

There are lovely places to camp on both the east and west sides of the lake – they are not organised campsites so be very careful to take your rubbish away with you.

Listvyanka   Листвянка

From Irkutsk the 65km run to Listvyanka through the forest is enjoyable for itself. If you haven't seen enough wooden architecture museums by now then it is worth stopping at the 47km mark to see the collection of relocated old buildings, dating back two or three hundred years.

The village of Listvyanka nestles between the hills and the lake. Dotted along the shore are wharfs for ferries, tourist boats and research ships. Ship repairs seem to be the main industry but increasing tourism may soon take over as number one.

Where to stay
Expensive
Baikal Hotel; tel: (3952) 29 03 91, 29 62 34, set on the hill above Listvyanka, has panoramic views across the lake to the mountains. It is one of the best tourist-class hotels east of Moscow, with comfortable rooms and

efficient plumbing. Coachloads of tourists come from Irkutsk but the plus of this is that the hotel offers an 'all singing, all dancing' floor show by a group in traditional costume accompanied by a balalaika band. Cheaper places are opening up all the time and there are pleasant (unofficial) camping places along the shore.

Security parking
A boom gate across the road leading to the Baikal Hotel is locked at night and parking is close to the hotel building.

Where to eat
The restaurant at the **Baikal Hotel** serves good Russian/Siberian and European food and very limited snacks are served on the terrace. You will meet the locals at the **Restoran Baikal**, near the hydrofoil terminal, and it is much cheaper.

What to see
Below the Baikal Hotel is the headquarters of the **Baikal Limnological Institute**, a branch of the Russian Academy of Science, which studies the extraordinary aquatic life of the Baikal area. The Institute Museum is open to the public and worth a visit. There are lovely walks over the hills along the lake, with spectacular views.

Boat trips on the lake can be arranged at the wharf or through the Baikal Hotel. The hydrofoil trip to Irkutsk takes an hour through interesting country.

Arshan Buddhist mineral waters spa
To reach this tiny village and Buddhist spa turn off the main M55 road 72km south of Irkutsk on to the A164 road to Mondi, following the Irkum River. After about 80km or so look out for a turn to the right to Arshan. At the spa you can bathe your eyes, drink various mineral waters at various temperatures and tie a ribbon round the tree of your choice. After cleansing the inner you, return to the Mondi road and turn right; a small road just before Zhemchug leads to two bath houses on the banks of the Irkum River where, for a few thousand roubles, you can have a mineral bath at the temperature of your choice. There is free camping (no facilities) close by but try not to negate the benefits of the spa by sharing your friendly fellow campers' vodka as we did.

IRKUTSK TO ULAN UDE

Route M55; distance 448km
Take the M55 round the southern end of Lake Baikal.

There are good camping spots along the southern shores of Lake Baikal off the road to Ulan Ude but you have to try a number of side roads crossing the railway before you find them.

Look out for buckets of raspberries, strawberries and blueberries, in season, along the roadside on the way to Ulan Ude in late July/early August. You have to buy the whole bucketful so have your bucket ready for the transfer.

Camping on eastern Lake Baikal
There are some beautiful camping places northeast of Ulan Ude on the Selenga River delta and others further north, reached by taking the road from Ulan Ude via Nesterovo. Beware of the treacherous wind which can spring up at night if you choose to camp on a bluff.

BURYATIA   Бурятия
The area from the north of Lake Baikal down the eastern side of the lake to the Mongolian border is the home of the indigenous Buryats. In looks very similar to Mongolians, the Buryats have a colourful history. Probably originating in Mongolia and migrating northwards, they claim Genghis Khan's mother came from the eastern shore of Lake Baikal and that the Buryats were part of the Golden Horde. Certainly today there are Buryats living on both sides of the border.

Until the Revolution, Buddhism was the recognised religion and there were around 50 *datsans* (monasteries) and perhaps 150 temples in Buryatia. As in other parts of Russia and the USSR, Stalin violently discouraged Buddhism, along with Christianity and Islam, destroying the datsans and temples. Only the Ivolginsk datsan, on the Ulan Ude to Naushki road, and the Atsagat datsan, 40km east of Ulan Ude, survived.

ULAN UDE   Улан Уде
Time Moscow +5 hours
Population 360,000
Ulan Ude, capital of the Buryat Republic and centre of the Buddhist religion in Russia, is a pleasant city. Approximately 20% of the people are Buryat. Dominating ploshchad Sovietov is a gigantic head of Lenin, giving the impression of a head on a platter.

The Trans-Mongolian line meets the Trans-Siberian railway at Ulan Ude and there is a big railway workshop and locomotive plant here.

Money
Binkombank, ul Tereschkovoi, at the fourth tram stop south from the Buryatia Hotel, will cash Visa or MasterCard travellers cheques and charge 4%. Mosbisnesbanka, ul Lenina 27, and the Buryatia and Geser Hotels have exchange bureaux.

Communications
Area telephone code: 30122

Mail and fax The main post office in ploshchad Sovietov also houses the fax office. Open 09.00–19.00.

Telephone The telegraph office, ul Lenina 105, is the place to make international phone calls. There is often a long wait but there are plenty of seats. Open 09.30 – 21.00.

Consulate

Mongolia 2nd floor, Hotel Baikal, ul Yerbanova 12. The consul is very friendly and has an English-speaking assistant. However, although he can issue Mongolian visas, naturally he has no control over the Russian side of the border. Do not assume that because your Mongolian paperwork is in order and you have a Russian double-entry visa your crossing will be smooth.

Where to stay
Inexpensive
Hotel Barguzin, ul Sovetskaya 28, tel: 2 57 46, is good value and has a stuffed bear in the foyer.

Hotel Baikal, ul Yerbanova 12, was in the process of having a facelift in 1996.

Moderate
The multi-storey tourist-class **Hotel Buryatia**, ul Kommunisticheskaya, 41a; tel: 2 19 02; fax: 6 34 61, took 15 years to build and opened in 1993. The ground-floor public areas are pink and red marble, transported all the way from St Petersburg, and gilt chandeliers hang from the ceilings. Unfortunately the cost of electricity has increased since the break-up of the USSR so sometimes only the light over the reception desk is on, leaving the rest of the foyer in gloom. The rooms are small but have bar fridges, television sets and tiny en suite bathrooms complete with toilet seats and hot (except in August) and cold running water. Very little English is spoken. Does NOT accept credit cards or travellers cheques.

Expensive
Hotel Geser, the old Communist Party hotel, ul Ranzhurova 11; tel: 2 81 51, where the service is friendlier than at the Buryatia, has tiny rooms with even tinier bathrooms which are not worth the more expensive rates. However, it has the advantage of housing the Buryat-Intour office; tel: 2 44 16, 2 69 54, which has English-speaking staff. Contact the Managing Director of Buryat-Intour, Rada-Bairma Jalsaraeva, for help in getting permission to drive into, and out of, Mongolia.

Security parking
A well-run security carpark on ul Sovetskaya, opposite the Buryatia Hotel, is quite close to all hotels.

Where to eat
Inexpensive
A pleasant little café on the ground floor of the **Hotel Baikal** serves tea, coffee and a selection of cakes and open sandwiches.

Moderate
If you need a change from Russian food, the **Seoul**, ul Lenina, ploshchad Sovietov, has good Korean food. The **Geser** restaurant has very loud live music but, if you are in the right mood, it is fun to either join in the uninhibited dancing or at least watch. On special occasions – birthdays or wedding parties – Russians are likely to make lively speeches, recite poems and even burst into song. The two restaurants at the **Buryatia** serve a mixture of Buryat and standard Russian dishes – ask for *poza* (Buryat meat dumplings) – and snacks are sometimes available at the coffee bar. **Café Boolyart**, 33 ul Lenina, is air-conditioned and offers tea and coffee, ice-creams, salads and light meals and a bar.

What to see
The dilapidated **Virgin Hodegetria Cathedral** (1745–85) houses an amazing collection of Buddhist artefacts gleaned from Buryat temples and monasteries closed or destroyed during the Revolution. It is only open to visitors on organised tours so contact Buryat-Intour; tel: 2 44 16, 2 69 54, at the Hotel Geser to arrange one.

The **Troitskaya Church** is a functioning Orthodox Church on the east side of town. Take a tram to ul Kubysheva and walk up the hill past some lovely old apartments and offices.

The **Ethnographic Museum** is one of the best open-air museums in Russia with a big selection of vernacular architecture. The Buryat exhibits include *gers* (yurts), clothing, everyday items and a still for making *kumyss* (fermented mares' milk).

Ivolginsk Datsan   Иволгинск Датсан
The Ivolginsk Datsan, 35km from Ulan Ude at the foot of the Khamar-Daban mountains off the A165 road to Kyakhta, is the centre of Buddhism in Russia. The main temple was built in 1972 and contains hundreds of Buddha images and *tangkas* (icon tapestries) rescued from other temples around the time of the Revolution. Pride of place in the museum beside the temple is given to a beautiful illuminated *Ganjur* (Buddhist scripture) written in Tibetan. The Dalai Lama, spiritual leader of the Gelugpa Buddhists, has visited Ivolginsk in recent years.

Always walk clockwise around Buddhist temples and prayer wheels and have a few coins ready as offerings. A donation to the monastery will be gratefully accepted as there is a vast amount of restoration work to be done in the Buryat area.

ULAN UDE TO THE MONGOLIAN BORDER

Route A165; distance 235km

Take the A165 out of Ulan Ude, past the road to the Ivolginsk Datsan, to Kyakhta if you have permission to drive into Mongolia. If you have to go by train turn right just before Kyakhta to Naushki, 34km. Many road signs from Ulan Ude to the border are in Roman script as well as Cyrillic.

Camping

There are lovely places to camp in woods and flower-strewn meadows between Ulan Ude and the border.

KYAKHTA Кяхта

At the southern end of this small town is the road border with Mongolia but, in 1996, it was not an international border and so was open only to Russians and Mongolians. Still, it's worth a try because the more demand there is, the more likely the rules will change. The only way for foreigners to cross with their vehicles is on the train, which is very expensive and takes days to arrange.

Where to stay

Inexpensive

Try to avoid spending time in this rather dreary border town. However, if you have to wait while trying to get your vehicle across the border there is a fairly awful hotel, the **Hotel Druzhba**, opposite the Militsiya office. Its only advantage is its position, as the Militsiya will put your car in a lock-up garage for you. A better bet is the **Hotel Tourist**, a pretty, traditional wooden cottage with blue shutters on ul Lenina, which has a locked yard to park in for a small fee.

Where to eat

Neither hotel has a restaurant but if you head for the small golden Lenin at the top of ul Lenina and veer right you will find the **Lotus Restaurant** which serves the usual Russian fare but in a pleasant room with a small bar.

NAUSHKI Наушки

The sister town to Kyakhta and the international border with Mongolia. Foreigners can cross here but only on the train. There is a 'guesthouse' in the railway station building, with multiple beds in each room and reasonably clean toilets.

Everybody – not least the very friendly Russians who try to get you across the border – hopes the rules will change in the next few months so that you can drive into Mongolia.

ULAN UDE TO CHITA

Route M55; distance 665km
A pretty road, the M55 runs parallel with the Khulok and Ingoda rivers.
There are good camping places on the river banks.
  It is a good sealed road – but don't trust the kilometre posts, they do not
compute!

CHITA   Чита
Time Moscow +6 hours
Population 370,000
Chita lies very close to Mongolia and China and there is much trade
across the borders. The city was established in the mid 17th century as a
Cossack outpost on the banks of the Chita River when Russia expanded
east. In 1825, after the failed revolution, a group of Decembrists was
exiled here. Later, when their families joined them, the revolutionaries
contributed to the development of the city and it soon became a thriving
commercial and agricultural community.
  Chita is beginning to encourage tourists and the standard of
accommodation and service in most of the hotels and restaurants has
improved greatly in the last two years.

Money
Bank Zabaikalskaya, ul Anokhina 81, will give cash on Visa and cash
travellers cheques. Open Mon–Fri 10.00–15.00.

Communications
Area telephone code: 30222

Mail Post office, ul Butina 37, on ploshchad Lenina

Telephone and fax Telegraph office at ul Chaikovskogo 24

Air connections International flights go to and from Beijing and Harbin;
internal flights serve Moscow.

Where to stay
Some of the hotels seem to cater for Chinese traders laden with huge
parcels of merchandise and show no interest in tourists. However, there is
still a range of hotels which are acceptable.
Inexpensive
The best value for money is probably the **Hotel Ingoda**, ul Profsoyuznaya
23; tel: 3 32 22. The staff are pleasant and helpful, the rooms very small
but clean and the plumbing works.

Close by is the **Hotel Dauria**, ul Profsoyuznaya 17, tel: 6 23 65/6 23 88,
where the receptionist is rude and the Change Bureau НЕ РАБОТАЕТ
(doesn't work).

Moderate
Hotel Oblispolkom, ul Profsoyuznaya 19, tel: 6 23 97, 6 52 70, is better than most, with large clean rooms, plumbing which works and pleasant staff. The only problem is it's often full but it would be worth phoning ahead and making a reservation if you can.

Hotel Zabaikal, Leningradskaya 36, tel: 6 45 20, is centrally located and has had a much needed face lift, inside and out, since 1994. The staff are trying, but are reluctant to end personal phone conversations to deal with tourists.

Security parking
If you are staying at Hotel Zabaikal it's worth asking Administration if you can park in their locked yard overnight. None of the other city hotels has security parking but there are several public security carparks, although they are much more expensive than in most other cities. The carpark in ul Petroskaya has proved safe, despite being close to the railway station.

Where to eat
Inexpensive
Café Tsyplata Tabaka, Ostrovskovo 20, serves a roast chicken set menu. The bar on the second floor of the **Ingoda Hotel** serves light meals such as *pelmeni*, coffee and wine, vodka etc.

Moderate
Restaurant Argun, ul Lenina 65, has a set menu and is one the best of a fairly uninspired bunch but closes at 21.00. Another worth trying is **Café Odessa**, ul Lenina 120, again with set menu and reasonable service.

What to see
The **Officers' Club**, ul Lenina 80, gives an interesting glimpse of Russian entertainment. There are eight full-size billiard tables and a great many chess tables – very noisy as the players punch their clocks every 30 seconds – on the second floor. The bar is open 12.00–23.00 except Mondays. If you have time to kill visit the **Military Museum**, ul Lenina 88, which gives a history of the Soviet Army in the region.

The streets near the station are lined with kiosks and stalls selling just about everything so stock up with bread, fruit and fruit juice as you leave.

CHITA TO CHERNYSHEVSK   Чернышевск

Distance 408km
Take the A166 to Aginskoe (Агинское) and Mogoitui (Могоитуи) where you turn left to Shilka and Nerchinsk. Turn left again to Chernyshevsk.

CHERNYSHEVSK TO SKOVORODINO (Сковородино) BY TRAIN

Time Moscow +6 hours

Until recently there was no road between Chita and Blagoveshchensk (1,730km), but by 1995 a massive road-building programme had shrunk the gap and the road was quite good as far as Chernyshevsk. Before putting your vehicle on the train find out whether the road goes through to Skovorodino.

We have heard of two motorcyclists who, in 1995, rode from Chernyshevsk to Mogocha but then, due to terrible conditions (thick mud), they had to go by train to Skovorodino. In 1996 the road became impassable at Chernyshevsk (408km from Chita) for approximately 700km and all vehicles went by train to Skovorodino which takes about 36 hours. The road from Skovorodino to Taldan was just passable in a 4WD but it may be necessary to stay with the train as far as Taldan if there has been much rain. The 1993 edition of the *Road Atlas* is blank from Mogocha to Skovorodino, indicating no road.

Although it may be possible to book ahead at Chita it is not necessary and within 24 hours of arriving at Chernyshevsk your vehicle should be on a *platforma* (open flat wagon) on the train. The train spends many hours waiting in sidings for passenger and, more important, goods trains to pass and there is no timetable. Do not stray far from the train as it will not wait for you. Think about this before you leave and make suitable food, water and toilet arrangements.

The cost in 1996 from Chernyshevsk to Skovorodino was $510 per vehicle for two on a platforma ($1,020 per platforma) – payment in roubles.

SKOVORODINO TO BIROBIDZHAN AND KHABAROVSK

Distance 1,700km

The 1993 edition of the *Automobile Road Atlas* does not show a road from Skovorodino to Magdagachi but a road-building programme is under way and the road now continues via Taldan. The road is shown as petering out again at Sivaki and not restarting until Mukhino but, in fact, there is a road of sorts all the way from Skovorodino to Svobodny. The roads are not numbered on this route and it is best to follow the 'main' road via Shimanovsk, Svobodny, Blagoveshchensk, Arkhara and Birobidzhan to Khabarovsk.

Road conditions vary from new tarmac to good gravel to ungraded tracks to quagmires where heavy road-building machines are attempting to make a road during the wet summer months.

Travelling east to west there is a GAI post on the western side of the Bureya ferry where all foreign vehicles are stopped, papers checked and details recorded. We assume this is aimed at catching illegal imports from Japan. The officials did not seem to know what to do about us and eventually we were told to carry on without our documents being recorded. Traffic going east was not stopped. From Taldan there are three roads to Skovorodino. Take the one through the town. Do not take the right-hand fork at the beginning of the town to the east (even though locals may direct you that way) as there is a broken bridge 160km from Taldan and if there has been much rain the Unakha River may be too deep to ford. Likewise do not take the road to Albazino as it runs close to the Chinese border and you will be refused entry at a barrier by Russian border guards about 60km from Taldan – only Russian vehicles are allowed to use this route to Skovorodino.

SKOVORODINO   Сковородино
Time Moscow +6 hours
Skovorodino is 33km east of the junction with the BAM railway and 20km west of the Yakutsk highway. Unload here to drive north to Yakutsk and Magadan or east to Khabarovsk.

TALDAN   Талдан
Time Moscow +6 hours
Population 7,000 approx
Taldan has little to recommend it; but if you are driving east to west and arrive during a wet spell you may be forced to spend some time here deciding whether to blow an exorbitant amount of roubles (the equivalent of approximately $1,000 to get to Chernyshevsk – dollars are not acceptable and there is no bank) on getting from here to anywhere else by train, or waiting for the rain to stop and the roads to dry out and/or the rivers to subside – unless, of course, the border guards persuade their superiors to see sense and allow foreigners heading west to pass through the border zone (with China) at Albazino in order to reach Skovorodino.

Taldan is a depressing place made worse if you have driven 60km back from the border where you watched cars you earlier pulled out of bogs drive past you as you tried to persuade the very charming young guards to let you through. It's a waste of time – they cannot, unless their officers give permission and, in our experience, this isn't forthcoming. They admit there is no problem with China but they have their orders.

There is no hotel at Taldan, no café, the stolovaya is closed, the two or three shops don't open until 09.00, but a treat is in store – the *Nova Magazin* sells excellent Belgian chocolate bars and German liqueur chocolates: surely the only luxury in town.

The Station Controller is very helpful but speaks no English so, unless your Russian is good, he may take you to visit an elderly schoolmistress who will translate his instructions and interrogate you to discover whether you have the necessary millions of roubles for the platforma. Even if you do speak Russian, or don't have the roubles, it's worth going to see her in her tiny library – literally walls of books – in her house on the hill. She was in the middle of giving an English lesson to five small boys when we arrived and any English children's books would be gratefully received.

MAGDAGACHI   Магдагачи
Time Moscow +6 hours
Population 20,000
This railway town, at first, seems like any other unprepossessing small town, but if you can find your way to the outwardly depressing hotel you are in for a surprise.

Communications
Area telephone code: 41653

Where to stay
Inexpensive
Hotel Russ, ul Lenina 25a, tel: 97 2 67, has a suite on the third floor which consists of two rooms and en suite bathroom, with no way of getting the water from the tap to the bath and a loo needing a more efficient cistern. However, the bedroom has comfortable beds, the sitting room has two armchairs plus table and tea-making facilities – actually you take the teapot down to the concierge on the ground floor.

Where to eat
The bar and restaurant open at 20.00 so put on what glad rags you may have if it's Friday or Saturday night and be prepared for another surprise. Through a padded door you enter a different world from the depressing small town outside. Excellent food, Moldavian wine and enthusiastic dancing await you in the elegantly furnished room – little curtained booths for four, a bright bar and smart, friendly barman and waiter who, if you're lucky, will ask you to dance between serving drinks and food. Again with luck, Valentina, the managing director of the Russ group of companies, and Vanya, her eight-year-old son, will be there to welcome you. Vanya will make a valiant effort to act as interpreter and the welcome is warm. Valentina owns seven or eight shops in the town and surrounding villages and is an enthusiastic supporter of the new political system.

BLAGOVESHCHENSK   Благовещенск
Time Moscow +6 hours
Population 212,000
On the border with China, at the confluence of the Zeya and Amur Rivers, Blagoveshchensk is the capital of the Amurskaya Oblast. Established in 1856 by the Cossacks, it rapidly became a commercial and administrative centre for the Far East. At this time the Amur valley was Chinese territory

but the Russians, taking advantage of the problems China was having with the British and French in the south, pushed through the Aigunski Treaty, ceding the area north of the Amur River to Russia in 1858. Blagoveshchensk is one of the most pleasant medium-sized towns in the Far East. The wide main street, tree-lined ul Lenina, runs parallel with Krasnoflotskaya promenade along the Amur River; and across the river the Chinese town of Heihe, with its high-rise buildings, looks much like any other modern city. There is much commerce between the cities now, although there have been a number of confrontations in the past including a bloodbath in 1900 when the Russians slaughtered thousands of Chinese in response to the Russian deaths in the Boxer Rebellion.

Communications
Area telephone code: 41622

Mail The main post office is on ul Pionirskaya.

Where to stay
Inexpensive
Hotel Yubileinaya; tel: 2 11 19, is centrally located on Lenin Square. Its restaurant is open only in the evening.

Inexpensive to moderate
Hotel Zeya, ul Kalinina 8, corner of Lenina; tel: 2 11 00, has well-furnished rooms with showers costing $50, while a luxury suite of three rooms, with large fridge, direct dial (Russia only) phones, and bathroom with bath and hot water, is only $10 more. Laundry can be done in 24 hours if you persist.

Security parking
Across a side street next to the Hotel Zeya in a public carpark.

Where to eat
Inexpensive
Kitaiskaya Kukhnya (Chinese), corner of Krasnoarmciskaya and Pionirskaya, owned by Chinese, serves good traditional Chinese food but is only open for lunch.

Café Otdykh, above the Kolosok bread shop at Zeyskaya 106, serves coffee, cakes and pastries.

Hotel Zeya has a stand-up café type buffet on level 4, open 07.00–20.00.

Moderate
The **Zeya** restaurant, in the Hotel Zeya, has rather severe service but quite good food.

The **Pelmeni Restaurant**, Hotel Amur, ul Lenina 122, has a picture of a big black pot on its sign. Good food, pleasant service and, on Friday and Saturday, live music and enthusiastic dancing.

What to see

The **Kraevecheski Museum**, ul Lenina 165; tel: 2 40 86, 2 24 14, is housed in a lovely old building. Natural history is on the ground floor and socio-political history on the first floor. Very good exhibits and friendly helpful staff make it well worth a visit. Open Tues to Sun 10.00–18.00.

Keen birdwatchers should visit the **Muriyovka National Park**, a private (non-government) park famous for cranes and storks.

A ferry runs across the Amur River to China and it may be possible to spend a day in Heihe without a visa.

Jewish Autonomous Oblast

This was set up in 1928 as a 'homeland' to settle the 'Jewish question'. People were sent from the Ukraine and Crimea to the Jewish Autonomous Oblast. By the late 1930s over 34,000 Jewish people had migrated from the west but today only a small percentage of the population claims to be Jewish.

BIROBIDZHAN   Биробиджан

Time Moscow +7 hours
Population 90,000
The capital of the Jewish Autonomous Oblast, Birobidzhan began as a station, Tikhonkaya, on the Trans-Siberian railway in 1912. At the foundation of the JAO in 1928 it became the capital of the region and in 1937 achieved city status. Although over the years many of the original settlers migrated to Israel and other places, the remaining Jews, somewhere between 7% and 10% of the population, have recovered a pride in their race and have started Hebrew schools and cultural organisations.

In June the streets were covered in white fluffy seeds from the poplars lining them.

Communications

Area telephone code: 42162

Where to stay
Moderate

Hotel Vostok, Sholom-Aleikhema 1, tel: 49 2 51. This is one of the best hotels in the smaller towns along the road. It has well furnished suites with large fridge, TV, and bathroom with bath and bidet. The water was warm rather than hot but the welcome was warmer. No English spoken but everyone was very willing to help and we made an international phone call with ease.

Security parking

Ask for directions at the Hotel Vostok.

Where to eat

There are a number of cafés as well as a restaurant in the **Hotel Vostok**. The Vostok has the all-too-often-encountered faint-carbon copy menu which makes deciphering more difficult than usual.

What to see

A room in the **Museum of Local Studies**, ul Lenina 25, illustrates the history of the Jewish Autonomous Oblast. There is a **Yiddish Music and Drama Theatre** and the Intour-Birodbizhan office, Sholom-Aleikhema 55; tel: 6 15 73, should have details of performances. Next to the Hotel Vostok is a big market.

BIROBIDZHAN TO KHABAROVSK

Getting to and from Khabarovsk is not as easy as you might imagine. There is, as yet, no road bridge over the Amur River. Although one is being built it looks as though it will be a few years yet before it opens – it's a massive undertaking over the 2km-wide river. In theory there are big drive-on ferries which leave from the 'ferry terminal' north of the city centre several times a day. Going east to west we arrived at the terminal in time for the 08.00 ferry on a Wednesday to be told no ferries would run again until Friday.

Another driver suggested a 'small ship' might go the following day, if anyone could wake up the skipper, but then a friendly young man beckoned us to follow him and several other cars along a track beside the railway line to where a small engine was pulling about 40 wagons loaded, with vehicles across the bridge. We found the office, paid 321,000 roubles ($60), and eventually left the east bank at midday – the ferry would have cost 25,000 roubles ($4.80), if it ever went.

Travelling west to east you should check at the ferry 'terminal' on the west bank to see if the ferry is functioning. If it's not then go back to the station at Priamurskii where a goods train will be taking vehicles across the rail bridge.

KHABAROVSK   Хабаровск

Time Moscow +7 hours
Population 610,000

A comparatively new town, Khabarovsk was established in 1858, at the confluence of the Ussuri and Amur Rivers, as a military outpost to reinforce the Russian hold on their newly acquired territory. Thirty years later Khabarovsk had become the capital of the Far Eastern Territories. During the 1890s the railway line was built south along the Ussuri River to Vladivostok. Until recently, travellers going east on the Trans-Siberian railway changed trains here to go to the port of Nakhodka because Vladivostok was a closed city.

Khabarovsk is an attractive town with wide tree-lined streets and 19th-century architecture giving it a surprisingly European atmosphere.

Money

Dalcredobank, Hotel Intourist, Amurski Boulevard 2, tel: 33 76 34, will cash travellers cheques and give cash advances in US dollars on MasterCard and Visa but charge 6% fee. Try the Credobank, ul Kim Yu Chena 45; tel: 21 04 06, instead.

Communications
Area telephone code: 4210

Mail The main post and telegraph office is on the corner of Muraveva-Amurskovo and Frunze.

Telephone and fax A smaller telegraph office on ul Sukhe-Batora has very helpful staff doing their best with one of the worst telephone systems in Russia. Send faxes or make calls from here and parking is easy.

Email The Parus Hotel, ul Schevchenko 5, tel: 33 39 30, 33 72 70, fax: 38 88 38, 33 89 26, boasts a Business Centre where you can connect your computer to send and collect email. It also has satellite phones and pleasant staff.

Courier services DHL, ul Muraveva-Amurskovo 4; tel: 33 08 57, 33 09 49, satellite tel: (50901) 600053.

Air connections International: Alaska Air to Alaska, Seattle and San Francisco; Asiana Air to Korea; China Northern Airlines to Harbin; Japan Airlines to Niigata. Internal flights serve Moscow, Kamchatka, Magadan, Sakhalin and Vladivostok.

Embassy and consulate addresses
China Chinese Consulate, Lenin Stadium; tel: 34 85 37, 39 98 90. Open Mon, Tues, Fri, 0.900–12.00

Japan Japanese Consulate, room 208, Hotel Sapporo, ul Komsomolskaya 79; tel: 33 26 23, 33 78 95

United States US and Foreign Commercial Office, ul Turgeneva 69; tel: 33 79 23, 33 69 23

Where to stay
Moderate
Hotel Amur, ul Lenina 29, tel: 33 50 43, 39 43 73, has a *banya* (Russian sauna) – pay in roubles.

Hotel Intourist, Amurski Boulevard 2, tel: 33 76 34, one of the better Intourist hotels in Russia, has a number of shops, an exchange bureau and a fairly good restaurant.

Expensive
Iris Hotel, ul Tikhookeanskaya 211, tel: 72 84 62, is, as usual, a long way from the town centre but very comfortable, with pleasant service. Leave the car here and catch a No 5 tram or a No 8 bus into town at the gate. Your car will be safe here if you leave it while you spend a few days sailing down the Amur River.

Very expensive
There are two pleasant small hotels: the **Sapporo**, ul Komsomolskaya 79, tel: 33 27 02, and the **Parus**, ul Shevchenko 5, tel: 33 39 30, 33 72 70, fax: 38 88 38, 33 89 26, which overlooks the Amur River.

Homestays
These are available with **Mrs Julia Chernjakova**, ul Bluher 10, Flat 19, but try to phone first (can be a problem with Khabarovsk phone system), tel: 21 75 29. Julia, a retired teacher, speaks English and her husband is an engineer. Bluher Street is close to the centre, not far from the river.

Security parking
At the Iris Hotel for 15,000 roubles ($3) per day. There is a security car-park near the Hotel Amur. It may be possible to park in the hotel yard at the Parus – ask the director. Security carparks around the city.

Where to eat
Inexpensive
The **Tower** café, ul Moscovskaya 2a, serves coffee and ice-cream, open 10.00–22.00, closed 16.00–17.00, with great views over the river.

Moderate
For Korean food try the **Seoul**, ul Kicpychni 4a, or the **Phenyan**, ul Karl Marx 108, both reasonably priced.

Café Sapporo, ul Komsomolskaya 77 (don't mistake its expensive sister across the road for this café), has a good atmosphere, pleasant service and interesting menu – definitely the best bet for lunch or a coffee break. Open 11.00–23.00, closed 16.00–17.00. Live music in the evenings.

Very expensive
The **Umihab**, top floor of Intourist Hotel, and **Sapporo**, ul Muraveva-Amurskovo 3 (top floor), are both Japanese restaurants. Food is not exceptionally good, and menu prices at the Sapporo are in yen not roubles. The **Harbin**, ul Volochavskaya 118, serves genuine Chinese food.

What to see
The **Kraevecheski Museum** (Regional History), ul Shevchenko 21, tel: 33 07 83, 33 08 64, gives a good overview of the Far East, including an

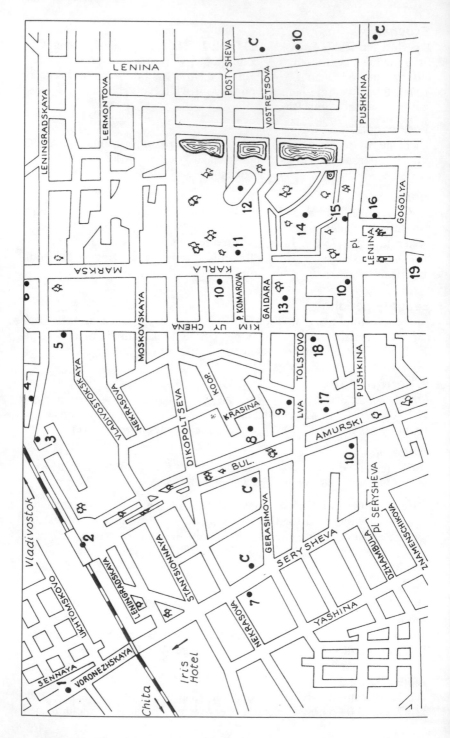

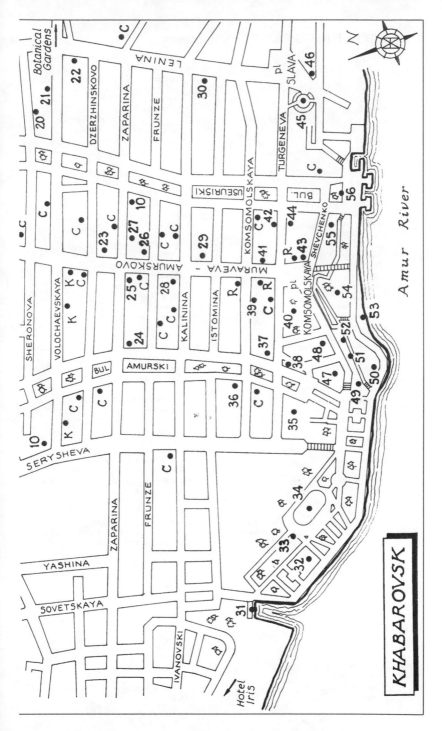

KEY TO KHABAROVSK   Хабаровск

1	Bus station (*Avtovokzal*)	Автовокзал
2	Railway station (*Vokzal*)	Ж-Д вокзал
3	Church	церковь
4	Advance purchase rail ticket office	Предварительная ж-д касса
5	Hotel Zarya	гостиница Заря
6	Hotel Turist	гостиница Турист
7	Far Eastern State Academy of Railway	Дальневосточная государственная академия путей сообщения
8	Hotel Mayak	гостиница Маяк
9	Summer Circus	Цирк
10	Book shop (*Knigi*)	Книги
11	Theatre of Musical Comedy (*Teatr*)	Театр музыкальной комдеии
12	Stadium Dinamo (*Stadion*)	Стадион «Динамо»
13	Gaidar Children's Park	Детский парк им. Гайдара
14	Park Dinamo	Парк «Динамо»
15	Hotel Tsentralnaya	гостиница Центральная
16	Government administration (*Dom Soveta*)	Дом совета
17	Market (*Rynok*)	Рынок
18	Hotel Amethyst	гостиница Аметист
19	Hotel Lyudmila	гостиница Людмила
20	White Theatre (*Teatr*)	Белый театр
21	Hotel Sever	гостиница Север
22	Hotel Amur	гостиница Амур
23	Drama Theatre (*Teatr*)	Театр Драмы
24	Aeroflot International	Аэрофлот
25	Cinema (*Kino*)	Кино
26	Central post office (*Pochtamt*)	Почтамт
27	Stamp shop (*Filatelia*)	Филателия
28	Tainy Remesla art store	Тайны Ремесла
29	Hotel Dalny Vostok	гостиница Далный Восток
30	Geological Museum (*Muzei*)	Геологический музей
31	Yacht club	Яхт-клуб
32	Open air pool (*Bassein*)	Открытный бассейн
33	Chinese Consulate (*Kulsulstvo*)	Китайское Кулсульство
34	Stadium Lenin (*Stadion*)	Стадион «Ленин»
35	Church of St Innocent (*Innokentevskaya*)	Иннокентьевская церковь
36	Aeroflot Domestic	Аэрофлот
37	Youth Museum	Южний музей
38	Literature Museum (*Muzei*)	Литературный музей
39	Hotel Sapparo	гостиница Саппоро
40	Odosa Park	Парк ОДОСА
41	Children's Theatre (*Teatr*)	Молодежный театр
42	Eurasia Trans Inc	Предприятие Eurasia
43	Amur Steamship headquarters	Управление Амурского речного пароходства
44	United States and Foreign Commercial Service Office	Американский Центр
45	Memorial complex of the Second World War	Мемориальный комплекс «Боаевая и трудовая славла»
46	Radio Centre	Дом радио
47	Hotel Intourist	гостиница Интурист
48	Museum of the History of the Russian Far East Military District (*Muzei*)	Музей истории Краснознаменного Дальневосточного военного округа
49	Casino Amur	
50	Tower (*Vyzhka*)	Вышка .
51	Museum of Local Studies (*Muzei*)	Краведческий музей
52	Concert hall (*Zal*)	Концертный зал
53	Beach (*Plyazh*)	Пляж
54	City park	ЦПКиО
55	Conference hall (*Zal*)	Конферекц-зал
56	River station (*Rechnoi Vokzal*)	Речной вокзал
R	Restaurant (*Restoran*)	Ресторан
C	Café (*Kafé*) or Bar (*Bar*)	Кафе или Бар
K	Canteen (*Stolovaya*)	Столовая

exhibit about the Soviet Gulag. Open Tues 12.00–17.00, Wed–Sun 10.00–17.00, closed Monday. The **Geological Museum**, ul Lenina 15, open daily 10.00–17.00, has an interesting display of minerals, including rocks from the moon. The **Military Museum**, ul Shevchenko 20, open 09.00–15.00, closed Monday, traces the history of the Russian army in the Far East.

The **Musical Comedy Theatre** has a season of pantomime – ask Intourist or your hotel for the current programme.

Pick a sunny day for a ferry trip on the Amur River or, if you have time, arrange a longer cruise down the river to visit a Nanai fishing village and see 11th-century rock carvings – remember to take insect repellent. A hydrofoil service runs up the river to Fuyuan in China – you don't need a visa if you return the same day.

There is a hydrofoil service daily to and from Komsomolsk-na-Amure (Комсомольск–на–Амуре).

An enterprising young skipper offers sailing excursions down the Amur. Ask for Gene (Yevgeny) at the Yacht Club or look for Anna at home at ul Kim-U-Chena 9a/131, Khabarovsk (no phone).

KHABAROVSK TO VLADIVOSTOK

Route M60; distance 760km

SAILING DOWN THE AMUR

We loaded our gear and plenty of food and drink on to the 8m fibreglass yacht, *Optimist,* and motored out into the river. There was very little wind but the outboard pushed us along with the help of the current and by lunchtime there was enough breeze to give us a spinnaker run. In June the evenings are long so we sailed until nine o'clock when Gene wound up the retractable keel and slipped the bow gently up on to a sandy beach.

The bank was thick with driftwood and very soon we had a huge fire blazing. Sitting watching the sun set, we drank a toast to the gods of the river in vodka and ate potatoes baked in their jackets while we waited for the fish soup to cook.

The next day Anna showed us some ancient petroglyphs near the Nanai fishing village of Sikacchi-Alyan – reindeer, fish and human faces – said to have been carved into the rocks many centuries BC. The teacher at the school was surprised to see us but delighted to show us the exhibits in the tiny museum.

The following day was Election Day and we visited a polling station in the village school – I don't know why we were surprised to find it was just like an Australian one. We asked if we could take photos and were surprised to be given permission. A few minutes later a door burst open and an elderly man, chest festooned with medals, shouted *'Nyet! Nyet!'* so we apologised and beat a hasty retreat. It was, after all, an area which supported the Communist Party.

It takes much longer to sail up the Amur than down because of the strong current so we shared the local bus back to Khabarovsk with several families. The children slept on their mothers' knees, the women talked quietly, two of the men, who had been celebrating all day, fell into a drunken stupor so did not disturb the other passengers, and everyone insisted the bus driver take us direct to our hotel.

GAIVORON Гаиворон

This is a tiny village west of Spassk-Dalnii where Dr Victor Yudin is studying the magnificent Siberian tiger. He and his wife, Lena, have a breeding pair, Niurka and Koucher, who had two cubs in 1995. Unfortunately Niurka did not produce any milk and one cub died but Victor and Lena hand-reared the other, Globus; he's now thriving and has been taken to Minnesota Zoo. The next litter (three cubs born in 1996) may, in the long term, be returned to the wild if a sanctuary can be found for them. See *National Geographic* 191/2, February 1997.

Victor and Lena can organise homestays in an A-frame cabin with basic facilities, or you can camp in a field behind the house. They can arrange tours to Lake Hanka to see some of the magnificent birds of the Far East, including orange herons but, most importantly, can teach you about the Siberian tiger which is in grave danger of extinction. Telephone first on (252) 7 42 99 but be prepared to persist – the phone is poor and Victor and Lena are often out working with the tigers. If you cannot contact them make sure you are self-sufficient when you call in to see them.

VLADIVOSTOK Владивосток
Time Moscow +7 hours
Population 690,000
The city was established in 1860, shortly after the settlement of Khabarovsk, as part of the push to command the east – even the name Vladivostok is derived from the Russian for 'to rule the East'. Since its inception Vladivostok has been a cosmopolitan place with European and Asian residents, and sailors and traders from around the world visiting the busy port on a regular basis.

It was a bastion of Tsarist support, holding out until 1922, two years after the White Army commander, Admiral Kolchak, was executed in Irkutsk. During the 1920s, Stalin killed and deported thousands of Chinese and in the 1930s a large transit camp was established to hold prisoners on their way to the infamous gulags in the north.

In 1958 Vladivostok, home port of the Pacific Fleet, became a closed city and people travelling on the Trans-Siberian railway had to divert to Nakhodka until 1992 when it was reopened to foreigners. Despite its turbulent history, Vladivostok is an attractive city built on the hills surrounding the Golden Horn Bay and Amursky Gulf.

Money
DalRybBank, in the DalRybVtuz building at ul Svetlanskaya 51a, tel: 26 71 97, fax: 22 89 49, has two automatic teller machines which accept Visa. Credobank, ul Aleutskaya 6, on floor 2, Maritime Terminal, tel: 22 22 64, 22 49 54, will give cash advances in dollars/roubles on Visa. Inkombank, ul Semenovskaya 26, will give cash advances on credit cards.

Communications
Area telephone code: 4232

Mail The main post office is on the corner of Morskaya and Verkhenortovaya, near the railway station.

Telephone and fax All the expensive hotels have satellite phones – at a price.

Email The Commercial Pacific Business Centre, ul Svetlanskaya 115, 4th floor; tel: 269 590, 266 372; fax: 266 372; email: cpl/vlad.wood and cpl@sovam.com. They also have an office in the grounds of the Vlad Motor Inn; tel: 215 871, 310 212; fax: 310 212. The company can arrange interpreter services, send faxes and arrange car hire.

Courier services DHL, Khabarovskaya 27 B, Floor 3; tel: 25 52 26, 25 52 52.

Media *Vladivostok News*, English-language newspaper, published weekly.

Air services International: Aeroflot has services to Japan and Korea; Korean Air to Seoul; Alaska Airlines to Anchorage and Seattle, via Magadan. Internal flights serve Moscow, Khabarovsk, Kamchatka, Magadan, Sakhalin and Yakutsk.

Embassy and consulate addresses
Australia ul Uborevicha 17, floor 4; tel: 228 628; fax: 228 778. Hon Consul General: Vladimir Dmitryevich Gavriluk.

Japan ul Mordovtseva 12; tel: 267 502/ 513/ 481, satellite phone: 7 50985 11001; fax: 267 541. Consul General: Hideki Asahi. Visa applications: Mon, Tues, Thurs, Fri 10.00–12.00

Where to stay
Moderate
Hotel Vladivostok, ul Naberezhnaya 10, tel: 22 22 08, has expansive views over the Amursky Gulf but is often full and is pretty run-down. One floor is reserved for foreigners but don't expect any service – they won't call you to the phone or even take a message for you.

A little farther up the road, on the opposite side, the **Hotel Amursky Zaliv**, ul Naberezhnaya 9, tel: 22 55 20, nestles into the cliffs. The rooms are clean and have small en suite bathrooms. Reception is below street level.

Expensive
Top of the range and very expensive, the **Hotel Versailles** (pronounced Ver-sah-les), ul Svetlanskaya 10, tel: 26 40 57, fax: 26 51 24, is housed in a sumptuously restored pre-Revolution building but don't expect service to match. However, if you have driven west to east – and have a

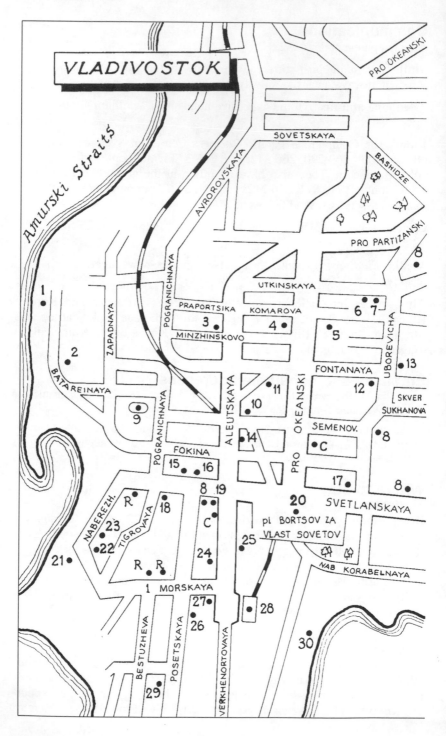

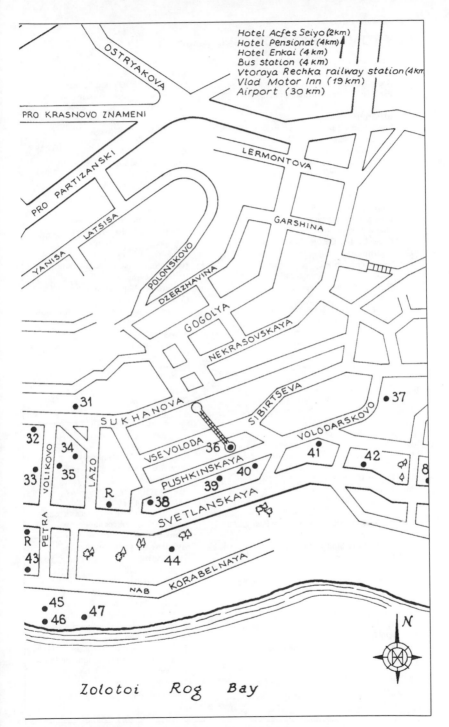

Hotel Acfes Seiyo (2km)
Hotel Pensionat (4km)
Hotel Enkai (4 km)
Bus station (4 km)
Vtoraya Rechka railway station (4km)
Vlad Motor Inn (19 km)
Airport (30 km)

Zolotoi Rog Bay

KEY TO VLADIVOSTOK   Владивосток

1	Oceanarium	Океанария
2	Beluga whales (*Kita*)	Кита
3	South Korean Consulate (*Kulsulstvo*)	Кулсульство Южной Кореи
4	Far East Business Institute (*Institut*)	Дальневосточный коммерческий институт
5	Market (*Rynok*)	Рынок
6	Former ecclesiastical council building (*Konsistoriya*)	Быв. духовная консистория
7	Former residence of Langelit	Быв. особняк Лангелитье
8	Book shop (*Knigi*)	Книги
9	Dinamo Stadium (*Stadion*)	Стадион «Динамо»
10	Border Guard Museum (*Muzei*)	Музей «Пограничников»
11	Japanese Consulate (*Kulsulstvo*)	Кулсульство Японии
12	Australian Consulate (*Kulsulstvo*)	Кулсульство Австраилии
13	Radio Centre (*Dom Radio*)	Дом радио
14	Hare Krishna restaurant	ресторан для вегетарианцев
15	Drama Theatre (*Teatr*)	Драматический театр
16	Green Lantern Cabaret House (*Kabare*)	Кабаре
17	Department Store (*GUM*)	ГУМ
18	Hotel Versailles and Casino Amherst	гостиница Версаиллес и казино
19	Museum of Local Studies (*Muzei*)	Краведческий музей
20	Victory of Soviet Power monument	Памятник «Борцам за власть Советов»
21	Hotel Amurski Zaliv and Casino	гостиница Амурский Залив и казино
22	Hotel Vladivostok and Indian Consulate (*Kulsulstvo*)	гостиница Владивосток Консульство Индии
23	Hotel Ekvator	гостиница Екватор
24	House of the Brynner family	Быв. Дом Брыннера
25	Picture gallery (*Galereya*)	Картинная галерея
26	Hotel Primore	гостиница Приморье
27	Central post office (*Pochtamt*)	Почтамт
28	Railway station (*Vokzal*)	Ж-Д вокзал
29	Aeroflot	Аэрофлот
30	Hotel at the Sea Ferry Terminal	гостиница в Морском вокзале
31	House Museum of Sukhanov	Дом-музей Суханова
32	Far Eastern University (*Universitet*)	Дальневосточный университет
33	Far Eastern Institute (*Institut*)	Дальневосточный институт
34	Gorky Theatre (*Theatr*)	Театр им. Горьково
35	Puppet Theatre (*Teatr*)	Театр кукол
36	Funicular railway (*Funikuler*)	Фуникулёр
37	Catholic Church	Католический костёл
38	American Business Centre	Американский коммерческий центр
39	Far Eastern Technical University (*Universitet*)	Дальневосточный технический университет
40	Pacific Fleet Military Museum	Музей Тихоокеанского флота
41	USA Consulate (*Kulsulstvo*)	Кулсульство США
42	Circus (*Tsirk*)	Цирк
43	Submarine Museum and Navy memorials	Мемориальный комплекс «Боевая слава краснознаменного Тихоокеанского флота»
44	Admiral Nevelski monument	Памятник адмиралу Невельскому
45	125th anniversary of Vladivostok monument (*Obelisk*)	Обелиск в честь 125-летия основания города Владивостока
46	Krasni Vympel Ship Museum	Параход «Красний Вымпел»
47	Local ferry terminal	Морской вокзал прибрежных сообщений
R	Restaurant (*Restoran*)	Ресторан
C	Café (*Kafé*) or Bar (*Bar*)	Кафе или Бар ____

fistful of dollars left – you might want to celebrate your final night here after you have got your vehicle safely into a container. Tariff includes breakfast.

About 19km north of the city at Sanatornaya, the **Vlad Motor Inn**, tel: 26 80 93, satellite tel: (509) 851 5111, fax: 26 83 51, satellite fax: (509) 851 5116, is home from home for ex-pats working in Vladivostok. In a woodland setting, close to the beach, good, if bland, food, comfortable rooms with tiled bathrooms, and MTV or CNN await you – but you are no longer/not yet in Russia! Built, owned and run by Canadians it has VCR rentals, a change bureau and a tennis court of sorts. Credit cards accepted. Tariff includes breakfast.

Security parking
Available in a small enclosed courtyard at the Versailles at night. There is a security carpark close to the Hotel Amursky Zaliv but it has a very low fence. Vehicles are safe in the guarded grounds of the Vlad Motor Inn. There are a number of security carparks around the city.

Where to eat
There are lots of restaurants and cafés in Vladivostok in all price ranges and varying in quality.

Inexpensive
Nostalgia Café, ul Pervaya Morskaya 6/25, tel: 26 78 13, is good value and has a gift shop as well.

Hare Krishna Café, Okeansky prospekt 10/12, serves vegetarian food in simple pleasant surroundings. Open 10.00–19.00 seven days

Moderate
The Vlad Motor Inn, ul Vosmaya 1, tel: 26 80 93, has typical North American fare – burgers, ribs, steak etc. Credit cards accepted.

Nostalgia Art Salon and Restaurant, in the same building as the Nostalgia Café, serves good Russian food.

If you are yearning for fish, both the **Okean**, ul Naberezhnaya 3, tel: 26 81 86, with views over Amursky Gulf, and the **Volna**, top floor of the Maritime Terminal, tel: 21 93 40, 21 98 60, with views over the harbour, offer seafood at reasonable prices.

Expensive
The Australian **Captain Cook Restaurant**, ground floor of Pensionat Hotel, ul Devyataya 14, Sanatornaya, tel: 21 53 41, serves a mixture of Australian and Russian food: even crocodile and kangaroo are sometimes on the menu. Credit cards accepted. A Russian friend recommends the **Svetlana**, in the city, for good but expensive Russian food.

What to see

The **Arsenyev City Museum**, ul Svetlanskaya 20, traces the history, ethnography and nature of the Primorski region with the usual collection of dusty stuffed animals and birds. Open Tues–Sun 10.00–18.30 (closed 15.30–16.00). The **Border Guards Museum**, ul Kolkhoznaya 17, as you might guess, traces the history of the border areas. Open Tues–Sat 09.00–17.00, closed last Friday in month. An old Lutheran Church now houses the **Pacific Military Fleet Museum**, ul Pushkinskaya 14. Exhibits illustrating the history of the fleet from the time of the Tsars to post World War II. Open Wed–Sun 09.30–17.45 (closed 13.00–14.00), closed last Friday in month.

The **C-56 Submarine** sank ten enemy ships in World War II, and is now high and dry on the waterfront; walk through at Korabelnaya Naberezhnaya. Open Wed–Sat, 09.00–18.00 (closed 13.00–14.00).

Catch a ferry from the Vokzal Priberezhnikh Soobsheniya to beaches and islands in the bay. Or you can hire a boat here for a trip around the harbour – a great way to see the fleet and get the city into perspective.

PUSHING THE BOUNDARIES

Foreign travellers are always anxious to claim to be the first to hike, ride or drive through remote parts of the world, often forgetting that the locals have been doing it for years. However, to be among the first foreigners in a particular area has a huge attraction for most serious travellers.

In 1991 Australian journalist George Negus led a television film crew with Russian advisers from Vladivostok to Moscow in four Mitsubishi Pajeros – probably the first foreigners to drive across Russia since the Revolution.

In 1994 David Thurlow and I drove our LandCruiser from Vyborg to Vladivostok – possibly the first unsponsored, unaccompanied foreign individuals to do so for many years.

In 1995 an Australian family shipped their Land Rover camper to England and set out for the Russian Far East. The Kincaids, academics Diana and Peter and their teenage children, Hilary and John, drove a huge loop from London across Siberia to Yakutsk and Magadan and back through the 'Stans, including a hair-raising few days in Tajikistan, to Europe, camping all the way. See overleaf for Hilary's description of the leg from Chernyshevsk to Magadan.

MAGADAN TO IRKUTSK IN WINTER

All these expeditions had to put their vehicles on the train for varying distances between Chernyshevsk and Svobodny and all had been travelling in summer. Gary and Monika Wescott, American photo-journalists and adventurers extraordinaire, drove from Magadan to

LONDON TO VLADIVOSTOK AND BACK

In 1995 my family and I drove from London, across Europe, through the Baltic States, across Russia to Magadan and then by ship to Vladivostok. From Vlad we drove back across most of Russia, through Central Asia, crossed the Caspian Sea (on the most noisomely awful ferry it has ever been my misfortune to experience), through the Caucasus and back across Europe to London. The journey took six months. Our objective was to reach Magadan (very far north, very far east, very cold, not much fun) by road. At the beginning we were purists – we would stick to the road come hell (Russian mosquitoes) or high water (no bridges). But there were a few places where purism gets you nowhere. The road from Chernyshevsk to Skovorodino was impassable in July 1995. You must put your vehicle and yourself on the goods train – on a flat car that does not stop. The road from Skovorodino north to Yakutsk is good – wide and relatively smooth. However, like most public works in Russia, it was probably state-of-the-art about thirty years ago and now could do with a little maintenance. A little way east of Yakutsk the road runs out. There is a track but it is only passable in the wintertime and then only by tank, so we caught a ferry for approximately 130km along the Aldan River.

The ferry leaves from the tiny village of Ust-Taata. It is subject to the usual timetable of major forms of transport in the CIS – namely that there is none and you must wait until it is full/loaded before it leaves. It goes to the largish village of Khandyga where the road begins again. The ferry (actually a barge and a punt) is impeccably kept. At that latitude and time of year true darkness does not fall until very late indeed – 10 or 11pm – and cruising along the wide, calm and clean river was very beautiful. I am a big fan of skies (this is why I love the outback) and these ones were huge and filled with all sorts of light and clouds that I haven't seen before or since.

The road from Khandyga to Magadan is relatively easy going. There are a few rivers with no bridges but with a good winch and a little dumb luck we were fine. The area is surprisingly populated – a hangover from the Soviet Union days of massive subsidies. Some of the locals are violently proud of their heritage, thumping their chest and exclaiming 'I am Siberian!' and gruffly asking (or perhaps telling) 'This is beautiful, yes?'

Magadan is a surprisingly attractive town. This is not to say it is beautiful – merely that it is not nearly as horrible as circumstances might have made it. Founded in the 1930s when gold was discovered in the Kolyma area, it was little more than a huge transit gulag for the first twenty years of its existence. It is thought that of the millions of people who were sent to the gold fields of Kolyma some 20 million prisoners were put to death or died of starvation, ill-treatment and torture during the Stalin era.

The far northeast of Siberia is, like the rest of Russia and Central Asia, definitely worth the trip. The landscape is beautiful – fairytale forests on the flat plains from Skovorodino to Khandyga and glacial valleys from there to Magadan. Like most areas full of space and solitude, it soothes the soul.

Irkutsk, in winter, via Susuman, Ust-Nera and Khandyga to Yakutsk. From Yakutsk they travelled sometimes on 'roads' and sometimes on the frozen Lena River via Sangyakhtakh, Khorinsky and Lensk to Ust-Kut on the BAM railway northwest of Lake Baikal. From Ust-Kut they took the road via Bratsk to Irkutsk. It took them nearly three months and they drove all the way, often in convoy with Russian trucks for safety, never once using a ferry or train.

Gary gives the following distances:

Magadan to Susuman – 633km
Susuman to Ust-Nera – 378km
Ust-Nera to Khandyga – 575km
Khandyga to Yakutsk – 414km
Yakutsk to Lensk on the river – 1,023km
Lensk to Markovo on 'winter road' – 1,039km (from Lensk back to the Lena
   at Markovo is a 'winter road' which is passable only when frozen)
Markovo to Ust-Kut – 122km
Magadan to Ust-Kut – port to pavement – 4,184km

The total mileage with side trips, Magadan to Ust-Kut, was 5,973km.

Although it sounds to us as if driving in winter in remote areas of Siberia
is for experienced professional drivers this is what Gary says about Turtle
Expeditions' adventure:

'From a purely mechanical standpoint, if you had an adequate food and
fuel supply, and adequate extreme cold weather gear (ours was good for
–100° F), the trip from Magadan to Ust-Kut could be done in practically
any good 4WD in a couple of weeks or less, without a convoy. The lowest
temperature we saw was –87°F (–63°C), and a week or more of –50° to
–60°F. It was a warm winter.

'There are also two other winter routes from Yakutsk, we were told; one
through Chita and one through Mirny, if one did not wish to drive the
Lena. Mirny might still be a closed city for foreigners, accessible only
with a permit.

'The previously unexplored trading route between Chadan and Kosh
Agach was, by any scale, the most challenging and beautiful leg of our
32,000km/11-month adventure.'

Chadan and Kosh Agach are in the southeast of the Altai Republic, close
to the Mongolian border.

For more information log on to the Turtle Expeditions' web site:
http://www.4x44u.com/pub/k2/am4x44u/whats_new/turtle.htm or contact
Gary and Monika direct on: 74464.1433@compuserve.com.

Chapter Five

Mongolia

Mongolia, land of Chinggis Khaan (Genghis Khan), hordes of horses, khulans (*Equus hemionus*) and takhis (*Equus przewalski*), yaks and bright white gers, is one of the last frontiers for adventurous travellers to discover. Once outside a 400km radius of the capital, Ulaanbaatar, many people still live a traditional nomadic lifestyle where the horse is king.

The positive side of the fact that there are problems crossing the road borders into Mongolia is that it is still unusual for foreigners to visit the country other than in tourist groups, and so you will receive a genuinely warm welcome from the people of the steppe.

Spelling of names varies as Russian influence declines. Ulan Baatar is now more often Ulaanbaatar, Genghis Khan has become Chinggis Khaan or sometimes Khan and many city street names have changed. We have tried to go with the Mongolian spelling wherever possible. Many towns and villages use a number of different names – the 'old' name meaning pre-revolution, as well as the post-revolution name and the 'new' name which may be the 'old' name or may be a new 'new' name. If you think this is confusing – you are right.

FACTS AND FIGURES

Despite being surrounded by two world powers, Russia to the north and China to the south, Mongolia has managed to resist colonisation.

Time

GMT +8 hours in the east, including Ulaanbaatar. The three western *aimags* (provinces), Bayan-Olgii, Uvs and Khovd, are GMT +7 hours (Ulaanbaatar −1 hour). Daylight saving begins on the last Sunday in March and ends on the last Sunday in September.

Population
Mongolia has a population of 2,317,000 (1996 estimate); population density 1.5 people per km^2.

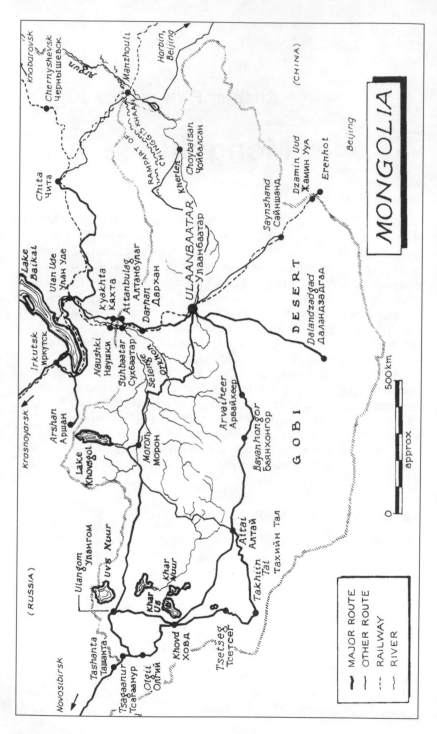

Capital
Ulaanbaatar, population 600,000.

GEOGRAPHY

Mongolia has a total area of 1,565,000km². It is a vast landlocked country as big as Britain, France, Germany and Italy combined. Until comparatively recently, when Inner Mongolia, now Chinese, and a large area of Siberia, now Russian, were part of its territory, it was even bigger. Surrounded by China to the east, south and west and Russia to the north, Mongolia is a land of rugged extremes. The Gobi Desert occupies approximately one third of the country, with the other two thirds being divided between steppe and mountain ranges. The average altitude is 1,580m. Only about 10% of the country, mostly in the northeast, is forested.

The highest peak, Tavan-Bogdo-Uli, reaches 4,374m in the northwest Altai Nuruu. Mongolia's two biggest rivers are the Selenge Gol, which rises in the Khangayn Nuruu mountain range and flows north into Lake Baikal; and the Kherlen Gol, which rises in the Khentii Nuruu mountain range northeast of Ulaanbaatar, and flows east across the border into Lake Dalai.

CLIMATE

Mongolia is known as the 'Land of Blue Sky', having a harsh continental climate with long, dry, cold winters and short, mild and relatively wet summers.

With its high elevations and terrain varying from desert to high mountain ranges, Mongolia suffers large daily and seasonal temperature swings. In summer the Gobi Desert's day temperatures often reach the high 30s Celsius, and sometimes even 40°C, followed by cold nights. Its altitude and distance from any ocean cause low humidity so the heat is more bearable. In winter freezing winds sweep down from the Arctic across Siberia bringing lows averaging –20°C to –35°C. In the Uvs Lake basin in north western Mongolia, the lowest temperature ever recorded is –58°C.

Temperatures on the steppe range from –50°C in winter to +20° or so in summer. Nights in summer are chilly but it is still pleasant to sleep under the stars in a medium-weight sleeping bag. In winter 10-gallon churns of water may freeze solid in gers overnight.

It is a land of summer rainfall, with precipitation ranging from 600mm in the high mountain ranges to below 100mm in the Gobi where there may be no rain at all for several years at a time.

NATURAL HISTORY AND CONSERVATION

Long before conservation became a buzz word, Mongolians protected wild animals from over-hunting. Marco Polo wrote of his travels in Central Asia in the 13th century:

'Mongolians prohibit hunting during birthing and weaning period of hare, elk, roe deer, gazelle and other animals by law. Therefore there are plenty of animals and wonderful opportunity for the increase of animals. Violators are strongly punished.'

Mongolia is committed to biodiversity conservation. With a population density of only 1.5 per km², and a tradition of semi-nomadic rural lifestyle, it would appear to be an ideal country for a successful conservation plan.

'Ecologically, Mongolia occupies a critical transition zone in Central Asia: here the great Siberian taiga forest, the Central Asian steppe, the high Altai mountains and the Gobi desert converge. Spared the harmful impacts of the unsustainable development that took place in many parts of the globe during the past 100 years, today many of these areas provide habitat for representative, and often rare, examples of the wild plants and animals of central and northern Asia. Wildlife species that have largely disappeared from the rest of the continent remain here, sometimes in relative abundance.'

Mongolia's Wild Heritage. See page 268.

Flora

Besides almost 150 endemic plants and 100 relict species, Mongolia's diverse vegetation includes many thousand species representative of neighbouring regions. Plants from the steppe of Kazakstan and Manchuria grow side by side and, in the north, trees and plants endemic to the Siberian taiga occur. The Mongolian *Red Book* lists over 100 rare or endangered plant species.

Fauna

Mongolia's fauna is representative of species from Central Asian deserts, the steppe and the Siberian taiga. Species to be found include 436 birds, 136 mammals, 75 fish, 22 reptiles, 8 amphibians and numerous invertebrates.

Species endemic to Central Asia include two birds, the Altai snowcock and Kozlov's accentor; eight reptiles; two fish, the Altai Osman and the Mongolian grayling; and a number of mammals including four species of jerboa, Brandt's vole and the Mongolian subspecies of the saiga antelope (*Saiga tatarica mongolica*).

You are likely to see a number of endangered and rare species if you spend any length of time in Mongolia. In the Dzungarian Gobi (Gobi B) alone you can expect to see herds of khulan (wild asses), Bactrian camels, black-tailed gazelle and Gobi naked-toed geckos.

National parks and natural reserves

There are four types of protected area in Mongolia:

Strictly protected areas

These are ecologically important wilderness areas of particular value to science and people. They are divided into three categories: **pristine zones**

– research only; **protected zones** – research and conservation; **limited use zones** – tourism, traditional religious activities, and some plant collecting. Hunting, logging and construction are prohibited. There are currently ten strictly protected areas.

National parks

These are wilderness areas with historical, cultural or environmental education value. Again they are divided into three categories: **core areas** – research and conservation activities; **ecotourism zone** – tourism, fishing, research and conservation; **limited use zone** – the above activities plus grazing, and construction is allowed with park permission. Four areas have been designated national parks.

Natural reserves

These are of four types: **ecosystem** – protecting natural areas; **biological** – conserving rare species; **palaeontological** – conserving fossil areas; **geological** – of geological importance. Certain economic activities are allowed provided they do not conflict with reasons for which the reserve was established. Seven areas are classed as Natural Reserves.

Natural and historical monuments

These have been established for the preservation of unique landscapes and historical and cultural sites. Many activities are allowed if they do not adversely affect the monument. There are five natural and historical monuments.

Approximately 12,300,000 hectares are protected under the above classifications. It is difficult to police them all on a small budget but Mongolians generally show enormous regard for their country. A recent problem is the proliferation of small Russian-built jeeps which are very popular in rural areas. As there are virtually no roads, drivers constantly pick new tracks which causes tremendous soil compaction and erosion. Short of a massive road construction programme, the problem seems insoluble.

Try to get the beautiful and informative booklet *Mongolia's Wild Heritage*, from which much of this information was gleaned. It should be available from the Ministry for Nature and the Environment, Khudaldaany gudamj 5, Ulaanbaatar 11; fax: 976 1 321 401. See *Further Reading, Appendix Three*.

HISTORICAL OUTLINE

Archaeological finds suggest Mongolia was inhabited 500,000 years ago. Mongolians remembered their more recent history in 1991 when they celebrated the anniversary of the establishment of the first Hun State in 209BC. This was also the first state, as opposed to tribal area, in Central Asia.

The Huns were descended from a number of nomadic tribes such as the Xianya, Hun yi and Di. Recognised as being as powerful as neighbouring Chinese states, the Hun State stretched from the Great Wall in the south to Lake Baikal in the north, and from the Hingan Hills in the east to the Ertis River in the west.

The Hun State lasted for nearly three centuries but in the middle of the first century AD it divided along north/south lines, with the southern Huns creating the states of Han and Xia while the northern Huns moved west, eventually settling in Eastern Europe in the 4th and 5th centuries. In the 7th century the area which had been the Hun State was overrun and occupied by the Chinese states of Xianbi and Jhou Jhan.

It appears that from the 7th to the 10th century Kyrgyz, Turkic and Uighur tribes inhabited Mongolia. By the 10th century a Mongolian-speaking tribe, the Kidans, dominated an area of northern China and created the Great Liao State. Liao was so powerful that the Chinese tribes of the area recognised its supremacy.

It was in the 11th and 12th centuries that the Mongol tribes became known as the Jalair, Kerait, Tatar and Whole Mongolia. They spent most of their time fighting each other until the late 12th century when Temujin, the young warrior king, succeeded in uniting the Mongol tribes under his leadership. In 1206 a *kuriltai* (great assembly) proclaimed him Chinggis Khaan (supreme ruler) and he used the occasion to create a mighty army.

To begin with, Chinggis Khaan concentrated on conquering neighbouring Chinese states; but later he moved west and by his death, in 1227, the Mongol Empire stretched from the Amur River in the east to the Aral Sea in the west and from the Yellow River across to Kashgar and Merv in the south.

His son, Ogodei Khan, ruled from 1227 to 1241, extending his empire from the Pacific Ocean to the Black Sea, western Russia, Ukraine and Hungary. Only his death prevented a Mongol invasion of Vienna. For five years after his death, Toregene, Ogodei's widow, acted as regent while her son, Guyu, and his cousin, Batu, quarrelled over who should succeed Ogodei. With the aid of his mother, Guyu won the dispute and ruled from 1246 to 1248.

A precedent having been set, Ogul-Gaimish, Guyu's widow, ruled as regent for three years after his death but failed to prevent Mongke, grandson of Chinggis Khaan through his son Tolui, becoming Khan. Mongke Khan proved to be a good administrator as well as a successful general.

After Mongke's death, the great Kublai Khan ruled for 34 years, until 1294. Second only to his grandfather Chinggis Khaan, Kublai was a great khan. Unlike Chinggis who made Karakorum (near present day Ulaanbaatar) his capital, Kublai Khan, admiring all things Chinese, set up his capital in Daidu (Beijing). He was the founder of the Yuan dynasty and one of China's great emperors. His descendants ruled China until defeated by the Min State in 1367 and Mongolia's domination of world trade and culture then ceased.

In the 14th and 15th centuries the people became divided into Eastern Mongols and Western Mongols (Oirat Mongols). In the 16th century the Eastern Mongols split again into Outer Mongolia (Khalh Mongolia) and Inner Mongolia and continued to fight each other.

In the 17th century the Manchurians conquered first Inner Mongolia and then Khalh Mongolia; and in 1757 Oirat Mongolia was subdued. The next 150 years saw the subjugation of Mongolians as the Manchurians isolated Mongolia from the rest of the world. In the early 1900s Bogdo Khan, a Khalh Mongolian, led a resistance movement aimed at reviving the Mongolian State; but it was summarily suppressed by the Manchurians in 1911. When, in 1919, China invaded Mongolia, violating the 1915 treaty between Russia, China and Mongolia, outraged Khalh Mongolians joined the national liberation movement with renewed vigour. In 1921 Mongolia was declared a 'republican monarchy' with the eighth living Buddha, the Bogd Haan, as nominal king; but three years later, in 1924, it changed to a Soviet-style republic.

The first democratic election was held in July 1990 and since then Mongolia has gradually moved towards a free market system.

POLITICS

From 1924 until the early 1990s the Mongolian People's Revolutionary Party (MPRP), effectively the Communist Party with a name change, ruled through the Council of Ministers and a ten-member Politburo.

However, on January 13 1992 a new constitution was adopted. The State Great Hural is a unicameral parliament with 76 seats. In June 1992 the first democratic election was held and the MPRP was returned to power.

President Punsalmaagiyn Ochirbat, who first became president in 1990, was re-elected in 1993 with 57.8% of the votes. According to the new constitution the president serves a four-year term and can only be re-elected once.

On July 1 1996 the MPRP lost the election and, for the first time in 72 years, communists no longer ruled Mongolia.

There are three main political parties: the MPRP, the Mongolian National Democratic Party (MNDP) and the Mongolian Social Democratic Party (MSDP). A coalition of the latter two parties became the government in 1996.

On May 18 1997 the results of the presidential election were declared. N Bagabandi, 47-year-old chairman of the main opposition party, MPRP, was elected the second president of Mongolia by 60.79% of voters.

ECONOMY

Although the economy was traditionally based on agriculture and, in particular, the breeding of livestock, the USSR encouraged and assisted Mongolia with the exploitation of considerable mineral resources until 1990.

Since the demise of communism the Mongolian government has gradually changed from central planning to a market economy but the loss of the USSR's financial support has created severe economic hardship.

PEOPLE

The majority of Mongolians, approximately 78%, are Halhas, with the remaining 22% made up of small ethnic groups such as Kazaks, Dorvod, Buryat, Chinese and Russian. Until the breakup of the USSR approximately 2% of the population was Russian but many have returned home in the past seven years. Kazakstan has been enticing Kazaks across the northwestern border since 1990.

A little over 50% of the population are urban dwellers.

Approximately 45% of the population is under 16 years of age.

LANGUAGE

Mongolian, an Ural-Altaic language of the same family as Finnish and Turkish, is the official language. Many people speak Russian having attended Russian universities prior to 1990. Likewise German is spoken by people who trained in East Germany. Not much English is spoken but it is the most popular language to study today.

The Cyrillic alphabet is used with the addition of two extra characters. Some road signs around Ulaanbaatar are also in Roman script. Names on tourist maps are written in Roman script but it's useful to buy one with names in Cyrillic too if you are travelling without a guide. It is advisable to take a guide if you want to leave the area around Ulaanbaatar.

Although Mongolian seems at first very difficult we met two Peace Corps workers who had become fluent within a year – they were the only foreigners in their respective villages so had little option.

RELIGION

Buddhism

The **Yellow Sect of Tibetan Buddhism** or **Lamaism** has been the traditional religion since the 16th century when Altan Khan acknowledged Tibetan Buddhism and gave the Tibetan religious leader the title *Dalai Lama*. Although the first Buddhist monastery was not built in Mongolia until 1586 Buddhists have been living in the area for 2,000 years.

From the revolution of 1921 to 1990 all religion was vigorously discouraged (as in Russia). Of 700 or more monasteries only four appear to have survived the destruction by the communist governments in the purges of the 1930s. Several Buddhist temples within a 400km radius of Ulaanbaatar have reopened but religion does not seem to play a very important part in the everyday lives of the people.

Christianity
A few fundamentalist Christian sects are trying to convert the people but they rarely leave the area around Ulaanbaatar.

Islam
In the northwest of the country Islam is making a tentative comeback amongst the Kazaks. Recently a mosque has been built in Olgii but, although people claimed to be Mussulmen, few seem to take their religion seriously enough to give up vodka.

Shamanism
A form of animism with shamans acting as intermediary between the people and the spirits, this was the religion of Mongolia until the 16th century. There are to this day more overt signs of Shamanism than of any other religion.

CULTURE AND THE ARTS
Dwellings
Mongolia is one of the few countries in Central Asia where people still live a nomadic lifestyle despite the extreme climate. To enable them to do this in comparative comfort Mongolians developed the *ger*, a circular tent-like structure similar to the *yurt*. Quick to erect and dismantle and easily transportable, in earlier days by camel but now more often by truck, the ger is warm in winter and cool in summer.

The walls are made from sections of collapsible birch lattice framework called *khana* in Mongolian. Each section is 2–3m long and 2m high and an average-sized ger has seven or eight khanas attached with leather thongs. The roof is made of light poles, *uni*, slotted into the top of the khanas and into a wooden cartwheel-like structure with a hole in the centre, called the *toono*, approximately 1m in diameter. Two upright poles

---

OVOO
At the top of every mountain pass you will see an o*voo* – a cairn, often with a flag on the top. Drivers stop their vehicles and everyone scrambles out to walk clockwise round the ovoo, tossing stones on to the pile as they go in thanks for a safe journey so far and in hope of continued good luck. Look carefully and you will see all kinds of offerings on the ovoo – flowers, empty vodka bottles, broken car components, sweet and cigarette packets and colourful pieces of glass and plastic.

Religious ceremonies take place at the ovoos at certain times of year. Buddhist monks chant prayers to the Mountain Spirit (sacred mountains have their own special prayers) asking for blessings of good health, good weather for the vegetation and an increase in their livestock and wildlife.

Digging of soil or removal of rocks, the killing of wild animals and fish, and polluting of the rivers, lakes and springs near an ovoo are strictly forbidden.

Ovoos are believed to have marked sacred sites in pre-Buddhist times when people practised Shamanism, a form of animist religion.

support the roof. The toono allows smoke from the central stove to escape and also creates a through draught in summer when the lower part of the felt wall covering is rolled up.

The outside of the khanas is covered in thick felt – one layer in summer but two or more in winter. Gers always face southeast because the wind comes from the northwest. The low wooden door, a trap for tall foreigners, opens inwards and has a flap for added protection from the weather. There are various taboos connected with behaviour when entering a ger. Traditionally people enter on the left, lifting the flap with their left hand, and leave on the right – to ignore this is to court bad luck. Never step on the threshold as that is considered a great insult.

The floor used to be made of as many hides as possible covered with felt and then sometimes a carpet. Now that weight is not such a consideration many gers have wooden floors covered with felt and carpets. If the family is well off the walls will be hung with carpets, more for insulation than for decoration. Furniture is quite basic – a few brightly painted wooden dressers and beds and suitcases or trunks. A favourite colour scheme for the furniture is orange with blue and yellow flowers.

As in the West the place of honour for guests is on the right side of the host. Cushions are placed in particular positions on the floor and it is considered bad manners to move them although, in our experience, Mongolians are so hospitable they will do anything to make you comfortable and welcome.

Art and sculpture

Mongolian painting started thousands of years ago as simple rock drawings but by the 8th century Uigher Buddhist painting was flourishing. In more recent years Mongolian painting has been influenced by European art. The 19th-century artist, Balduugiin Sharav, is perhaps Mongolia's most famous artist and his picture, *One Day in Mongolia*, the best-known Mongolian painting.

In the Bronze Age nomads built graves from slabs of rock on which they carved the outline of animals – these became known as 'deer' or 'reindeer stones'. They erected similar stone monuments to mark special sites, not necessarily graves. The most interesting stones are divided into three sections, the top band having engravings of the sun and moon, the middle band depictions of leaping deer and the bottom section weapons, hooks and other utilitarian objects. Occasionally the upper section shows a human head or face.

One of Mongolia's most famous sculptors, Undur Gegeen Zanabazar, sculpted 21 *tare* (consorts of Buddha) portraying the beauty of Mongolian women in the 17th century. Zanabazar greatly influenced later sculptors such as S Choimbol and N Jambai.

Modern sculptures, such as the monument to D Suhbaatar, a hero of the revolution, by S Choimbol, symbolise the continuing veneration of Mongolian heroes by the people.

Literature

Mongolian epics go back to the 12th and 13th centuries and tell the stories of ancient heroes. Mongolians claim their epics *Geseriada* and *Jangar* rank with the *Iliad*, the *Odyssey* and the *Mahabharata*. Traditionally passed down orally from generation to generation, they are now recorded in the national script.

Music and singing

Mongolian folk songs can be divided into two types – 'long song' and 'short song'. Short songs are the 'lightest' and mainly about daily life and activities. Long song is the classic form of Mongolian singing – usually songs of love for one's horse, homeland or beloved. They are called 'long' because of the slow arching of their phrases.

The Chandmani district of Khovd aimag is famous for its *khoomi* 'singing'. This is a rare and difficult form of biphonic or harmonic singing where the singer produces and modulates two distinct notes at once. It has an almost magical quality which once heard can never be forgotten.

Wind, strings and drums are also traditional Mongolian musical instruments but the one most visitors are familiar with is the *morin khuur*, a two-stringed 'violin' with a carved horse's head scroll and horse hair strings and bow, often played to sound like horses galloping across the steppe.

A compact disc, *Enchanting Mongolia: traditional Mongolian music*, produced by Stefan Körbel, PF 106, 10266 Berlin, Germany, and recorded in Ulaanbaatar in 1993, is on sale in Ulaanbaatar. It is an interesting introduction to the music of Mongolia but cannot hope to recreate the atmosphere of the music in its original setting – the mountains and valleys of Mongolia.

PLANNING AND PREPARATION

See also Chapter One

When to go

Weatherwise, from late May to October is the best time of year for driving across Mongolia – any earlier or later and you may be cut off by sudden snowstorms. July and August are the wettest months which can make driving difficult on unsealed roads. However, regardless of the weather, try to be in Mongolia for *Naadam* – the festival which coincides with National Day, or more accurately days, on 11–13 July. (See page 155.) Naturally this is peak tourist season but, with your own transport, you can pick a country town which is much more fun than Ulaanbaatar. We were in Arvaiheer (sometimes spelt Arbaykheer) for Naadam and were the only foreigners there.

Maps

There are many reasons why you should buy several maps of Mongolia although there are not many available. Many towns and villages seem to have two names – the pre-revolution one and the later one – and some are changing back again or even have new names; there are also several different ways of spelling or transliterating names. Road signs, when there are any, may be signifying the aimag, of which there are 18, rather than the town.

Much of the information on aeronautical charts seems to be out-of-date but they at least show mountains, rivers and other physical features in the right place although the accuracy of roads and tracks leaves much to be desired.

Maps of aimags, scale 1:1,000,000, can be bought at the shop in the Museum of Natural History, corner of Sambuu and Suhbaatar Streets, Ulaanbaatar.

Documentation
Visas
These are available from Mongolian Embassies or Consulates in Beijing, London, Sydney and Washington. When applying for visas make it clear that you will be driving your own vehicle and ask about a permit for the car. You may be told you must get this through a travel agent in which case contact an Ulaanbaatar travel agent and ask them to arrange for a guide to meet you at the station in Suhbaatar. If you have a guide you will get through the voluminous paperwork much more quickly as no-one speaks English in the immigration and customs offices. Guides cost approximately $50 per day plus accommodation if you stay in hotels.

Travel agents in Ulaanbaatar
Nomads, Room 20, Peace and Friendship Building, Peace Avenue, (mail address: P.O. Box 1008), Ulaanbaatar; tel/fax: (976 1) 328 146; email: nomads@magicnet.mn. These are specialists in adventure travel and can arrange horse and camel riding treks, mountain climbing and bird-watching expeditions.

Mongolian Adventure Tours Co. Ltd., Bayangol Hotel, Block A, level 2, Ulaanbaatar; tel: 312 095.

Juulchin, Bayangol Hotel, Block B, Ulaanbaatar; tel: 312 095; fax 320 246. Ask for Mr Batjargal.

Vehicle documentation
Similar to Russia and the rest of the CIS. See *Chapter One*, page 22. Take registration papers showing proof of ownership, international driver's permit and insurance papers.

Insurance
Third party insurance was not available in Mongolia in 1996. Shop around before you leave home – you may find a company prepared to insure you at a reasonable premium.

Full medical insurance is essential as hospitals are running down due to lack of funds and evacuation may be necessary if you suffer a serious illness or accident.

Embassy and consulate addresses

Australia Honorary Mongolian Consul General, Mr Sean Hinton, 112/189 Philip Street, Waterloo 2017; tel/fax: (02) 9319 4797. Phone for appointments to see the Honorary Consul General.

China Mongolian Embassy, 2 Xiushui Beilu, Jian Guomen wai, Beijing; tel: (10) 532 1203

France Mongolian Embassy, 5 Ave Robert Schuman 92, Boulogne, Billancourt, Paris; tel: (1) 4605 2812, 4605 2318

Germany Mongolian Embassy, Botschaft der MVR, 1157 Berlin Karlshirst Fritz, Schemkel Strasse 81, Berlin; tel: (30) 509 8954; Bonn office (228) 402 727

Japan Mongolian Embassy, 21–4 Kamiyamacho Shibuya ku, Tokyo; tel: (3) 469 2088, 469 2092

Russia Mongolian Embassy, Spaso Peskovskii per 1/7, Moscow; tel: (095) 229 67 65. Mongolian Consulate, ul Lapina 11, Irkutsk; tel: (3952) 4 23 70, 4 22 60. Mongolian Consulate, 2nd floor, Hotel Baikal, ul Erbanova 12, Ulan Ude

United Kingdom Mongolian Embassy, 7 Kensington Court, London W8 5DL; tel: (171) 937 0150, 937 5235, 937 5238; fax: 937 1117

United States Mongolian Embassy, 2833 M Street NW, Washington, DC 20007; tel: (202) 333 7117; fax: 298 9227. There is also a Consulate General in New York.

Warning Make sure you have double-entry Russian visas if you intend to re-enter Russia.

Customs and immigration

Everyone entering Mongolia must fill in a customs declaration form at the border. Declare all valuable items such as cameras and computers to avoid problems when leaving the country. Keep receipts for any souvenirs bought in Mongolia in case Customs ask for them on the way out.

All the usual things are prohibited imports – guns, explosive items, drugs, pornography.

At the Mongolian border, Customs complete a form in triplicate for motor vehicles entering the country and return one sheet to the owner. This must be handed back to Customs on leaving the country.

Health and safety
Health

There have been outbreaks of cholera. If in doubt, peel it, boil it, cook it or forget it. Immunisation doesn't help.

Safety

Take all the usual precautions without becoming paranoid. On many occasions in small towns I parked the LandCruiser in security parks some distance from the hotel and walked back alone in the dark without feeling in danger. Often it is impossible to find somewhere to camp where you are not very obvious – there are not many trees on the steppe. Sometimes local horsemen would ride over to check us out but we were never disturbed. It is a good idea to ask if you can camp beside gers if there are any in sight.

Photography

Guards at Suhbaatar railway station shouted at us when they saw our cameras but otherwise there seemed to be no problems.

Communications

Country telephone code: 976

Mail, telephone and fax

Even very remote settlements have post offices and telephone services. If the telephone service is impossible from a particular area, and you desperately need to make a call, try to persuade the telephonist to use the fax machine which is likely to have a direct dial facility. Mail services are slow but seem to be reliable.

Email

Data Communications Systems Company Limited, Negdsen Undestnii Street 49, Ulaanbaatar 46; tel: 976-1-312 063, 327 309, 312 065; fax: 320 210; email address: info@magicnet.mn or ganbold@magicnet.mn

Media

Newspapers *Mongolia*, published by 'Ardyn erkh', is an English-language tourist newspaper with information about accommodation, tourism, restaurants, entertainment and travel connections. On sale at most tourist hotels.

Television international channels are available in hotels.

Email news service is available by subscription from Mongolia, with an option of daily news (Mon–Fri) with two pages, or weekly news with four pages every Monday. For further details, contact ganbold@magicnet.mn

Air connections

International flights go to and from China, Japan and Russia; internal flights to and from most of the *aimag* capital cities.

Roads

46,700km of which 1,000km are sealed and the rest vary from occasionally graded gravel to unmarked tracks.

Railways

1,750km. Apart from two short branch lines, this is the Trans-Mongolian line. Leaving Russia at Naushki the first town in Mongolia is Suhbaatar. The Mongolian/China border is at Barkhoyn, southeast of Ulaanbaatar.

Electricity
220 volt, two-pin European-type plug

IN MONGOLIA
Driving in Mongolia
Drive on the right.

Rules of the road
These are as in Russia and the rest of the CIS. Driving in Ulaanbaatar is quite an experience. Drivers do obey the traffic lights (usually) but otherwise it's a free-for-all with pedestrians coming in last. If you want some fun, stop when you find people trying to use zebra crossings. The response is interesting – the pedestrians are confused, other drivers are so astounded they occasionally stop too, and tourists have been known to shriek their thanks.

Road conditions
Statistics tell us there are 1,000km of paved and 45,700km of unpaved 'highways' in Mongolia.

Apart from a few hundred kilometres of sealed road around Ulaanbaatar, the roads vary from a few graded gravel stretches, to areas where the unmade track spreads for kilometres across valleys, to single-vehicle, narrow, twisting rock paths through mountain passes. This is real 4WD stuff and should not be attempted in anything less robust. Russian jeeps, originally produced for the military forces and now a healthy export, appear to be tailor-made for the terrain but larger Japanese vehicles suddenly become ungainly monsters.

Having said that, if you are keen to experience driving in the wild then this is the country for you. You will be rewarded by spectacular scenery, wonderful camping and friendly hospitality from the people who live in the high country in their gers.

Police
Unlike in the CIS there are no police barriers on the outskirts of towns. The police were helpful in small towns, allowing us to park in their guarded yards.

Fuel
There is usually a fuel station on the outskirts of the towns but nothing in between. Unleaded petrol was not available in 1996. Fuel is cheap despite the vast distances it has to be transported by 'road'.

Workshops and motor car agencies
No specialist brand agency had set up in 1996. In Ulaanbaatar, Sanshiro Co Ltd, tel/fax: (1) 38 50 59, is a joint Japanese/Mongolian company

workshop staffed by Japanese mechanics who specialise in 4WD but will work on any vehicle. Their workshop is very clean and well organised and the manager and staff are particularly interested in overland vehicles. English is spoken and we highly recommend them. It is hard to give an exact street address but head for the power station and turn left after the Hotsh Bank – best to ring and get directions first.

Spares
Take your own. See *Chapter One*, page 7.

Security parking
There are security carparks in Ulaanbaatar but in the smaller towns you may have to ask the police to allow you to park in their yards.

National holidays and festivals

January 1	New Year's Day
End of Jan and beginning Feb	Tsagaan Sar (Lunar New Year) The Mongolian calendar operates in five cycles of 12 years, each cycle being named after an element – earth, water, fire, ice or wind – and each year bearing the name of an animal. The Lunar New Year celebrations last for three days. It's a time for parties and much *airag* (fermented mare's milk) and *arkhi* (distilled from fermented cow's milk) is consumed.
July 11–13	Naadam Although this festival originated many centuries ago, Naadam more recently celebrated the People's Revolution of 1921 and consists of sporting events such as archery, wrestling and horse-racing. The biggest festival is held in Ulaanbaatar but every aimag capital and many smaller towns and villages stage their own celebrations. It's also a time for families to get together and catch up on the gossip.
November 24	Republic Day

Money
100 mongo = 1 togrog
Visa, American Express, Diners Club and some other credit or charge cards are accepted at many tourist hotels in Ulaanbaatar but not in the country. Visa is the most commonly accepted. The Trade and Development Bank in Ulaanbaatar will give cash advances on Visa and cash travellers cheques.

Shopping
There are a number of Western-type supermarkets in Ulaanbaatar but the stores where the locals shop and the markets have a fair selection of goods at very reasonable prices. Look out for imported and local cheese, yoghurt and other dairy produce.

NAADAM

For no apparent reason the stadium suddenly cleared leaving three couples, shiny with sweat, wrestling without an audience. The mob, on horseback, in jeeps and on foot, moved briskly down the hill to join the crowd already scanning the horizon with narrowed eyes. A long plume of dust, travelling as fast as a bush fire, appeared some 5km to the south.

A lone policeman, mounted on a small motorbike and blowing a large whistle, desperately circled the area around the finishing post, trying to clear the way for the approaching horses. The judge, in dark suit, black high boots and a black leather cap, manoeuvred into position carrying the large red, blue and gold Mongolian flag.

The first two horses careered up the hill, neck and neck, riders' legs and arms flapping madly as they urged their steeds on. The flag dropped and the boy in the red-and-blue shirt was declared the winner. Neither rider showed much emotion at the end of the gruelling 25km bareback race and there was only a muted cheer from the crowd.

Almost immediately another group of 50 horses set off at a jog-trot for the neighbouring village for the start of the next race. Some of the mums and dads accompanied the riders, giving racing instructions as they went, and a couple of jeeps full of officials escorted the group to ensure fair play.

The crowd returned to the stadium to watch the wrestlers once more. Several pairs of wrestlers, wearing *gutuls*, traditional long leather boots with turned-up toes, a *zodog*, a bolero-like jacket with long sleeves that left the chest bare, and *shudag* (skimpy satin trunks) entered the field. They were accompanied by their seconds who wear *deels* (traditional robes) and hats. Before the bout begins the combatants perform the eagle dance which shows off their physique and also acts as warming-up exercises.

At the other end of the stadium a target was erected consisting of 360 small leather rings attached to a wall 40–50cm high by 4m long. Several men took up positions on either side and began to sing the *ukhai*, a traditional song, urging on the archers and signalling the results of the shooting. Both women and men take part in the archery competition with the women shooting from 60m and the men from 75m.

Souvenirs

Traditional hats, *deels* (men's robes) and boots, cashmere and camel-hair sweaters, small watercolours, model gers, pipes, and soft toys will remind you of your trip. Avoid the hotel shops; it is much more fun to go to the markets and local shops and far better value. Department stores in Ulaanbaatar stock traditional clobber at reasonable prices and the locals are delighted to see you trying on their gear.

Gifts

Take cigarettes and snuff for the men, sweets, books and toys for the children, and scarves and souvenir books of your country for the women.

Food and drink
Water

Take the usual precautions. Bottled water is available in Ulaanbaatar but in rural areas you should boil and/or filter drinking water – or drink imported beer which is available in the meanest village shop.

Drinks

Suutei tsai (salt tea) is universally served – made with two-thirds water and one-third milk (sheep's, goat's, cow's or mare's) heated in a big wide pan until boiling, when tea 'leaves', grated from a block of tea, and salt are sprinkled on top. A jug or small saucepan is dipped into the pan and the tea is then poured back from a great height to mix the brew. It is rarely served with sugar. Mongolians insist on drinking hot tea with their food 'to dissolve the fat' from the mutton and claim to suffer terrible indigestion if they don't.

Coca-Cola, Pepsi and other bottled drinks are sometimes available.

Alcohol

Imported beer and vodka are on sale in the humblest kiosks and shops throughout Mongolia.

Every ger has a skin bag of *airag* brewing beside the door to be stirred in passing. It is a not unpleasant drink and, having a low alcohol content, not likely to make you drunk – provided your host hasn't laced it with vodka or distilled it into *shimiin arkhi*, a highly potent alcoholic drink.

Food

The prospects are not good for vegetarians. The staple diet is mutton and flour, in the form of dumplings, or rice, with little variation. When you are invited to visit a family ger in the country you are likely to be offered *aaruul*, which our guide described as dried yoghurt – it has the look and texture of Parmesan cheese and a slightly tart flavour if your teeth are strong enough to gnaw a bit off.

Bansh is a Mongolian version of Siberian pelmeni, boiled dumplings stuffed with ground mutton, sometimes served in soup and sometimes on their own.

Dairy products made from sheep's milk can be very good. The yoghurt is delicious and doesn't need the sugar you may be offered; *öröm*, cream crust from sheep's milk, is interesting and quite pleasant if offered with small doughnutty biscuits.

Bread is not universally available so buy it when you can or make damper.

Likewise buy any fruit and vegetables, including potatoes, when you see them – it may be a while before you get another chance.

Accommodation
Camping

There are wonderful places to camp all over the country – just pick your spot on a mountainside, by a stream or lake. People are friendly but not intrusive. Out on the steppe there are gers run as cafés which will also allow you to put down your sleeping bag; there is not much privacy but it's a great way to experience the Mongolian way of life.

Hotels

In Ulaanbaatar there are a number of tourist-class hotels of varying quality and cost. Every aimag capital has at least one hotel – most with plumbing which leaves much to be desired.

Homestays

Ask your guide if he knows a family who take paying guests; or travel agents in Ulaanbaatar may be able to help.

Arts and entertainment

Most of the aimag capitals have theatres but, because the population shrinks in the summer months when people move out to their gers, there are few performances from June to September. In Ulaanbaatar short concerts of traditional music are put on for tourists; these are worth going to, and you may also be lucky and hear country people singing the 'long' and 'short' song out on the steppe.

GETTING THERE AND AWAY

Naushki or Kyakhta (Russia) – Altanbulag – Suhbaatar

In 1996 the railway line between Suhbaatar and Naushki, 235km south of Ulan Ude, was the only international border crossing between Mongolia and Russia and, until the old commie general in charge of the border retires, it is likely to remain so. This causes pain, grief and dollars for trans-continental drivers because the only way to get across the border is to put your vehicle on the train. (Strangely we were allowed to drive from Altanbulag back into Russia at Kyakhta on our return; see page 172.)

There is no international border crossing at the Mongolian/Chinese border in the west either, so currently it is not possible to cross into or from Xinjiang Province. If and when this changes, an interesting route to and from Europe and western Russia will be via Kashgar and the Torugart Pass in Kyrgyzstan but, until then, there is no direct route.

As very few foreign vehicles attempt to cross into Mongolia you may need the help of a travel agent in Ulan Ude. See page 150. The staff in the privatised Intourist offices in the Hotel Geser speak English and are very helpful. After several abortive attempts to drive across the border we realised we would have to put the car on the train. The station master at Naushki did not seem to know how to obtain a flat-top wagon and so Intourist organised one for us. Loading was difficult due to the difference in height between the wagon and the platform; and we had to comb the area for timber to use as ramps and wedges and wire to tie down the vehicle for the very slow 25km trip to Suhbaatar.

See also *Chapter Four*, page 115.

Road conditions

The road from the Russian border at Kyakhta/Altanbulag to Suhbaatar, should you be lucky enough to drive into Mongolia, is narrow but with a good sealed surface.

SUHBAATAR Сухбаатар

Time as Ulaanbaatar (GMT +8 hours)

Suhbaatar is the capital of Selenge aimag; and the excitement of the day here is when the Moscow train arrives at the station. The border guards turn out in force; no-one is allowed on to the platform unless they are boarding the train; sniffer dogs laconically cock their legs against the bogeys; and guards scramble over the roofs of the carriages. It is an action-by-action repeat of the performance when the train from Beijing reaches Naushki. In Naushki bags of pelts are removed from the train and taken into the Customs House – whether they're being confiscated or being valued for duty, who knows? What the Mongolians are looking for we never discovered but the procedure on both sides seems to reflect the antagonism between the two countries.

Where to stay

Inexpensive

Selenge Hotel, across the road from the station, is the usual small-town place. Otherwise there is a 'guesthouse' in a building on the station itself.

SUHBAATAR TO ULAANBAATAR

From Suhbaatar to Darhan and on to Ulaanbaatar the road is sealed but with some corrugations and many pot-holes.

DARHAN Дархан

Time as Ulaanbaatar

Population 85,000

On the main road to Ulaanbaatar and about 125km south of the Russian border, Darhan is the second biggest city in Mongolia and is the industrial centre of the country. A steel mill, jointly financed by Japan, recycles scrap, mostly imported from Russia where there is an abundance of it. There is also a big tanning and leather garment manufacturing industry here.

Communications

Area telephone code: 037

Health

Be aware that in 1996 there was an outbreak of cholera which put the city into quarantine for weeks. Do NOT drink the water – it's not a great place to spend more than one night.

Where to stay
Moderate
Darhan Hotel, which seems to be the only hotel, is on the outskirts of town. It has the usual fairly clean small rooms with bathroom (but no hot water in the summer) and service or lack of it – the receptionists are very friendly and helpful, the dining-room and bar staff the opposite.

Security parking
Available under the hotel

Where to eat
The restaurant at the **Darhan Hotel** has edible food but terrible service.

ULAANBAATAR Улаанбаатар
Time GMT +8 hours
Population 600,000
Altitude 1,350m
The capital of Mongolia, Ulaanbaatar shows the usual Soviet influence – vast civic squares suitable only for displaying the armed strength of the government on National Day, tall chimneys and huge lagged pipes carrying hot water from a central plant to the city. Despite this it has an atmosphere all its own and is quite appealing. Where else would you see horsemen, in traditional national dress, riding through the city regardless of the chaotic traffic?

The city is surrounded by four mountains which, beside being romantic, enclose the pollution from the power and hot-water plants within the valley.

Money
The Trade and Development Bank, tel: 312 641, open Mon–Fri 09.30–12.30, Sat 09.30–11.30, will give advances on Visa and also change travellers cheques. There are branches of various banks in tourist hotels, the State Library, the National Historical Museum and the central post office. Most tourist hotels accept some credit cards.

Communications
City telephone code: 1

Mail The main post office is on Peace Avenue on the west side of Suhbaatar Square. Open Mon–Fri 09.00–18.00, Sat 09.00–15.00. The post office at the Hotel Ulaanbaatar can arrange to send express mail. Most tourist hotels sell stamps and will post letters and cards for guests.

Telephone and fax Both the international telegraph office and the fax offices are in the main post office building.

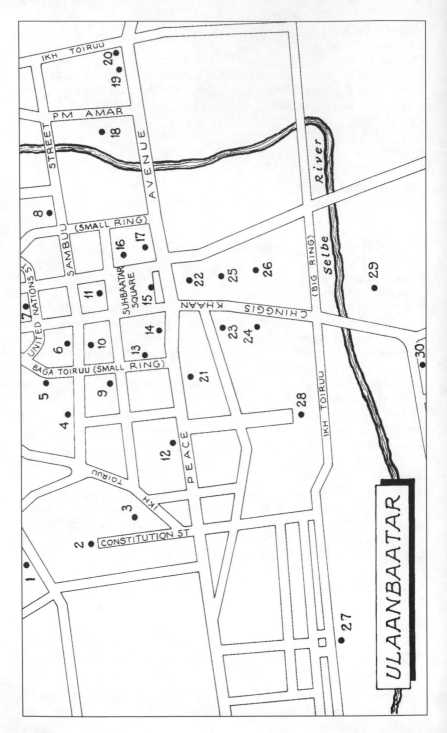

KEY TO ULAANBAATAR	Улаанбаатар

1 TV Centre
2 Gandantegchinlen Monastery
3 Hunting Trophy Museum
4 Ministry of Trade/Juulchin Foreign
     Tourism Corporation
5 USA Embassy
6 State Central Museum
7 German Embassy
8 Chinese Embassy
9 Fine Arts Museum
10 Museum of the Revolution
11 Parliament House
12 State department store
13 Mongolian Airline office
14 Central post office
15 Suhbaatar Monument
	16 State Academic Opera and Ballet
	      Theatre
	17 Ulaanbaatar Hotel
	18 Chinggis Khaan Hotel
	19 New Capital Hotel
	20 UK Embassy
	21 Russian Embassy
	22 Choijin Lama Temple Museum
	23 State Academic Drama Theatre, D
	      Natsagdorj
	24 Bayangol Hotel
	25 Central Exhibition Hall
	26 Nairamdal Park
	27 State Circus
	28 Railway station
	29 Central stadium

Emergency telephone numbers
Fire   01
Police   02

Email Magicnet seems to be the provider. Try contacting them on: info@magicnet.mn or ganbold@magicnet.mn or tel: 312 063.

Air connections International flights go to and from Beijing and Moscow; internal flights to and from Tsetserleg, Olgii, Bayanhongor, Bulgan Choibalsan, Mandalgov', Altai, Ondorhaan, Khovd, Moron, Dalanzadgad, Arvaiheer, Baruun Urt, Ulaangom and Uliastai. Flights to and from aimag capitals vary in frequency from daily to weekly.

Foreign embassy and consulate addresses
Canada Canadian Embassy, Beijing. 19 Dongzhimenwai Street, Chaoyang District, Beijing 100600; tel: 86 10 532 3536; fax: 532 4072
China Sambuu Street; tel: 20 955, 23 940
Germany United Nations Street, 270613 Ulaanbaatar; tel: 323 325, 323 915, 320 908; fax: 323 905
Russia Peace Avenue; tel: 25 207, 27 071
Turkey Ulaanbaatar; tel: 313 992
United Kingdom Peace Avenue; tel: 51 033
United States Big Ring; tel: 29 095, 29 639

Where to stay
Ulaanbaatar has a surprisingly large selection of hotels in varying price ranges.

Moderate
New Capital Hotel, set betside the British Embassy on Peace Avenue, is good value for money – perhaps due to the fact that a famous Mongolian surgeon ate a bad egg (Chinese, of course) there in 1995 and subsequently died of salmonella poisoning, causing the hotel to close for some months.

Surprisingly, it reopened under the same name. Takes Visa and American Express cards as well as travellers cheques.

Expensive
Bayangol Hotel, Chinggis Khaan Orgon Chuloo 28, tel: 312 255, fax: 326 880, caters mainly for tourist groups and it can be hard to gain attention if you are on your own (especially in the restaurant) but it has all the usual comforts – hot water, bar fridge, TV with CNN and Star (sports etc) and telephone – and is close to the centre of town.

Hotel Chinggis Khaan, Prime Minister Amar's Street, tel: 313 380, fax: 358 067, is the newest hotel in town and has the advantage of security parking under the hotel.

Very expensive
Ulaanbaatar Hotel, Suhbaatar Square 17, is in the centre of town and if you are simply looking for comfort after weeks of mutton and rice you could do worse and hang the expense.

Security parking
The Chinggis Khaan is the only hotel with security parking. If you are staying at the Bayangol Hotel, care of Juulchin, they will let you park in their huge depot for a few dollars – the problem is it's quite a hike from the hotel. Alternatively there is very cheap security parking at various carparks around town. There is also parking beside the New Capital Hotel.

Where to eat
All the big hotels have restaurants of varying quality and price. The Korean restaurant at the **Rainbow Club**, tel: 329 032, in the Office of the Youth Centre on Youth Avenue, serves food 09.00–21.00 and the karaoke bar is open 21.00–06.00. **Praha**, as you might expect, serves Czech food and is open 11.00–20.00.

What to see
The **Museum of Natural History**, Sambuu Street, will give you an idea of what flora and fauna to expect as you travel deeper into the country. The skeletons of the trabosaur and duck-billed dinosaurs from the Gobi desert are impressive. Closed on Tuesdays. **Gandantegchinlen** (Gandan Hiid), Constitution Street, tel: 3 360 167/360 3554/360 258, a Buddhist monastery built in 1840, was kept open as a show-place for foreigners during the communist years. Now the monastery is fully functional once more and visitors are welcome.

Try to catch a performance of the **Jamuha Art Company** or the **Tumen Eh Song and Dance Ensemble** at the Institute of National Culture and Rest, tel: 327 279/326 020 or ask at one of the tourist hotels.

ULAANBAATAR TO ARVAIHEER (ARBAYKHEER)

Distance 460km
Take the main road to the west from Ulaanbaatar heading for Lun; and at the junction keep left for Ulaanbulag. The right turn will take you to Harhorin (Karakorum), the 13th-century capital of the Mongolian empire. Good sealed road.

ARVAIHEER   Арвайхззр

Time as Ulaanbaatar
An easy run southwest from Ulaanbaatar with lovely scenery, Arvaiheer is the capital of the Ovorhangai aimag. It is a typical small Mongolian town with not much of interest to visitors unless you are there for the Naadam, when you are likely to be the only foreigners.

Communications

Mail and telephone The post office is opposite the town hall, across the divided road.

Air connections Flights go to and from Ulaanbaatar.

Where to stay
Inexpensive
Hangai Hotel has the usual floor plan but a bad case of concrete cancer makes it even less inviting and the plumbing is abysmal. Do not venture out on to the tiny balconies – they are rotting faster than the main structure and are hazardous.

Moderate
Bayanbulag Hotel, on the same side of the road as the post office, is all that the Hangai is not – new, clean, light, comfortable but, alas, with no hot water in summer.

Security parking
In a locked yard on the east side of the town hall.

Where to eat
Inexpensive
Both hotels have restaurants. The dingy **Hangai** restaurant served mutton and rice with a few vegetables which was very cheap and quite good, washed down with a can of imported beer. The **Bayanbulag** had a pleasant bar, stocked with several different brands of imported beer, and a restaurant which served good mutton-and-vegetable soup followed by mutton and rice.

What to see
The **Gandan Muntsagian Hiid** (Monastery), which was destroyed in 1937, but was rebuilt and opened in 1990. The Museum, if you like stuffed animals.

ARVAIHEER TO BAYANHONGOR

Distance 210km
The road is sealed for the first 10km, then it's a case of picking your own rough to very rough track. Follow the power lines but try not to get diverted to a village off the main track. Can take up to seven hours from Arvaiheer to Bayanhongor.

The road conditions from here onwards deteriorate rapidly but the magnificent views more than compensate.

BAYANHONGOR   Баянхонгор

Time as Ulaanbaatar
Population 20,000
Bayanhongor is the capital of the aimag of the same name. It is a dreary town which looks as if it was built around a slag heap but perhaps the state of the hotel coloured our vision.

Communications

Post and telegraph office This is in the main street before the square.

Airport Flights several times a week to and from Ulaanbaatar.

Where to stay
Inexpensive
Nomgon Hotel – it took an hour to find someone to let us in but it wasn't worth the effort; it was dirty and run down. We would have been far better off camping had it not been pouring with rain. There used to be two hotels in Bayanhongor but in 1996 the Negdelchin had closed and looked deserted.

Security parking
After several dud leads we realised there was no security parking to be found and our guide insisted on sleeping in the car outside the hotel. A busload of Mongolian tourists arrived after us and their driver slept in his bus too.

Where to eat
Inexpensive
The **UEG Restaurant** (sign in English) and bar next to the police station seems to be the only place to eat. It serves mutton-and-vegetable soup, mutton and rice and Danish, German or Singaporian beer.

BAYANHONGOR TO BAYDRAG RIVER

Distance 140km
It is approximately five and a half hours' driving from Bayanhongor to the Baydrag River bridge. There are at least two ways from the high country

down to the river but neither is clearly shown on current maps so the choice will depend on your guide, or your instinct if you don't have a guide. One way is very rough along a rocky dry river bed and the other very winding but not so rough.

The wooden bridge over the Naryn river about halfway between Bayanhongor and the Baydrag River was washed away in a flood at the end of June 1996 but, provided the river is not in flood, it is possible to ford it a few kilometres downstream.

There are many lovely places to camp beside the Baydrag. On the west side a group of gers offer food and basic accommodation. If you stop here you may be lucky enough to find someone who will lead you to Wild Goat Place – a superb campsite beside a mountain stream. Please don't persist if no-one offers to show you the way; it is a sacred site as well as being a very fragile environment and the local people do not want to turn it into a tourist spot.

BAYDRAG RIVER TO ALTAI

Distance 270km
The road from Baydrag River to Altai takes around seven hours and winds through the mountains before dropping down into the long valley leading to Altai.

ALTAI Алтай
Time as Ulaanbaatar
Population 15,000
Altai is the capital of the Gobi-Altai aimag. If you are going down through the Altai Mountains to visit the *takhi* (Przewalski horses) then you must get your supplies here. The shops are not well stocked but by visiting each in turn you should be able to find enough to keep you going for a couple of weeks. As usual most shops have vodka, imported canned beer, cigarettes and sweets; you may have to hunt around for potatoes and other basic commodities.

Communications
Area telephone code: 065

Mail and telephone It is sometimes possible to telephone from the post office to the west of the town square. The telephone operators, in the exchange behind the post office counter, wear shiny purple blouses and are very helpful but connections through the old-fashioned switchboard system were difficult to make.

Fax There is direct dial from the little fax machine in the telephone exchange which works well.

Airport There are regular flights from Ulaanbaatar to Altai.

Where to stay
Inexpensive
There is only one hotel in Altai, the **Zendmen Hotel**, which has clean rooms, friendly staff and the usual pathetic plumbing. If by this time you are desperate for a warm 'shower' nobody minds if you take a saucepan and your camping gas stove into your room. An attractive alternative is a small group of tourist gers about 5km west of Altai – head for the red-and-white antennae to the left of the road to Khovd. The gers are decorated and furnished in traditional style and the family running the camp is friendly and knowledgeable about the area.

Security parking
Opposite the hotel at the side of the police station. There is no fence but if you get there first you can park right outside the duty officer's window.

Where to eat
Surprisingly there are two places, both inexpensive, to eat – the **Zendmen Hotel** has a dining-room and serves the usual mutton soup followed by mutton and rice. Ask for vegetables well ahead and you may be lucky. Russian wine is sometimes available at the bar.

The **Sutai Restaurant** to the south of the post office was once a grand place but has seen better days. With its amazing pressed aluminium ceiling, parquet floor, filthy tablecloths, upright chairs with bright yellow loose covers, and shocking-pink 'tropical' drapes with palm-tree and sailing-boat motif, it's the place for a special night out. The food, mutton and rice, is not as good as at the hotel but you are likely to meet more locals here.

What to see
Sutai mountain, at over 4,000m, on the Khovd aimag border, is the highest in Gobi-Altai and is a challenge if you are a climber.

ALTAI TO TAKHIIN TAL

Distance 271km
There are many reasons to visit the southwest corner of Mongolia: the flora and fauna, the takhi, the spectacular scenery and the sense of penetrating one of the few areas in the world which are truly off the beaten track.

The drive from Altai to Gobi B National Park, in the Dzungarian Gobi, where the takhi are being reintroduced to their native land, is an adventure in itself. Take the Khovd road out of Altai for 32km and then turn off to the left, following the power lines. Leave a village, possibly Sharga, with large antennae to your right. After 85km you will come to a bridge over a small river (clean water) and a few gers. From here drive southwest, heading for a range of bald mountains with a frieze of vegetation around the foothills.

MONGOLIAN PICNIC

A picnic had been arranged for the day after we reached Takhiin Tal. There were several reasons to celebrate – the birth of a son to Sukhbaatar, the director of the Takhi Reintroduction Centre, and his wife; the winning of a horse-race by the 11-year-old daughter of Sukhbaatar's assistant; and the birth of a foal to one of the Australian-bred takhis.

We gathered on a patch of bright green grass at a bend in the stream which ran through the rugged Altai Mountains. Soon a lad appeared on horseback driving a flock of sheep and goats towards us. An old man got unsteadily to his feet and picked out two young, glossy black goats.

With the minimum of fuss, the goats were slaughtered, skinned and cut up on the skins. Nothing was wasted; even the intestines and stomach were emptied, washed in the stream and stuffed with the liver and kidneys. Meanwhile dry dung was gathered for a fire to heat special flat stones, and water was fetched and mixed with sheep's milk in a big aluminium bowl for tea.

By the time the stones were hot the butchering was finished. Layers of stones and meat were placed into a big metal milk churn. The water and sheep's milk were boiling and salt and tea-leaves, hacked off a solid brick of Georgian tea, were sprinkled on top. A woman mixed the tea by scooping it up in a small saucepan then pouring it back from a great height.

Everyone sat in a circle on the grass. The medal won in the horse race was placed in a shallow silver dish filled with vodka, and handed on a blue scarf to the elder. He dipped his fingers in and sprinkled a few drops into the air in a traditional libation before drinking and passing it back. The dish was topped up and handed to the next man who drank, placed a bank note between the dish and the scarf, and returned it to the host and so on until everyone – men first and then the women – had drunk.

The meat was passed round by hand, our hosts making sure we tried all the delicacies and exhorting us to 'Meat eat!', followed by small Chinese bowls of broth. Then the serious drinking began and the men started to sing the two traditional songs – the 'long song', so named because the notes are held for a long time, and the 'short song' which is easier to sing. Both felt as old as time – about horses, the land, nature – and have been sung since the era of Chinggis Khan.

At 145km you will reach the village of Tögrög where fuel is available. Take the road up behind the fuel station and at the junction at the top of the hill go straight down into the valley and along the valley floor. The road is narrow and rough and climbs through rocky passes to 2,500m at an ovoo (see page 147) 32km from Tögrög. Follow the power lines for 57km to Bugat.

Continue southwestward up the valley through sheer rock passes, with sparkling streams running down the centre of the track, for 69km to Takhiin Tal. The 271km trip takes eight to ten hours.

TAKHIIN TAL   Тахийн Тал

This is a small section of Gobi B National Park devoted to the reintroduction of the takhi. There are big herds of khulan and black-tailed gazelle in this part of the Gobi Desert.

Communications

The Takhi Reintroduction Centre has an office in Ulaanbaatar, 'Baigali' ordon, Ulaanbaatar 38; tel: (1) 362 064; fax 360 067.

The post office, with satellite dish, 70km from Takhiin Tal at Bugat, is the nearest public telephone. Sometimes the radio telephone at Takhiin Tal works.

Where to stay

Stay in the DIY gers past the office or camp beside them. Water is available from the river and there are clean pit latrines.

Security parking

Unnecessary in this wilderness area.

What to see

The takhi, khulan, black-tailed gazelle, saiga antelope and wild Bactrian camel as well as unusual birds, reptiles and flora are waiting for the keen photographer. Sunrise is the best time to see khulan.

Explore the surrounding area but avoid the border with China as the border guards are very territorial.

TAKHIIN TAL TO KHOVD

Khovd is 474km from Altai along the main road but from Takhiin Tal there are a number of different ways to reach the town. However, unless you have a guide or a GPS and accurate large-scale maps, it is safer to return to the main Altai–Khovd road even though it is much longer and slower.

The alternatives are to drive up to the Takhiin Tal airfield and follow the concrete kilometre boundary posts to number 80, turn right and follow the track to the village of Barlag situated at a T-junction. Apparently both ways lead to Khovd – the left goes through the villages of Bor-Uzuur and Uyench to meet the road from Tsetseg to Lake Khar-Us. The right-hand track heads northeast through very rough country in the Altai Mountains – challenging driving.

If you take the right-hand track stop about 130km from Takhiin Tal at a large ovoo to throw an offering on to the pile and thank your guardian angel for your safe arrival at this magical place. Pause and meditate; for surely moments like these are the reason that you travel so far.

After another 90km or so Tsetseg Nuur (Wildflower Lake) will come into view and, as the route has taken about nine hours of tough driving, you may want to camp either by the lake, mosquitoes permitting, or on a hillside facing the magnificent 3,752m snowcapped Ulaan Sunduy uul.

The village of Tsetseg, like many villages in remote areas of Mongolia, is almost deserted in summer when the inhabitants move their gers out to the hills to be close to their flocks. It is, therefore, difficult to get information about the best route to take. Should you see other vehicles or motorbikes flag them down and ask the way.

As usual there are two routes from Tsetseg to Khovd. One goes over the mountains to the northeast and the other, which locals say is the better road, a bit west of north along the valley floor. Road conditions on the latter vary from good sandy track to corrugations to rocky surfaces. If anything they deteriorate as the road nears Khovd, with some of the worst corrugations in western Mongolia. Some road work being undertaken near the town in 1996 may have improved the last few kilometres. Tsetseg to Khovd takes about five and a half hours.

In the area near Tögrög (not the Tögrög in Gobi-Altai aimag), about 90km southeast of Khovd is Tsenherin Agui, meaning 'three blue caves', in which are cave paintings said to be 15,000 years old. The caves are about 15km off the track. Don't forget to take torches.

KHOVD Ховд
Time Ulaanbaatar –1 hour
Population 35,000
The capital of the aimag of the same name, Khovd is the largest town in the west of Mongolia. The city lies along the Buyant Gol (river) in a green valley dotted with white gers, horses and flocks of sheep and goats. Many of the inhabitants move a few kilometres out of town and live in their gers for the summer months.

Money
There is a bank which will change dollars into togrogs.

Communications
Area telephone code: 043

Mail The post and telephone exchange office is in the main street.

Airport There are flights several times a week to and from Ulaanbaatar.

Where to stay
Inexpensive
Buyant Hotel, tel: 3860, situated opposite the theatre, is clean and comfortable although there is no hot water in summer.

Khovd Hotel, on the other side of the theatre, is rather run down.

Security parking
In a locked yard behind the Buyant Hotel.

Where to eat
The restaurant at the **Buyant Hotel** serves mutton and rice and delicious mutton-and-vegetable soup. Stalls sell small refreshing watermelons and very small apples in June.

What to see

Khovd is a historic city which was established by the Manchu in the 18th century. The ruins of the mud walls of the city of Sangiin Herem are rapidly disappearing back into the earth but you can still see part of the wall to the north of the town.

The Sunday Market is memorable for the recycling of old-fashioned water-filled radiators half buried to mark out parking areas. Most of the stalls were selling poor-quality Chinese clothing but look out for blackcurrants and other fruit in season. For relaxation you can have a game of pool or join a group playing a Mongolian version of two-up.

KHOVD TO OLGII

Distance 230km

The run from Khovd to Olgii (seven to eight hours) takes you through some of the most beautiful country in Mongolia. Snowcapped mountains, brilliant blue lakes and lots of birds – elegant white-naped cranes, swans, kingfishers and cormorants – plus a 'good' road make the drive memorable.

OLGII   Олгий

Olgii is the capital and, indeed, the only town of the Bayan-Olgii aimag. The majority of the population of the aimag are Kazak. They say that from the 1840s their nomadic forebears began to bring their flocks to the mountain pastures of the area in summer, returning to Kazakstan and Xinjiang province of China for the winter.

Islam, with the aid of Saudi Arabia and the Muslim World League, is beginning to re-establish itself and a small mosque has been built. However, the Kazaks do not stick to strict Muslim law and, like their brothers in Kazakstan, enjoy their vodka.

Our Mongolian guide said he found it hard to understand the Kazaks even when they spoke Mongolian and the problem appeared to be mutual.

Olgii has an air of mild prosperity and a number of small factories manufacture clothes, boots and belts, furniture and even carpets.

Communications

Area telephone code: 071

Mail and telephone The post office and telephone exchange is opposite the Tavanbogd Hotel.

International airport Flights go to and from Ulaanbaatar and also Almaty, capital of Kazakstan.

Where to stay
Inexpensive

Tavanbogd Hotel, named after the highest mountain in Mongolia, is not the best in Mongolia but possibly not the worst either. Not very clean, a disgusting bathroom and no hot water but there was running cold water – it ran constantly through the lavatory. If there is a party of tourists in town the hotel fills up. We heard rumours of other better hotels, including the **Sansar**, but we did not have time to check them out.

Security parking

Ask at the police station if you can park in their large enclosed yard. One night we were charged a few togrogs by the policeman who opened the gate, the other night there was no charge.

There is an enclosed yard beyond the mosque but 'the man with the key' was missing.

Travel agent

A good contact is Mr Meduhan, of Altai Tour Company; tel: (home) 21 79 or (office) 21 69; fax 12 44. Although he does not speak much English he can make hotel bookings and arrange horse treks and climbing trips. Get Juulchin in Ulaanbaatar to phone him in case of language difficulties.

Where to eat

The **Tavanbogd Hotel** has a restaurant which serves the usual fare but if you ask you may get some vegetables with the mutton. Unfortunately one of the nights we were there 'the woman with the key' was missing but we eventually got dinner at 21.30.

What to see

The museum is worth a visit – make sure you go up to the third floor to see the exhibition of Kazak culture.

Try to arrange a visit to a family ger near Olgii. Kazak gers are a different shape from traditional Mongolian ones, having a steeper roof and only one centre pole. They are usually lined with panels of brightly coloured wool woven around reeds and have hand-embroidered felt or cotton rugs on the floor.

OLGII TO TSAGAANUUR/TASHANTA BORDER

Distance 137km

It is 110km to the Mongolian side of the border over rugged mountains and along valleys with rivers and lakes. The Mongolian officials at the border post are very friendly and helpful but until the Tsagaanuur/Tashanta crossing is declared an international port it is unlikely the Russian officials at Tashanta, 27km through no man's land, will let you through.

There are several ways back to Ulaanbaatar from Olgii. Apart from the route we had used via Khovd and Altai, another heads north to Nogoonuur, then east to Ulaangom, close to Lake Uvs, whilst another

MONGOLIAN/RUSSIAN BORDER AT TASHANTA

We were sad to be leaving a country which we had come to love but excited at continuing our journey. Following the usual lengthy immigration and customs form-filling rituals at Tsagaanuur, the chief of the border offered to come with us to the Russian post, ensuring there would be no problems. After the Russian refusal to let us drive into Mongolia we were feeling anxious but hopeful. We had made a number of contacts in Olgii; all insisted on accompanying us and all were confident they could get us across the border.

It's 27km from one post to the other with a Russian army barricade about halfway. Here the NCO rang through to ask whether he should let us pass. He got permission and we continued over the rough corrugated dirt track until we reached the Russian border post. Our Mongolian officer was greeted like a long lost friend by, we assumed, his magnificently uniformed (bright blue with masses of gold braid) counterpart. We began to believe we would be allowed to cross back into Russia here.

Alas! He was the chief customs officer and had no other authority. The Russian officer-in-charge of the border was a very pleasant young man who told us he would have to telephone Moscow. Intourist in Ulan Ude had promised they would get permission for us to re-enter Russia at Tashanta so we felt fairly confident all would be well. After half an hour or so the officer returned. Apologetically he explained that the general-in-charge of the Russian/Mongolian border at Chita had refused us permission. We tried to persuade him to ring Moscow or Intourist in Ulan Ude – he was sad but unyielding. David discreetly showed he had US dollars but, despite all the stories we had been told of officials demanding bribes, we had certainly found an honest officer.

There was nothing for it but to return to Olgii with a very disconsolate band of 'helpers'. Our Mongolian officer-in-charge was chagrined, having lost face, our guide was disappointed as he had hoped to fly back to Ulaanbaatar next day; and we were depressed at the thought of being 4,000km and three weeks behind in our schedule now we had to drive all the way back to Suhbaatar.

Back at the Mongolian border our guide said he must look after our 'helpers' by buying them dinner. We were exhausted and wanted to drive straight back to Olgii as it was now within an hour of darkness and we didn't fancy driving over the track at night. Our guide was adamant so we agreed we would go ahead and they would catch up with us in their jeep before we had a chance to get lost. 'Looking after' the group turned out to be getting blind drunk on vodka. Left alone, we took a wrong turn and landed up a two-hour drive to the west of Olgii at the small town of Biluu at dusk. The place seemed deserted but eventually we found a man who directed us back along the flooded road we had arrived on. As we left town we met a lad on horseback. He leaped off his horse and into the LandCruiser with his sack of rice before we could protest, telling us he would be our guide.

Darkness fell and the full moon rose as we wound our way up and down through the mountain range separating us from Olgii. Our 'guide' grunted assent when we queried the way and then appeared to go to sleep. After a while there was much shuffling in the back seat, the window was opened and the lad stuck his head out. At last I realised he was carsick. Whether it was vodka or nerves or a stomach upset we never discovered but he guided us back to Olgii, intimated he wanted to stop at a crossroads and jumped out of the car. Tossing the heavy sack on to his back, he waved cheerfully and disappeared.

It was nearly midnight when we reached the Tavanbogd Hotel. Just as we were falling into an exhausted sleep, the door burst open and two of our 'helpers' stumbled in; David pushed them out into the corridor where they stood, swaying gently, while we retired to bed. Next day our guide arrived, very much the worse for wear, with a cock and bull story about running out of petrol. We didn't want to know.

LAKE KHOVSGOL

John Lee, leader of an Australian Toyota Club expedition in 1996, warns: 'Lake Khovsgol is magnificent; it is as beautiful, or more so, as Lake Baikal. The problem is the ranger, or the "Chief" ranger, Jambal, who visited us on our first night and fined us for camping where we were told it was OK to camp by the English-speaking ranger at the entrance to the Khovsgol National Park. He took our guide's passport and forced us to move to another place about 10km further north, where he found us and "fined" us again for not camping in the correct spot. This he does to most people who do not stay in the "tourist camps", where extra charges are levied, and the facilities are grotty. This was the first example of "rob the tourist" we had experienced in Mongolia. We discussed these "fines" with him, which varied up and down – 20,000 togrogs for four vehicles, to US$100 per person, then down to 10,000 togrogs (US$1=500 togrogs). Finally we only had to pay another daily charge for the national park, but, unbeknown to us, our guide paid 10,000 togrogs "fine", or could we call this something else? The average wage is US$18/week in Mongolia. I hope the Jambal is replaced very soon, or disposed of in some way!'

goes back to Khovd and then north to Ulaangom. From here the road goes east to Moron, south of Lake Khovsgol.

From Moron there is a track up the west side of the lake and lovely places to camp. We were warned that the roads across the north of Mongolia quickly became impassable after rain due to washed-away bridges. At the northern end of the lake there is a border-crossing into Russia which is worth enquiring about. If it's still not classed as international, then you will have to go to Ulaanbaatar via Bulgan and so back to the train at Suhbaatar; or you may be allowed to cross by road from Altanbulag to Kyakhta.

Hopefully these silly border regulations will be changed before long.

ALTANBULAG   Алтанбулаг

This nondescript small town lies 24km east of Suhbaatar over a narrow sealed road with a reasonable surface. At one time there must have been much traffic crossing the border here. Now it is mainly people returning to Russia with bags, baskets and boxes of cheap Chinese clothing to sell in the markets.

Vehicles have to wait at the gates for permission to enter the border area before being signalled to drive in and park over an inspection pit. After you have filled in a number of forms in the office the Customs officers at the border post are likely to tell you to bring all your luggage into the Customs Hall. You will protest, smile, protest some more and eventually take the most sympathetic one by the hand and lead her to your vehicle, shrugging your shoulders hopelessly. Soon an officer will come out and, after a cursory inspection, let you through. At least that was our experience and we hope you are as lucky.

Part Three

THE 'STANS
Kazakstan • Kyrgyzstan
Uzbekistan • Turkmenistan

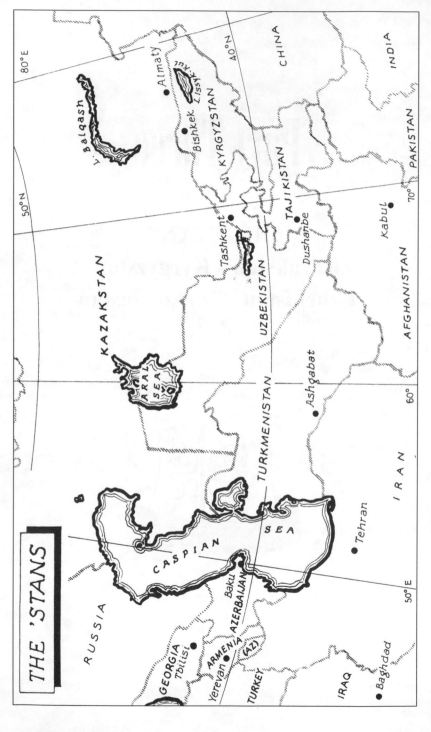

THE 'STANS

GETTING TO AND FROM THE 'STANS

Russia to Kazakstan

The Russian/Kazak border just south of Veseloyarsk, on the A349 from Barnaul to Semey, is informal. We told the guard we were tourists going to Semey and were ushered through without being asked to show any documents. After a few kilometres we were stopped at a Kazak police post and, after showing our car registration and the pink-and-green Russian customs form, we were free to go.

China to Kyrgyzstan

In 1996 we had planned to enter Xinjiang Province from Kazakstan at Korgos, then to drive to Urumqi, Turpan and Kashgar, entering Kyrgyzstan via the Torugart Pass. For this we had to apply to the China International Travel Service for a vehicle permit, which a guide would bring to the border. The guide would accompany us while we were in China. Unfortunately, due to difficulties leaving Mongolia and a mechanical breakdown, our permit had expired by the time we reached Kazakstan and we did not have time to wait another two weeks for a new permit.

See also Erik Korevaar's experience cycling over the Torugart Pass in *Chapter Seven.*

Turkmenistan to Iran

Crossing at the Artyk/Lotf Abad border is a serious business and took us four hours. Although I wore loose trousers, a long-sleeved loose shirt and a big scarf, covering head and shoulders, I was told I was not suitably dressed for a woman in Iran so I sat in the car while David went from office to office trying to make sense of the procedures.

Eventually he came back to the car but had to wait while a welcoming ceremony was arranged. He was taken to a large room where an *imam*, in full ceremonial gear, welcomed him to the Islamic Republic of Iran 'in the name of God', and then David was handed a short speech of thanks in English, also 'in the name of God', which he had to give. He was then presented with a large parcel, in colourful fancy paper; when we opened it much later we found it contained a big bag of pistachio nuts, a bag of toffees and a beautiful saffron flower.

We were then free to leave but a man insisted on coming with us to the gates, about one kilometre away. After we had passed the first guard post he told us to stop and handed David a bill (in Farsi, of course) for $120, claiming, in broken English, to have been our 'agent'. As we were now in no man's land between guard posts we found there was little we could do but protest vociferously before paying him, 'in the name of God'.

I should stress this was the only Iranian who was anything but friendly and helpful to us during the few days we spent driving through Iran to Turkey.

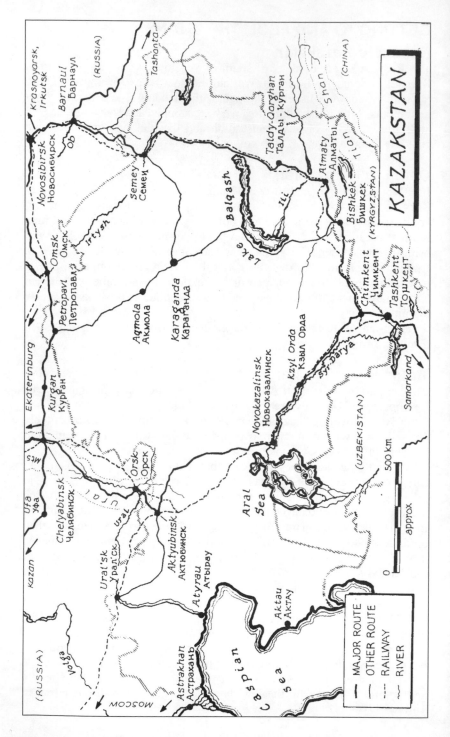

KAZAKSTAN

(RUSSIA)

Krasnoyarsk, Irkutsk

Barnaul Барнаул

Tashanta

(CHINA)

Novosibirsk Новосибирск

Ob

Taldy-Qorghan Талды-Курган

Atmaty Алматы

Tian Shan

Semey Семей

Irtysh

Omsk Омск

Bishkek Бишкек

(KYRGYZSTAN)

Petropavl Петропавл

Balqash

Ili

Lake

Ekaterinburg

Kurgan Курган

Aqmola Акмола

Karaganda Караганда

Chimkent Чимкент

Tashkent Тошкент

Kzyl Orda Кзыл Орда

Syr Darya

Samarkand

Ufa Уфа

Mts

Chelyabinsk Челябинск

Orsk Орск

Novokazalinsk Новоказалинск

(UZBEKISTAN)

500 km

Ural

Ural'sk Уралćск

Aktyubinsk Актюбинск

Aral Sea

approx

kazan

Volga

Atyrau Атырау

Aktau Актау

0

(RUSSIA)

Astrakhan Астрахань

Caspian Sea

MOSCOW

MAJOR ROUTE
OTHER ROUTE
RAILWAY
RIVER

Chapter Six

Kazakstan

Spelling of names varies as Russian influence declines, eg: Semipalatinsk is now Semey. We have tried to use the Kazak spelling, with the Russian version in parentheses the first time the name is mentioned, wherever possible. However spelling is changing all the time – sometimes just changing the K to a Q, as in Qazaqstan; it should be noted that Kazakstan (not Kazakhstan nor Qazaqstan) is still the official spelling at present.

Kazakstan is much bigger than the four other 'Stans combined. Its close proximity to Russia, combined with the comparative fertility of its steppe, led to colonisation as early as the 18th century. Unfortunately for the Kazaks, its size, long border with Russia (6,846km) and low population density (6.3 per km^2) also made it the ideal place, from the Russian point of view, to become the nuclear testing-ground of the USSR. In 1989 the Nevada-Semipalatinsk Movement organised massive anti-nuclear protests which resulted in the cessation of all nuclear testing in the Semey area.

FACTS AND FIGURES

Time
GMT +6 in eastern Kazakstan, including Almaty, +5 hours in western Kazakstan and +4 hours in the far west.

Population
17,376,615 (July 1995 estimate)

Capital
Almaty (Alma-Ata)

GEOGRAPHY
Kazakstan has a total area of 2,717,300km^2 and a land area of 2,669,800km^2. Second only in size to Russia in the CIS, Kazakstan is a vast, mainly flat

country bordering China, Kyrgyzstan, Russia, Turkmenistan and Uzbekistan as well as the Aral and Caspian Seas. It stretches from the Volga in the west to the Altai Mountains in the east, and from western Siberia in the north to the deserts of Central Asia in the south. The terrain varies from crop-growing steppe in the north to arid desert in the south. The Tian Shan mountain range, with peaks up to almost 7,000m, and the Zhungar Ala-Too, with peaks to 5,000m, form its boundaries with China and Kyrgyzstan.

The president plans to move the capital from Almaty, in the extreme south of the country, to Aqmola (Akmola), a little north of the centre of Kazakstan, in 1997. It is a very expensive undertaking but makes sense in the long term.

CLIMATE

Kazakstan has a continental climate, cold winters and hot summers, with temperatures varying according to latitude and altitude. For instance in Almaty average temperatures range from –10°C in winter to the high twenties in summer; and although Semey and Akmola have summer temperatures similar to those of Almaty, in winter they drop to –20°C or even lower.

Annual rainfall also varies with altitude and averages from below 100mm in the desert to 1,600mm in the Altai Mountains, with 250–300mm on the steppe.

NATURAL HISTORY AND CONSERVATION

Approximately 2.5% of the land is designated as either protected or a national park and reserve. Kazakstan is desperately short of funds to run its conservation programme. Cultivation of environmentally fragile areas of steppe has caused soil erosion and over-stocking has aggravated the situation.

Nature reserves

Kurgaizhino Nature Reserve, approximately 150km southwest of Akmola in northern Kazakstan, covers a cluster of lakes set in arid steppe. Geologists suggest that the largest lake, Lake Tenghiz, is the remains of an ancient sea. It is the habitat of numerous species of waterbird including gulls and sandpipers. A large breeding colony of flamingos, which migrate to the Caspian Sea, inhabit the lakes, as do pelicans.

Aqsu-Zhabaghly (Aksu-Dzhaballinskiy) Nature Reserve is set in the foothills of the Western Tian Shan on the Kyrgyzstan border. It is the home of bear, ibex, snow leopard and wonderful birds of prey, though you are more likely to see the birds than the mammals.

HISTORICAL OUTLINE

Kazakstan was for thousands of years an area inhabited by warring nomadic tribes, winning and losing battles, slaughtering and being slaughtered.

In 1969 archaeologists excavated a mound beside the Yesik River and found a treasure trove of gold artefacts, an iron sword, a dagger inlaid with precious metals, a silver spoon and many other artefacts dating back to between the 5th and 9th centuries BC. The most exciting find was a suit of gold which must have belonged to the chief of the Sak tribe. Alexander the Great was repelled by the Saks during the 4th century BC, one of his few defeats, illustrating the courage of the Saks.

The southern area of Kazakstan was on the Silk Route and was settled by traders while the rest of the country continued its nomadic way of life. In the 5th to the 8th centuries AD the south became part of the Turkic empire but by the mid-9th century the Samanids were in control.

In the early 13th century Genghis Khan conquered Kazakstan on his way to Europe. On his death a huge area including north and west Kazakstan became part of the Golden Horde ruled by Genghis Khan's grandsons. The southern and eastern area came under the command of Genghis Khan's son Chaghatai's command.

It was not until the 16th century that Kazaks emerged as an ethnic group. Gradually over the next 300 years Russia began to dominate the area. The abolition of serfdom in the mid 1800s led to such an influx of peasants from Russia and Ukraine that Kazaks gradually became a minority in their own country.

As well as voluntary immigrants many dissidents were exiled to Kazakstan including Dostoyevsky and the Ukrainian artist and writer Taras Shevchenko.

In 1916 the Kazaks rebelled against the Russians who were settling their land. In the ensuing battles over 150,000 people were killed and the Kazaks were subjugated.

After the October Revolution in Russia civil war broke out in Kazakstan followed by three years of independence. However, despite aid from foreign powers, the White Army was defeated by the Red Army in 1920 and Kazakstan became part of the Turkestan Republic. It was not until 1936 that Kazakstan became a Soviet Socialist Republic within the USSR.

At the time of the Revolution there was a big exodus with thousands of Kazaks moving into China, Mongolia and neighbouring countries. In the years between the Revolution and the collapse of the USSR, families from Russia and other communist countries poured into Kazakstan, to work in the newly established industrial cities and the nuclear industry and to cultivate the steppe, depriving many Kazaks of their traditional nomadic way of life.

Kazakstan achieved independence on December 1 1991, after the collapse of the USSR, and became a member of the CIS.

POLITICS

Shortly after the breakup of the USSR Kazakstan was proclaimed a democratic state. In January 1993 a new constitution was adopted and Kazakstan became a democratic republic with a presidential system. The executive president is also the head of state and is elected for a five-year term. He/she cannot be president for more than two terms. President Nursultan Nazarbayev has been in office since 1990 and in 1995 held a nationwide referendum which extended his term until 2000.

Parliament is unicameral with elections for the Supreme Council held every five years – the next one is due, in theory, in 1999. However, in March 1995, the Supreme Council was dissolved following a Constitutional Court ruling that the 1994 elections were invalid. The Council of Ministers (cabinet) is appointed by the prime minister. Prime Minister Akezhan Kazhegeldin was elected in 1994.

ECONOMY

Kazakstan is enormously rich in oil, gas and other minerals. The government encourages joint ventures with the West to exploit these resources. For example the Yuzhneftegaz State Joint Stock Company is involved in joint ventures with Turan Petroleum (Canada) and Germmunai (Germany) in the Kumkol oilfield.

Kazakstan, as part of the USSR, had a big agricultural and defence machine-manufacturing industry producing tractors, heavy earth-moving equipment, tanks and other machines. After the demise of the USSR the bottom fell out of the market for such machinery.

Annual inflation skyrocketed in the early 1990s but by 1995 was down to around 20%.

PEOPLE

Descended from bellicose Huns, tough Turks and militant horsemen warrior Saks, Kazaks lived a nomadic lifestyle for hundreds of years. Russians began to move into the area from the 18th century, followed by Ukrainians and other Europeans.

Since 1991 the government has been enticing Kazaks to return from Mongolia, China and other countries to bolster the population. There has also been an exodus of Russians and others from the former USSR.

Ethnic division is now approximately Kazak 44.3% (up from 41.9% in 1991), Russian 35.8% (from 37%), Ukrainian 5.1% (from 5.2%), German 3.6% (from 4.7%), Uzbek 2.2% (from 2.1%), Tatar 2% and other 7%.

LANGUAGE

Qazaq (Kazak) is the official language of Kazakstan but is generally only spoken by the Kazak population. Russian is an official language of

Wedding party, Khiva, Uzbekistan

KYRGYZSTAN
Above: *Donkey drawn haycart, Issyk-Kul*
Below: *South side, Issyk-Kul road*

LOCAL PRODUCE
Above: *Buying apricots at Issyk-Kul, Kyrgyzstan*
Below: *Melon sellers, Turkmenistan*

UZBEKISTAN
Above: *Pakhlavan Mahmud Mausoleum, Khiva*
Below left: *Madrasah nadir, Divan-Begi, Bukhara*
Below right: *Detail of madrasah, Khiva*

administration and public documents are supposed to be in both languages. The Russians are asking for Russian to be a joint official language as most business – government as well as private – uses Russian rather than the Qazaq language. Written in Cyrillic script from 1940, there is now a move to change it to the Roman script and some road signs are in both.

RELIGION

Sunni Muslim 47%, Russian Orthodox 44%, Protestant 2%, other 7%: those are the official figures but, although there are many new mosques being built, Kazaks are quite relaxed about religion. Few of the Muslims have given up alcohol and women do not wear the veil. It seems unlikely that after 70 years of religious repression 100% of people would adhere strongly to any particular religion.

CULTURE AND THE ARTS

Art and crafts

Magnificent gold ornaments and jewellery have been crafted in Kazakstan for thousands of years.

Handmade Kazak cotton and silk wall carpets and wool and felt floor carpets are used to this day for insulation as well as for decoration in yurts.

Literature

Abay Kunanbayev (1845–1904) is Kazakstan's greatest literary figure. Poet, musician, translator, philosopher and politician, he has a saying for every occasion in his prose work *A Book of Words*. As you drive through Kazakstan you might well ponder his words:

'In bonds of minutes which mortal bodies still enthrall
On bumpy roads you endeavour to escape a fall
Speak not of dissolution for the words he saith
Will live forever and confound death.'

PLANNING AND PREPARATION

See also Chapter One

When to go

Generally speaking, May to September is the best time to drive in Russia and Central Asia. In Kazakstan in August there are sometimes quite severe dust storms, exacerbated by smoke from grass fires, which can cut visibility and make driving hazardous.

Maps

Your bible, the *Automobile Road Atlas*, covers all of the CIS. Both Hallwag and Kummerly & Frey publish maps which cover Kazakstan.

Documentation
Visas
You are likely to need visas for the 'Stans although, in theory, a CIS visa gives you automatic transit through neighbouring countries. Once again try not to allow yourself to be tied down to dates of entry and exit when you apply for a visa. Explain that you are driving your own vehicle through many countries and that you cannot offer an exact date. As visas for the CIS are very expensive the embassy officials will probably give you a visa for X number of days or weeks from the date of entry – they do not want to lose a sale.

As we were staying in Kazakstan for more than three days we were told by our embassy we should register and pay a fee at OVIR, despite having very expensive visas. We duly went to the office but the place was so chaotic we left without registering and were not asked for registration papers anywhere in Kazakstan.

Vehicle documentation
As all other CIS countries. See *Chapter One*, page 22.

Insurance
As for Russia and other CIS countries – try to get a comprehensive policy, including third party, for your vehicle before leaving home.

Go for the best medical insurance you can afford in case you have to be evacuated.

Embassy and consulate addresses
Australia Kazakstan Consulate, 123 Darling Point Road, Darling Point, Sydney, NSW 2027; tel: 9362 4819; fax: 9362 8049

China Kazakstan Embassy, Beijing; tel: (1) 532 6182; fax: 532 6183

France Kazakstan Embassy, 59 rue Pierre Charron, F-75008 Paris; tel: (1) 4561 5200; fax: 4561 5201

Germany Kazakstan Embassy, Lassauxstrasse 1, 53424 Remagen; tel: (2642) 3071/2/3; fax: 938 325

Iran Kazakstan Embassy, Tehran; tel: (21) 801 5371; fax: 254 6400

Kyrgyzstan Kazakstan Embassy, Moskva 161, Bishkek; tel: (3312) 224 557; fax: 225 463

Russia Kazakstan Embassy, Chistoprudny bulvar 3A, Moscow 101000; tel: (95) 208 9852; fax: 208 0832, 208 2650

Ukraine Kazakstan Embassy, Kiev; tel/fax: (44) 290 7722

United Kingdom Kazakstan Consulate, 33 Thurloe Square, London SW7 2DS; tel: (0171) 581 4646; fax: 584 8481

United States Kazakstan Embassy, 3421 Massachusetts Avenue, NW, Washington, DC 20008; tel: 333 4504–7; fax: 333 4509

Uzbekistan Kazakstan Embassy, Holida Samatova 20, Tashkent;
tel: (3712) 333 705; fax: 336 022

Customs and immigration

When entering from or exiting a CIS country, customs and immigration formalities were virtually non-existent in 1996. However, depending on your priorities – whether your time is more important than your budget – you may be advised to obtain visas before you arrive at the border in future.

Communications

Country telephone code: 7

Mail

Like the rest of the CIS, the postal service is slow but cheap.

Telephone

Calls to Russia and the CIS are classed as inter-city so you do not need a country code. Dial 8, wait for the dial tone then dial area code and number. For international calls dial 8, wait for dial tone then dial 10 followed by country and area codes and number. For assistance from an English-speaking operator dial 062. It is possible to call America collect from the CIS by ringing AT&T in Moscow: (095) 155 50 42. The same number accepts AT&T phone cards.

Faxes

Most post offices have fax facilities although in the bigger towns it may be in a separate building. Faxes are expensive because of the poor telephone system – the operator rings the recipient to see if the transmission was legible and if not sends it again (and again, and again).

Email

Connection to Sprintnet or another provider is sometimes possible. Use the same plugs as for Russia – five-point for old type phones and the RJ for modern ones. Ask the business centre at expensive hotels if you can connect through their phone system if you have problems.

Courier services

DHL have an office on the corner of Abai and Rozybakiyev, Almaty.

Media

English-language newspapers are *All over the Globe*; tel: 338 403; *The Almaty Herald*; tel: 339 031; *Economics Today*; tel: 334 408.

Foreign English-language newspapers can be bought at Hotel Almaty and other tourist hotels.

Air connections

There are international flights to and from Austria, China, Germany, Netherlands, Pakistan and Turkey. Flights to and from Russia and CIS: Ashgabat, Moscow, St Petersburg, a number of cities in Siberia, and Tashkent. Flights to and from Osh and Karakol in Kyrgyzstan but none to Bishkek – there are connecting coach services. Most cities are connected to Almaty by internal flights at least once a week and the larger centres more often.

Railways

Covering 14,460km, with connections from Almaty to Tashkent and Bishkek, Urumqi, Moscow and Novosibirsk.

Electricity

220 volt, two-pin European-type plugs.

IN KAZAKSTAN

Driving in Kazakstan

Drive on the right.

Rules of the road

These are as in Russia and the rest of the CIS. See *Chapter Three*, page 57. Road signs quite often in Roman script as well as Cyrillic.

Road conditions

Approximately 83,000km are paved and gravelled, 81,000km unpaved. Most of the roads you are likely to use will have a reasonable surface but if you want to be more adventurous you will find plenty of 'off the beaten track' tracks.

Police

There are GAI posts on the outskirts of towns, as in the rest of the CIS. In our experience Kazaks in uniform seem to be friendly, helpful and pleasant to deal with.

Fuel

Leaded petrol and diesel are cheap and readily available. Unleaded petrol was not available in 1996.

Workshops and vehicle agencies

As in Russia and the CIS, sophisticated workshops are rare. For addresses see *Appendix Two*.

Security parking

There are security carparks in Almaty. For other towns take local advice but, if in doubt, ask the police.

National holidays

January 1–2	New Year
March 8	International Women's Day
March 22	Nauryz (Traditional Spring holiday)
May 1	Kazakstan People's Unity Day
May 9	Victory Day (World War II)
August 30	Constitution Day (1995)
October 25	Republic Day (1990)
December 16	Independence Day

Money

100 tiyn = 1 tenge

Alem Bank in Almaty and regional centres say they will cash American Express, MasterCard and Visa travellers cheques and give cash advances on Visa and MasterCard. Check at the head office in Almaty as to whether all regional branches offer these services. Most tourist-class hotels accept these cards.

Shopping

Western-type supermarkets are springing up in Almaty. Tinned fruit and meat, bottled water, French wine, European and even Australian beer, biscuits from Britain, in fact almost anything you may need or be yearning for is available.

Souvenirs

Look out for cotton or silk colourful *tus-kiiz* (wall carpets), bedspreads, horse and camel bags, and quilts – they will remind you of Central Asia when you get home.

Food and drink
Water

Tap water in Almaty is safe to drink. Good bottled water is on sale at street kiosks and shops. Boil or filter all drinking water outside Almaty.

Drinks

Chai (tea) is drunk with milk in Kazakstan. Instant coffee is served in most tourist hotels and restaurants – only the most upmarket places produce 'real' coffee. Western bottled soft drinks are available in the towns.

Alcohol

Vodka is the alcohol of choice all over the CIS. As in all of Central Asia toasts are often offered so have a phrase or two ready for your turn. Imported wine and beer are on sale in Almaty. *Qymyz*, fermented mare's milk, is a not unpleasant, mildly alcoholic drink offered on the steppe.

Food

You will find the usual meat, mutton or occasionally horsemeat, and flour, dumplings or noodles of Central Asia; but here fruit and vegetables are grown too and make a pleasant change. Aubergine (eggplant), squash and potato as well as the ubiquitous (except in Mongolia) cucumber and tomato salad are often served.

There are markets in every town and these are the places to stock up with fresh food for the road.

Accommodation
Camping

As usual take care to camp away from the road where you cannot be seen by passers-by. It is safest to ask if you can camp beside a farmhouse in the country.

Hotels

Hotels vary in price and degrees of comfort and service. Once out of Almaty and tourist hotels the plumbing is not good.

Homestays

In Almaty these can be arranged through HOFA. For addresses see *Chapter One*, page 30.

GETTING THERE AND AWAY
Barnaul (Siberia) to Semey

Route A349; distance 437km

Take the A349 from Barnaul, approximately 437km to Semey, crossing the border with Russia near Veseloyarsk. The A349 is bumpy and corrugated in patches but has only a few potholes. (For Barnaul see also *Chapter Four*, page 103.)

SEMEY (Semipalantinsk)   Семей

Time as Almaty (GMT +6 hours)

Population 342,000

The first town of any size you meet when entering Kazakstan from the north, Semey is close to both the USSR underground nuclear testing site and the space station.

Communications

City telephone code: 3222

Mail The post office is on Dulatov koshesi.

Telephone and fax The telegraph office is on Shakarim Qudayberdiev prospekt.

Where to stay
Inexpensive
Despite its air of faded modern opulence, it's hard to beat the **Irtuch Hotel** for comfort and value for money. Hot water both night and morning, plumbing that works and comfortable beds are yours for a few dollars.

Security parking
There are several carparks within a couple of minutes' walk of the Irtuch Hotel and, in the one behind the hotel, small boys will wash your car for a couple of dollars.

Where to eat
The restaurant on the ground floor of the **Irtuch Hotel** serves the usual hotel fare but cooked rather worse than usual. However it's served with a smile.

What to see
Dostoyevsky Museum, ploshchad Lenina, open 09.00–18.00 daily. Dostoyevsky spent five years in the army garrison at Semey as the second half of a ten-year sentence, commuted from the death penalty, in the mid-19th century.

SEMEY TO TALDY-QORGHAN (KURGAN)

Route M38, A350; distance 878km
Take the M38 from Semey for 163km before turning right on to the A350 near Georgievka. Follow the signs for 189km down the A350 to Arguz. The road is sometimes dual, sometimes single lane, all sealed. From Arguz, continue on the A350 for 526km to Taldy-Qorghan.

This is a long day's drive (13 hours) through the desert. Although the road surface is generally good, in places it is narrow and at certain times of year a howling wind threatens to blow your vehicle off the road – it's even worse for drivers of huge semi-trailers as they fight to keep a straight course. The wind creates sandstorms which, together with smoke from burning off fields of wheat stubble, reduces visibility to a few metres.

There is nowhere to stay, other than camping, between Semey and Taldy-Qorghan. Arguz is quite an attractive town in a valley oasis but the guesthouse had closed in 1996. About 188km from Taldy-Qorghan the road runs through a fertile valley and villagers' stalls line the roadside selling apples, tomatoes, grapes, plums and apricots.

TALDY-QORGHAN (Талды-Курган TALDY-KURGAN)
Time as Almaty
Population 125,000
A pleasant town with tree-lined streets. It is worth spending some time exploring the Zhungar Alatoo range to the east of Tekeli, 45km east of Taldy-Qorghan.

Communications
Area telephone code: 32822

Where to stay
Inexpensive
The appearance of **Hotel Taldy-Koorgan** (sic) belies the state of the rooms. Still, there is hot water night and morning and the linen is clean. More expensive than the Irtuch at Semey but much more run down.

Security parking
Beside the Hotel Taldy-Koorgan.

TALDY-QORGHAN TO ALMATY

Route A350; distance 243km
The good sealed road winds down an escarpment to the River Ili which has been dammed to form Lake Qapchaghay. About 50km from Almaty, Café Karligash, built beside the road overlooking the lake, is a favourite with long-distance drivers and serves fresh lake fish baked with tomatoes and herbs, ice-cream, melon and instant coffee.

ALMATY Алматьу
Time GMT +6 hours (+7 daylight saving)
Population 1,176,000

Money
The Alem Bank Kazakstan, on the corner of Dostyk prospekt and ul Karasat, tel: 507 726, 611 812, 509 501, fax: 615 704, 531 260, will give cash advances on Visa and MasterCard. Many banks will cash travellers cheques and there are a great many exchange bureaux around the city. Most of the tourist hotels accept payment by credit card.

Communications
City telephone code: 3272

Mail Central Post Office, 134 ul Bogenbai batyr, corner of Baiseitovoi. Open 08.00–19.00.

Telephone and fax Republican Telegraph, ul Panfilov 129, for international calls, fax and telex office. Open 08.00–23.00. Central Telephone Office, 100 ul Zhibek Zholy, corner of ul Panfilov, for local and long-distance calls. Open 08.00–20.00.

Emergency and useful telephone numbers:

Fire alarm	01
Police	02
Ambulance	03

Cooking gas alarm	04
Taxi service	058
City phone free info	09
Airport information	541 555
Currency exchange rate	323 869

Email Sprintnet is an efficient carrier for email. If you are prepared to queue, the National Library, tel: 696 163, gives free access to the internet.

Couriers DHL, 157, Abaya Avenue, tel: 509 416, fax: 509 417, offer an efficient international courier service and have very pleasant and helpful staff.

Air connections International flights go to and from Austria, China, Germany, India, the Netherlands, Russia and the 'Stans, Turkey and connections to the rest of the world; internal flights go to and from about 20 cities in Kazakstan.

Foreign embassy and consulate addresses

Australia 20A Kazbek Bi Street, corner of 8th March Street, Almaty 480100; tel local: 639 418, 639 514, satellite tel: (327) 581 1600, 581 1603; fax local: 2581 1601, satellite fax: (327) 581 1601

Canada 34 Vinogradov; tel: 501 151; fax: 581 1493. Also represents Canadians in Kyrgyzstan, Turkmenistan and Uzbekistan from this office.

China 137 Furmanov; tel: 634 966, 639 291; fax: 639 372

France 173 Furmanov; tel: 507 110, 506 236, 627 412; fax: 506 159

Germany 173 Furmanov; tel: 506 155, 506 156, 506 157; fax: 506 276

Iran 119 Qabanbay Batyr; tel: 677 846, 675 055; fax 642 754

Italy ul Karbek B1, 20; tel: 639 814/804; fax: 639 636

Kyrgyzstan 68A Amangeldy; tel: 633 305, 633 309

Mongolia Kazybek Bi, corner of 8th March; tel: 601 723, 601 733

Pakistan 25 Tölebaev; tel: 331 300, 333 548; fax: 331 300

Russia 4 Zhandosov; tel: 446 644, 446 491; fax: 448 223

Tajikistan 70 Yemelev; tel: 611 760, 610 225

Turkey Töle Bi 29; tel: 613 932, 618 153; fax: 618 519

United Kingdom 173 Furmanov; tel: 506 191, 506 192; fax: 506 260

United States 99 Furmanov; tel: 507 621, 507 623; fax: 633 88

Uzbekistan 36 Baribaev; tel: 618 316, 617 886 (visas); fax: 611 055. The visa section of the embassy is only open 15.00–17.00. You have to wait on the street outside the embassy as no more than three people are allowed in the office at one time. Park in the street. Visas take up to two weeks to process and you have to nominate your date of entry. A visa valid for more than two weeks takes some negotiating.

Where to stay

Cheaper hotels than those mentioned below can be found in the *Almaty Guide* which is published quarterly and is available at hotels, museums and shops.

Moderate

Hotel Almaty (it has changed its name, along with the city, from Alma-ata) ul Kabanbai, corner of ul Panfilov; tel: 630 943, where room prices seem to rise the higher the floor but include an excellent breakfast. Rooms on the fifth floor have private bathroom, hot water night and morning, TV and international direct dial telephone, if rather eccentric lighting arrangements. Ask for a room at the front as the restaurant and casino at the back can be very noisy. In the same range is the Astana International Hotel, corner of ul Satpaev and ul Baitursynov; tel: 501 214.

Expensive

Hotel Kazakstan, ul Kurmangazy, corner of ul Dostyk; tel: 619 906, and the **Hotel Otrar**, ul Gogol; tel: 330 075.

Very expensive

The super deluxe **Marco Polo Rachat Palace**, ul Satpaev 29; tel: 473 630.

Security parking

Security carparks have sprung up as more and more expensive European, Japanese and Korean cars hit the streets. There are three very close to the Hotel Almaty. The expensive hotels have their own carparks.

Where to eat

These vary from expensive and good to cheap and bad – not necessarily bracketed that way.

Inexpensive

A small open-air café, the **Anacy**, in the park off ul Abylai khan, behind the Hotel Almaty, serves the usual chicken and 'steak' but also a very passable spaghetti bolognese which, with tomato salad and imported beer, costs a few dollars. The **Konguterskaya** cake shop and bar, corner of ul Panfilov and ul Bogenbai Batyr, sells an assortment of small cakes, coffee and tea as well as the hard stuff.

Moderate

Shenyan Restaurant, Bögenbay Batyr 136, serves Chinese food in a pleasant atmosphere. Open for lunch and dinner.

Expensive

The **Vienna Café** in the Rachat Palace Hotel serves espresso coffee and cakes but does not open until 11.00 – it is just across the road from the State Art Museum.

Recommended for a special night out, the **Trattoria Paradiso**, pr Abai 17, tel: 616 920, has an Italian chef and an extensive menu with lots of shellfish and pasta and a short but adequate wine list. The head waiter is delightful, a young Dudley Moore. Open for lunch and dinner.

Avoid the vastly overpriced **Restaurant Issyk**, in the Hotel Almaty, at all costs. Both frozen fish and chicken, encased in breadcrumbed batter, were almost inedible; a mixed salad was just acceptable, and the snooty manageress delivered a tiny serving of caviar, unordered, and then expected us to pay $35 for it, bringing the bill to over $120 – good try but she misjudged these old hands.

What to see
The **Central State Musem**, Furmonov 44, Samal –1, tel: 642 390, 644 477, is well worth a visit – look for the traditional Kazak musical instruments. Open 10.00–18.00, Wed–Mon. In the same building is the **Museum of Gold and Jewelry**, tel: 645 455, with its astonishing 5th-century BC Sak Warrior's gold suit.

The **State Museum of Art**, Satpaev 30A, across the road from the Rachat Palace Hotel, has an interesting collection of contemporary Kazak art – the Kazak Applied Art section is particularly good. The **Art Gallery** on the corner of ul Jambool and ul Jeltoksan is also worth a visit.

The **Central Farming Market**, between ul Pushkin and ul Jibek Joly, is fun to wander through – and good for stocking up with fruit and vegetables before you move on.

MEDEU Медеу AND SHYMBULAQ Шымбулак
Telephone code is the same as Almaty: 3272
Before the breakup of the USSR the ski fields of Shymbulaq, only 15km southeast of Almaty but 2,300m above sea level, were used for Eastern Bloc winter sports competitions. The competitions are no longer held but people from the 'Stans and Russia still come to enjoy the skiing. There are two chair-lifts which work at weekends during the summer as well as all week during the ski season. A third is under construction and due to open in 1997. A large skating rink, 1,700m up in the mountains at Medeu, is usually open from October to May. There are spectacular walks in the mountains with views back down to Almaty.

Where to stay
Inexpensive
Above the Hotel Medeu, at 2,300m at the foot of the chair, is the **Hotel Shymbulaq**. Its good-sized rooms have views of the mountains, private bathrooms with hot water (for limited periods night and morning), large comfy armchairs and small TVs. There is a card phone on the ground floor for international calls.

Moderate to expensive
The **Hotel Medeu**, tel: 502 007, across the road from the skating rink, has a selection of rooms, all of which are well furnished with ISD phones and

TV (BBC, CNN etc) and have modern bathrooms attached. Reopened in 1995 after an extensive refurbishment by the joint Kazak-Turkish owners, it has enthusiastic staff and is a pleasant place to stay only 15 minutes from Almaty. Visa, MasterCard and Eurocards accepted. There is an exchange bureau on the ground floor.

Moderate

Further up the mountain above Hotel Shymbulaq, at 2,800m, is the **Otel Tyook-Su**, tel: 502 702, a wooden chalet-type building with open fire. Rooms are tiny except for the one on the top floor which has a minuscule en suite shower and loo. Price includes breakfast but, as only the top room has a shower, it is not cheap. Nevertheless the atmosphere is very pleasant and Igor, the manager, helpful and friendly.

Security parking

There is a fence and guarded gates at the Hotel Medeu. Park outside the Shymbulaq and Tyook-Su with confidence – there are two barriers between the mountains and the town below.

Where to eat
Inexpensive

There are a number of snack-bars and shaslik stalls around the ice rink. No food is served at the Hotel Shymbulaq but a café at the end of the hotel building is open 10.00–22.00, serves good hot food and has a few bottles of excellent, reasonably priced French and cheaper Italian wine. The bar in the building at the bottom of the chairlift is a surprise and serves the best food in Shymbulaq although the service is on the slow side – still, if you're sitting outside in the sun, admiring the view, it probably won't worry you. Ask for the chicken served on a bed of fresh herbs if you're hungry.

Moderate

The food at **Tyook-Su** is typical Kazak/Russian and there is a shaslik 'stove' set up outside.

Expensive

Hotel Medeu has a pleasant restaurant as well as a snack bar.

What to see

Nature at its most glorious. Walks up the mountains as energetic as you choose. Ride up to the top of the chairlifts – don't forget to get off at the top. Mountain climbing – guides available, ask in Almaty or at your hotel.

ALMATY TO BISHKEK

Route M39; distance 236km

The main road from Almaty to Bishkek, the M39, runs to the north of the Ala Too mountains. Bishkek is a mere 17km from the Kazakstan border.

Although it is wise to have a visa – particularly if you have foreign registration – you may not even be stopped at the border crossing. In 1996 there were no customs or immigration formalities, just registration by police which took a few minutes. We crossed this border twice and were stopped once but drove straight through on the second occasion.

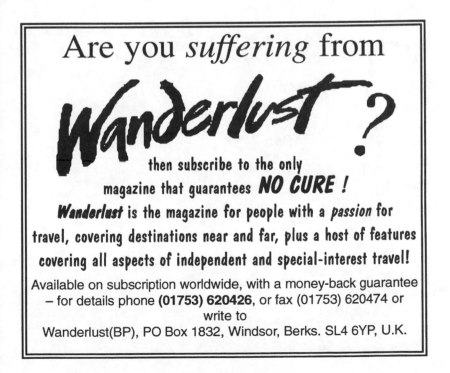

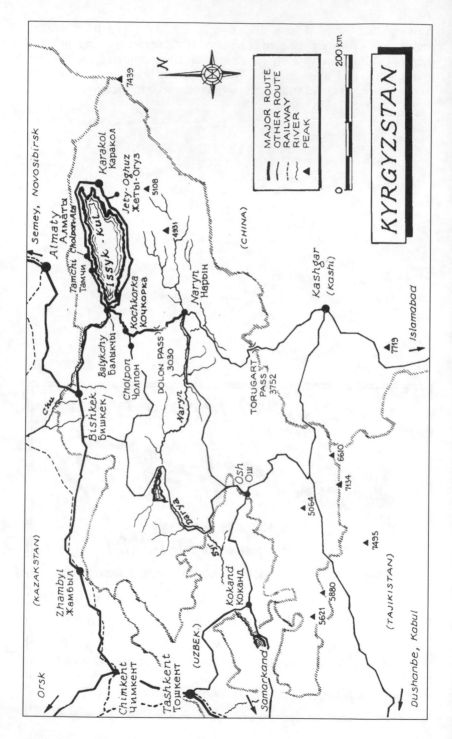

Chapter Seven

Kyrgyzstan

Kyrgyzstan is a small country of mountains and lakes, home to 80 ethnic groups. Up in the mountains, away from the towns, people still live a semi-nomadic lifestyle.

There is surprisingly little tourism considering the beautiful countryside, the friendliness of the people and the location – neighbouring Uzbekistan and Xinjiang Province of China, both of which are increasingly popular adventure tourist destinations.

FACTS AND FIGURES

Time
GMT + 6 hours

Population
Estimated 4,540,000 (July 1995). In recent years the urban population has decreased due, in part, to increased emigration.

Capital
Bishkek, population 613,200

GEOGRAPHY

With a total area of 198,500km² and a population density of 23 per km², Kyrgyzstan is one of the smallest countries in the CIS. It is a landlocked country bordering China, Tajikistan, Uzbekistan and Kazakstan. Its borders were imposed by the USSR after the Revolution, creating fingers of Uzbekistan and Tajikistan poking in from the west – or fingers of Kyrgyzstan protruding into those countries from the east, depending on your point of view.

Kyrgyzstan is a mountainous country, with an average altitude of 2,750m. At 1,607m, magnificent Lake Issyk-Kul lies framed between the snowcapped Tian Shan and Ala-Too mountains in a fertile valley to the east of Bishkek. At 170km long, 70km wide and averaging 229m deep it claims to be the world's second largest alpine lake – the biggest being Lake Titicaca in Peru. The highest peak of Tian Shan, Pik Pobedy, is 7,439m. Tian Shan creates a natural boundary with both China and Kazakstan. The main rivers are the Chu, flowing along the Kazakstan border, and the Naryn which runs the length of the country.

CLIMATE

The climate varies throughout Kyrgyzstan according to the altitude. Some of the higher mountain peaks have permanent snow while in midsummer the lower areas average between 30°C and 40°C at midday.

In the Fergana Valley region in the southwest the climate is subtropical but in the northern foothills it is temperate.

HISTORICAL OUTLINE

People of the Sak (Scythian) tribe were the earliest known inhabitants of the area from about the 6th century BC. The Sak resisted the invasion of Alexander the Great in the 4th century AD but were eventually overrun. It appears that the present-day Kyrgyz people originated in the Yenisei River region of Siberia. The movement south began around the 10th century to avoid Mongol raiders and gathered momentum during the years of Genghis Khan and his successors.

The Kyrgyz state began to form in the 16th century as the people united to defend their land from three powerful neighbouring empires – the Kharakhanid, Mongol and Chinese. After the Manchu defeat of the Mongols in the 18th century, the area was ruled by the Kokand Khanate until the 19th century when the Russians moved south following their conquest of Tashkent in 1865.

The Russians, as usual, began to settle families on the land and in 1916 the Kyrgyz revolted but their attempt to regain their land was defeated. The people suffered badly in the 1920s and 30s as nomads were forcibly settled during collectivisation. Nor were the Kyrgyz spared Stalin's purges.

It was only in 1926 that Kyrgyzstan became a semi-autonomous state when the Russians renamed many areas, arbitrarily dividing up the 'Stans. In 1936 Kyrgyzstan became part of the USSR.

After the demise of the USSR in 1991, Kyrgyzstan declared its independence.

POLITICS

In 1990 Askar Akayev, a physicist, President of the Academy of Sciences and a People's Deputy of the USSR, had been elected President of Kyrgyzstan. In 1991, six weeks after the Kyrgyz Supreme Soviet declared Kyrgyzstan independent, he was re-elected president in the first democratic elections.

With the new constitution adopted in May 1993, it was necessary to hold a referendum to confirm the presidential powers. This was done in January 1994.

After the 1995 elections the legislature became bicameral. The Assembly of Legislatures, a 35-member house, and the Assembly of Representatives, a 70-member house, must hold elections no less than every three years.

There are six or more political parties.

ECONOMY

One of the smallest and poorest countries in the CIS, Kyrgyzstan's economy has suffered severely since the demise of the USSR. Trade was almost entirely with Russia and other former Soviet republics until 1990 but since then the economy has shrunk by over 50%. Nevertheless Kyrgyzstan has managed to control rampant inflation, embrace privatisation and reduce the decline in productivity in the last two or three years.

Self-sufficient in oil, coal and gas, having significant deposits of minerals such as mercury, antimony, tin, tungsten and bauxite, and with the potential for hydroelectric power, Kyrgyzstan still needs considerable investment to create a reasonable standard of living for its people.

PEOPLE

Between 50% and 60% of the population is Kyrgyz, 21% Russian and 13% Uzbek, with Ukrainian, German, Tatar and many other ethnic minorities. These numbers are changing as Russian families return to Russia claiming Kyrgyz discrimination against them.

LANGUAGE

Kyrgyz has been the official language since the breakup of the USSR. However, the majority of people in the cities also speak Russian and notices and signs are often in both languages, sometimes with a third spelling of place-names in the Roman alphabet. There have been some protests from the Russian citizens who want Russian to be a second official language.

RELIGION

Nominally Sunni Muslim but, as all religion was suppressed during the communist era, it is hard to know how many people seriously follow Islam.

CULTURE AND THE ARTS

The lengthy verse epic *Manas,* and other heroic poems describing myriad horsemen, standards flying, spears gleaming, bows and arrows at the ready, galloping across the steppe and up and down the mountains, have been passed from generation to generation. But they are not just myths; they also record the country's history from early times as well as the people's desire for freedom and happiness. Nowadays a pale imitation can be heard in theatres in Bishkek but you'd be lucky to hear the real thing.

PLANNING AND PREPARATION
See also Chapter One

When to go
May to September are the best months to travel in Central Asia but, as Kyrgyzstan is in the centre, timing will depend on your route and any problems you may have on the way.

Maps
The *Automobile Road Atlas* covers Kyrgyzstan. A 1:1,300,000 map of Kyrgyzstan, with interesting information on the reverse, is published by the International Foundation 'Discovery of Kyrgyzstan', 6 Kamskaya Str, Bishkek, Kyrgyz Republic 720020; tel: (3312) 427 615; fax: 225 432, 427 615.

Documentation
Visas
You are likely to need visas for the 'Stans although, in theory, a CIS visa gives you automatic transit through neighbouring countries. See *Chapter One*, page 18. Once again try not to allow yourself to be tied down to dates of entry and exit. Explain that you are driving your own vehicle through many countries and that you cannot offer an exact date. As visas for the CIS are very expensive the embassy officials will probably give you a visa for *x* number of days or weeks from the date of entry – they do not want to lose a sale.

The Kyrgyzstan Embassy in Almaty will issue visas while you wait.

Insurance
It is best to get vehicle insurance before leaving home which covers all the countries on your planned route plus any deviations you may choose, or be forced, to make. We were unable to get third party insurance in Kyrgyzstan. Medical insurance is as for the rest of the CIS. Make sure you have top travel insurance cover for health as well as for loss of luggage.

Embassy and consulate addresses
China Kyrgyzstan Embassy, Ta Yuan Diplomatic Office Bldg, Chaoyang District, Beijing; tel: (10) 532 6458/532 4180; fax: 532 6459
There is no Kyrgyzstan representative in Kashgar.

Germany Kyrgyzstan Embassy, Hockreuzallee 117, 53175 Bonn; tel: (0228) 310 694; fax: 475 863

Kazakstan Kyrgyzstan Embassy, Amankeldi koshesi 68A, Almaty; tel: (3272) 63 33 09; fax: 63 71 90

Russia Kyrgyzstan Embassy, ul Bolshaya Ordynka 64, Moscow 109017; tel: (095) 237 44 81; fax: 237 44 52

Turkey Kyrgyzstan Embassy, Boyabat Sokak 11, 06700 Ankara; tel: (312) 446 84 08; fax: 311 99 21

Turkmenistan Kyrgyzstan Embassy, pr. Saparmurada Turkmenbashi 13, Ashgabat 744000; tel: (36300) 46 88 04/29 25 39

Ukraine Kyrgyzstan Embassy, vulitsya Kutuzova 8, 252000 Kiev; tel: (044) 295 53 80; fax: 295 96 92

United Kingdom Visas are handled by the Kazakstan Consulate, see page 184

United States Kyrgyzstan Embassy, 1511 K Street NW, suite 706, Washington, DC 20005; tel: (202) 347 3732/3733; fax: 347 3718

Uzbekistan Kyrgyzstan Embassy, Mustaqillik maydoni 5, Tashkent; tel: (3712) 39 45 43; fax: 39 16 78

There is no Kyrgyzstan representation in Australia.

Customs and immigration
As in all of the CIS, in theory, a valid visa for one country automatically gives a three-day transit visa in the others. There were no formalities entering or leaving Kyrgyzstan in 1996 but if you plan to stay more than a few days it may be as well to get a visa when you are in Almaty.

Health and safety
Health
No vaccinations are required but polio and tetanus, and probably hepatitis A, diphtheria, typhoid and rabies, would be wise. Prescription drugs: as for the rest of CIS. Make sure you have supplies of any you may need and carry your prescriptions with you.

Safety
Take all usual precautions, particularly around exchange bureaux and at night. There are reports of unfriendly people in the area around Naryn. Be particularly careful not to camp where you can be seen from the road. See page 214.

IN KYRGYZSTAN
Communications
Country telephone code: 7

Telephone
It's the usual unreliable system. Calls to Russia and other CIS countries are trunk calls so no country code is used. For international calls, in theory

dialling 062 will connect you to an English-speaking operator who will book your call. For inter-city and CIS calls – dial 8, wait for the dial tone, dial area code and number. Only local calls can be made from street phones using zhetons bought from post offices and kiosks.

Emergency telephone numbers

Calls are free from street phones.

Fire	01
Police	02
Emergency medical care	03
Gas repair service	04

Mail and fax

Post and fax services are available at most post offices. Faxes are expensive because of the poor telephone system – the operator rings the recipient to see if the transmission was legible and if not sends it again (and again, and again).

Courier services

DHL, tel: 29 29 34, and TNT, tel: 25 09 85, have reliable but expensive document and parcel services to and from Bishkek.

Email

In Bishkek the possibilities are endless. The NLPUB (National Library) in Bishkek writes in its homepage:

'Who are users of NLPUB ??? Maybe Aliens? Or Computer Wizards and Magicians??? No!!! They are just people – mere mortals: students, teachers, and ordinary parents of the children studying abroad.

Here they have a nice opportunity to escape any problems with the 'snail mail' and really enjoy their correspondence. If you search for a friend for your whole life, you may search him right here, sitting by computer.. If you want to marry, feel free to come, and all the Internet Wedding Catalog is here to serve you. If you're a student or a teacher, be sure that Internet is the most appropriate thing. Here are many people from different countries.

We let people to use e-mail for FREE!!! That's why our net is called FREENET.

Our E-mail is the only thing with the help of that they can correspond with their relatives and friends, and get some information about how to raise their profile in teaching English, business, International Relationships and so on. That's why they are so grateful to us. Also it's a very convenient place for them to gather, because sometimes our Internet Station is the only place where people from abroad can find each other in our big city. And of course, for our students it's a place where they can meet very interesting people, practise their skills in speaking a foreign language with native speakers, discuss their studying problems and ask for advice.'

Don't say we didn't warn you.

Media
An English-language newspaper is the *Kyrgyzstan Chronicle*. Published weekly.

Roads
22,600km paved and gravelled, 7,700km unpaved.

Railways
370km. Line joins the Almaty to Tashkent main line in Kazakstan.

Air connections
International flights go to and from Russia, Turkey and Uzbekistan; internal flights to and from Jalal-Abad, Karakol and Osh.

Electricity
220 volt, two-pin European type plugs.

Driving in Kyrgyzstan
Drive on the right. See also *Chapter Three*, page 57.

Rules of the road
These are the same as for the rest of the CIS. Be extra careful on the narrow, winding mountain roads and watch out for mini landslides.

Fuel
There were some problems with diesel supplies in 1996 so fill the tank whenever possible. There appeared to be no shortage of leaded petrol. Unleaded petrol was not available in 1996.

Workshops and agencies
Agencies for Japanese and European vehicles are opening up in CIS capital cities but, as in Russia, do not carry spare parts. See *Appendix Two*.

Spare parts
Bring your own.

Security parking
Available in Bishkek and the bigger towns.

National holidays

January 1	New Year
January 7	Christmas
March 8	International Women's Day
March 21	Nooruz (Muslim New Year, Day of Vernal Equinox)
May 1	International Day of Solidarity among Workers
May 9	Day of Victory over Fascism
June 13	Kurban Ait (Day of Remembrance)
August 31	Day of Independence

Money
100 tiyins = 1 som

Credit cards and travellers cheques
Tourist class hotels in Bishkek accept Visa and American Express cards. Several banks in Bishkek will change travellers cheques.

Shopping
Shops are beginning to stock imported Western-type food though you may have to hunt around more than in Almaty. There are several markets to choose from in Bishkek. The Osh Bazaar, off the Tashkent road, on Beyshenaliyeva, is probably the most interesting.

Fresh fruit and vegetables are available on roadside stalls in the country during summer. The stalls are usually run by older women who insist on selling by the bucketful. Don't hesitate; the sun-ripened apricots at the eastern end of Issyk-Kul will spoil you for all others!

Imported beer and cigarettes are sold in most shops and on the street.

Souvenirs
TsUM is the place to buy Kyrgyz men's hats – the high white felt *kalpaks* and the fur-trimmed *tebbetey*. The shop in the Museum of Applied Arts has *shyrdaks* (felt-appliqué rugs) for sale and you can also find them at the markets.

Food and drink
Water
If you cannot find bottled water, boil or filter all drinking water.

Drinks
As in all the 'Stans, *chai* (tea) is the popular drink. There is a traditional ceremony for serving tea to guests in Central Asia. After making a pot of green tea, the host pours tea into a small china cup, returning it twice to the pot, before offering it to the guest.

Soft drinks are available in the towns.

Alcohol
Kyrgyz Shampany Joint Stock Company specialises in the production of quite drinkable sparkling wines and brandy. Vodka is cheap and readily available everywhere. Imported beer is on sale in towns. The inevitable *kymys* (fermented mare's milk) is also drunk in the spring and summer and is only mildly alcoholic, provided it hasn't been tampered with.

Food
Kyrgyz food is very similar to Mongolian. *Laghman* (similar to Chinese noodles), *manty* (mutton dumplings), *plov* (rice pilaf) with *naan* (the local flat bread) and *kyrtyldak boorsok* (unsweetened pastries) are the traditional Kyrgyz dishes.

Accommodation

Camping

There are some wonderful camping spots around Issyk-Kul and in the surrounding mountains. Try to spend a night or two beside the beautiful alpine lake, Song Kel (sometimes spelt Song-Kol or Son Kul).

Hotels

Accommodation varies from the massive Issyk-Kul Sanatorium, nicknamed the Aurora, and tourist-class hotels in Bishkek, to less imposing establishments. Most towns of any size have at least one hotel but unless it is a resort town, the standard of accommodation is not good.

Homestays

Around Issyk-Kul many families move out of their houses in the summer to rent them to holidaymakers while others offer rooms in their houses and will provide meals. This makes a pleasant change from third-rate hotels. HOFA (see *Chapter One*, page 30) can arrange homestays in Bishkek.

GETTING THERE AND AWAY

There are several roads into Kyrgyzstan from Kazakstan besides the direct M39 Almaty to Bishkek route which is well signposted. An alternative crossing is at Kegen to the east of Almaty. The A353 turns east off the A350 at Sarozek, about 78km south of Taldy-Qorghan. Continue for approximately 177km before turning south at Koktal (18km west of Zharkent). It is 150km to Kegen and another 36km to the Kyrgyzstan border. From here there are several roads to Karakol – the A362 via Tup is the main road but we were told the route via the lush Karakara valley and Novovoznesenovka was more beautiful. Both routes are fairly rough and meet the A363, the circular road around Lake Issyk-Kul.

Perhaps the most spectacular route into Kyrgyzstan is from Kashgar, in the Xinjiang province of China, via the Torugart Pass. The A365 reaches over 3,500m and there is a lot of traffic in both directions. From the Pass it is roughly 190km to Naryn where the road turns west to Jalal-Abad or continues north to Balykchy, on the western tip of Lake Issyk-Kul, and Bishkek. Lake Song-Kel, high in the Moldo-Too mountains, is a magic place to camp.

Coming in from Uzbekistan there are several routes, of which the most straightforward but least interesting is along the main road, M39, from Tashkent to Bishkek.

The A373 through Kokand and the Fergana Valley, entering Uzbekistan at Osh and then continuing to Jalal-Abad (Dzhalal Abad), is a spectacular way to enter, or leave, Kyrgyzstan.

At the time of writing Tajikistan is unsafe for travellers apart from the ancient city of Penjikent just across the border from Samarkand. However, if things improve an interesting route would be to take the M41 from the capital, Dushanbe, as far as the A372 junction, 16km beyond Komsomolabad. Then continue to Osh either via the A372 or, if things are peaceful and you have time, via the M41 scenic route via Khorog and over the Kyzyl Arm Pass.

ALMATY TO BISHKEK

Distance 236km

From Almaty take the M39 which runs west, parallel to the Ala-Too mountain range. It is a good highway, much of it dual carriageway. There was no formal customs or immigration border post in 1996 and you are unlikely to have a problem crossing into Kyrgyzstan.

BISHKEK Бишкек

Time GMT +6 hours
Population 613,200

Bishkek, the capital of Kyrgyzstan, is a mere 17km from the border with Kazakstan. Although its history goes back to 1825 when the Uzbek Khan of Kokand erected a small clay fort on the banks of the Chu River on the Silk Route, it was not until 1878 that the town of Pishpek was established by the Russians as the district capital. After the Russian Revolution it was renamed Bishkek and, in 1924, it became the administrative centre of the Kyrgyz Autonomous Region. It suffered another name change in 1926 when it became Frunze, after Mikhail Frunze, the revolutionary hero born in the city in 1885. The city reverted to the name Bishkek in 1991.

It is an attractive city, situated 750m above sea level in the foothills of the snow-capped Tian Shan mountain range, with lots of parks, tall poplars and oaks, and beds of brightly coloured flowers.

Two intriguing legends surround the name Bishkek. One claims that many years ago, when moving camp, the Khan's (king's) wife forgot her *bishkek*, an implement for making kumys. The bishkek was very precious as it was studded with jewels and the Khan was angry. He sent 40 men back to look for it but they could not find it. Too frightened to return and tell the Khan they settled at the campsite which became Bishkek.

The second, and less romantic, legend is that five mighty knights found the land so beautiful that they fought over its possession. *Besh* is the Kyrgyz word for five and *bek* means knight.

Money

Maksat Bank in the Hotel Dostuk can arrange telegraphic transfers from overseas banks but it takes several days. Hotel Dostuk will give cash advances on Visa and MasterCard but charges 5%.

Almost every other shop in Soviet Street seems to be an exchange bureau. Rates vary – some will accept early (pre-1990) US$100 bills, refused by hotels and banks, but give a slightly poorer exchange rate.

Fuel

There are a number of modern, hi-tech fuel stations in Bishkek. In the summer of 1996 only one, on Toktogul Köchösü, had diesel.

Communications

City telephone code: 3312

Mail The main post and telephone office is on Soviet Street between Choy prospekt and Kiev Street. Open 08.00–17.00. Stamps can be bought at tourist hotels, bookstores and kiosks.

Telephone International and long-distance calls can be made from the main post office. If you have problems you can use the satellite telephone and fax at Kyrgyz-Concept, Razzakov 100.

Fax Facilities are in the main post office.

Email The National Library offers free email services but you may have to queue. Igor Moskin of Kyrgyz-Concept email, root@meyerim.bishkek. su, writes as follows:

'I can inform you about our e-mail services.

We have about 300–400 clients. Main part of them use IP connection (SLIP or PPP protocols) and IBM compatibl computers. Using MAC here is difficult a little because we don't have technical support centr for MAC and cannot fix hardware problems. We offer WWW, e-mail, FTP, gopher and IRC services. Our WWW is http://www.bishkek.su, but it is russian page.'

Igor is a useful contact who can book accommodation, find interpreters and help obtain visas.

Air connections International flights go to and from Russia, Turkey and Uzbekistan. Bishkek is only about three hours drive to Almaty and connections to Europe and China. Internal flights are to and from Jalal-Abad, Karakol and Osh.

Foreign embassy and consulate addresses

Canada See Kazakstan address on page 191
China Toktogul 196, tel: 222 423
Germany Razzakov 28, tel: 22 48 03, 22 4811, 22 88 78; fax: 620 007, 228 523
Iran Razzakov 36, tel: 226 964
Kazakstan Moskva 161, tel: 224 557
Russia Razzakov 17, tel: 221 775
Turkey Moskva 89, tel/fax: 620 500
United Kingdom No representation – try Almaty or Tashkent
United States Erkindik 66, tel: 222 693, 222 777

Where to stay
Inexpensive
None of the cheaper hotels had security parking in the vicinity.

Moderate

Until the Ake Keme opened, the **Hotel Dostuk**, tel: 28 42 78, was the best hotel in town. Now it has had to drop its prices to compete with its rival. Small but comfortable rooms with tiny bathroom, on the top floor, have views of the mountains. Good buffet breakfast included in tariff. Visa and MasterCard accepted. The rooms have satellite ISD (expensive) and local telephones, TV with nine stations including BBC and CNN, air-conditioning and bar fridges.

Expensive

Ake-Keme Hotel, tel: satellite phone 620 278, or city phone 483 853, a Turkish/Kyrgyz joint venture, is the newest and most expensive hotel in Bishkek and is some way out of town, at 93 Mir Avenue, on the road to the old airport. Room rate includes breakfast.

Security parking

There are a number of security carparks in Bishkek. The staff at the one next to the Hotel Dostuk took great interest in our travels and made sure we were parked close to the guard's hut.

Where to eat

Restaurants at both the **Ake-Keme Hotel** and **Hotel Dostuk** are overpriced. The Hotel Dostuk has two restaurants – in theory. The first-floor restaurant was either closed or being used for wedding receptions and other functions on the four occasions we tried to get in. The **Arizona**, on the ground floor, serves quite good Western-type food.

In the centre of town there are numerous small cafés serving *laghman* (similar to Chinese noodles) and *plov* (rice pilaff). For authentic Chinese food cooked by Chinese chefs try the **Flamingo Restaurant**.

What to see

Museum of Applied Art (sometimes called Museum of Fine Art), Soviet 196, has a nice collection of Kyrgyz jewellery, embroidery, felt rugs and other traditional items. Open Tues–Sun 09.00–17.00. The **State Historical Museum**, to the north of Ala-Too Square, has a display of yurts, carpets and applied arts and crafts. Open Tues–Sun 09.00–18.00, closed 13.00–14.00. **Frunze Museum** houses the original Frunze family home – a humble thatched cottage – and is devoted to the exploits of Mikhail Vasilievich Frunze, hero of the revolution, who was born in Bishkek in 1885. There are sometimes other exhibitions on the upper floors.

BISHKEK TO BALYKCHY (Балыкчы) AND LAKE ISSYK-KUL

Route A365; distance 175km

Take the sealed A365 from Bishkek to Balykchy, close to the lake, where the road divides, allowing you to continue eastward along either the northern or the southern side of the lake. If you choose the northern side, then just west of Balykchy you come to a big GAI post and barrier where all cars are stopped and must pay an 'ecology fee' – tourist price US$15, locals pay 35 som ($3). Make sure you get a receipt.

Fuel can be scarce in this area so fill up before you leave Bishkek and try to keep your tanks topped up. Diesel was available on the road south of the lake but not on the northern road.

LAKE ISSYK-KUL Ысык–Кол (Иссык–Куль)

It is a misnomer to put 'Lake' before Issyk-Kul because *kul* is Kyrgyz for lake, but the name on maps is usually either Lake Issyk-Kul or Oz Issyk-Kul. (*Ozero* is Russian for 'lake'.) Issyk-Kul means Hot Lake because the water never freezes. The ancient name was Tuz-Kul meaning Salty Lake – the water contains minerals and is said to have curative properties. Mongolians call the lake Temurtu-Nor which means Iron Lake and yet another name is Dzhytty-Kul or Fragrant Lake.

The lake is 170km long and 70km wide. Over 80 rivers and streams flow into it but none leave.

Magnificent views of the lake from the road can be distracting for the driver so pull in sometimes to enjoy the scenery – the locals drive fast and cannot understand why you are going so slowly. Wooden stands hung with bundles of small dried fish line the roadside – we found it very fiddly trying to get the miniscule bits of flesh away from the bones but locals assured us 'it's very good with beer!' The north side of the lake is the most popular because of its sandy beaches, safe swimming and spectacular views of the snowcapped Terskey Ala-Too mountain range.

On the south side it is more difficult to get down to the lake but there are equally spectacular views and a number of good red sand beaches. The road passes a number of Muslim cemeteries built on hillsides. Watch out for metal yurt skeletons topped with shining crescents with graves beneath, set against snowy mountain backdrops.

All around the lake, in the mountain foothills as well as on the shore, are mineral springs and the whole area was a great centre of tourism for people from all over the USSR. Now Russians prefer to go to Bulgaria, Turkey and Greece and many sanatoriums have closed.

TAMCHI Тамчы

This small village on the north side of the lake, approximately 39km west of Balykchy, has many private homes offering accommodation for a few dollars per day. Often the family moves into rooms beside the main house and rents the rooms in the house to holidaymakers. Some offer meals and others have a kitchen for guests' use. The down side of this is that the 'conveniences' are down the garden path and there is no hot water but, as the lake is only slightly salt, swimming takes the place of bathing.

A classy alternative (moderate) is the **Otel Zamok**, tel: (31942) 43 363 – a tiny castle built of uncut stone complete with small swimming pool and tennis court. Try to book ahead if you want to stay here as it gets booked up with CIS holidaymakers in the summer months.

CHOLPON-ATA Чолпон-Ата

This is a small town on the lake shore, once the centre of many sanatoriums where tourists from the USSR came to recuperate after the rigors of the northern winter, now a shadow of its former glory.

Communications

Town telephone code: 243

Mail and telephone At the post office.

Where to stay
Expensive
Cholpon-Ata is the home of the famous **Issyk-Kul Sanatorium**, nicknamed the *Aurora* (after the famous battleship) because of its vast size; tel: 4 48 70/9 53 89. If you feel like a mud bath or taking the waters in the grand Russian style, this is the place to do it. Tariff includes three meals.

KARAKOL (PRZHEVALSK) Каракол

Time as Bishkek
Population 80,000
Established in 1867 as a garrison town and later renamed Przhevalsk, after the great 19th-century Russian explorer who died here in 1888, Karakol reverted to its original name in 1991 when Kyrgyzstan became an independent state. It is now becoming an increasingly popular setting-off point for climbing and trekking trips.

Communications

City telephone code: 31922

Mail, fax and telephone The post office is on ul Kalinina.

Email Sergey Pyshnenko, email: root@glob-x.karakol.su, may be able to help you.

Where to stay
Inexpensive
Mountain Rescue Services, Fuchika ul 119, tel: 2 30 15, have a wooden chalet with a few double rooms used by climbers but if they have space you are made welcome. It is also possible to camp in the grounds. Hot showers (ask for the water heater to be turned on) and meals are available.

Moderate
Komplex Isyk-Kol, Fuchika ul 38, tel: 2 07 11, 2 95 73, set in pretty woodland has been refurbished recently and is good value for money, with singles, doubles and triples – standard or luxury (two rooms and private bath). There's a sauna and restaurant in the grounds.

Security parking
Both the Mountain Rescue and Komplex Issyk-Kul are in fenced grounds.

Where to eat
There are a number of cafés and restaurants in the town and a good little market where you can stock up with fresh vegetables, fruit and bread.

What to see
If you have visited, or plan to visit, the Przewalski horses at either Takhiin Tal in Mongolia or the Ecocentre Gazelle at Kagan, Uzbekistan, then you will be particularly interested in the Przewalski Memorial and Museum above the Mikhaylovka inlet. Turn off the main road about 7km west of Karakol on the north lake road, then, at two yurts, turn right up an avenue of poplars. There is a large carpark on the left but unless other cars are there continue up the road and park at the gates.

Set in extensive gardens the simple grave and memorial, topped with a magnificent eagle, overlook the erstwhile top-secret torpedo research centre. The museum is well worth a visit as it illustrates the four major expeditions Przewalski undertook through China, Mongolia and Tibet between 1870 and 1885. It is ironic that having survived these extraordinary travels he, so the story goes, drank water from the Chuy River when hunting tigers and contracted typhoid from which he died, aged 49.

Ask Valentin Derevyanko, at his travel agency in the Karakol Hotel, 8 Novorosslyskaya Street, tel/fax: 2 23 68, 2 30 36, email: valentin @glob-x.karakol.su, to help you organise a horse or yak trek into the mountains or a climbing expedition, or for information about homestays. If you are lucky he may tell you how to find Kootuldo, the man who hunts with eagles in the Tian Shan mountains on the south side of the lake. For a small fee you can camp in Kootuldo's garden or even sleep in his house.

At KRD Tian Shan, tel: 26 489, email: root@glob-x.karakol.su, Sergey Pyshnenko can arrange homestays and organise treks into the mountains.

KARAKOL TO BALYKCHY

Distance 220km
If you followed the northern route to Karakol then it makes sense to return along the southern shore.

NIKOLAI PRZEWALSKI

Nikolai Przewalski was born in 1839 in a village near Smolensk in Western Russia, the first son of a sickly army officer, Mikhail Przewalski, who had been pensioned off at the age of 32. The Przewalskis were descended from Cossacks and Poles. His mother, Yelena, daughter of Aleksey Karetnikov, a serf who had become a landowner through service to the Tsar, was a very strong young woman who insisted on marrying impecunious Mikhail Przewalski against her father's wishes. She ruled her family of three sons (a second son, Vladimir, was born in 1841 and the third, Yevgeni, in 1843) with the aid of an equally strong nursemaid, Olga Makaryevna, who later became their housekeeper, until Mikhail Przewalski died in 1846. Eight years later Yelena married again and had a daughter and two sons by her second husband.

It was his weak but educated uncle, Pavel, who taught young Nikolai to shoot and hunt in the countryside near Smolensk – pastimes he enjoyed until he died. As soon as he left school Przewalski joined the army and, at 18 years of age, was commissioned in the Polotsk Regiment. The following year he resolved to become an explorer and applied for a transfer to the Amur district of Siberia, which had that year been ceded to Russia by China. His first expedition was in 1867–8 when he explored the Ussuri River and Lake Hanka. He crossed into Korea at Keiko before turning north via Vladivostok and Olga (then St Olga) and then inland again to Beltsova. Despite, at times, appalling conditions Przewalski collected many plant specimens which he sent to the St Petersburg Botanical Gardens.

However, it wasn't until 1871 that Przewalski set off on his first Central Asian expedition, which took him from Kyakhta (now the Russian-Mongolian border post, south of Ulan Ude) through Urga (Ulaanbaatar) to Kalgan, Kuku Nor, Mur Usu and back to Kyakhta. An incident at Kuku Nor was to shape the rest of his explorations and even his life. The Tibetan ambassador, who was staying at a Mongolian camp on his way back to Lhasa after ten years in Peking, invited Przewalski to visit the Dalai Lama. Unfortunately he was running out of money and, with the Tibetan winter approaching, he could only continue for half the 1,660km to Lhasa before turning back. After a gruelling return trip he reached Irkutsk in October 1873.

The next two years were spent in St Petersburg and Otradnoye, his childhood home, writing up the expedition, lecturing and drumming up support to mount a three-year expedition to Lhasa and on into India. By mid June 1876 he was on his way and in August he had reached Khorgos, on the Kazakstan/Chinese border, and crossed into what is now Xinjiang Province. A year later he was back at Kulja having reached Lob Nor to the southeast in time for the spring bird migration. When he reached Charkhalyk, the closest settlement to Lob Nor, he was amazed to hear he was not the first Russian to visit the lake – a group of Old Believers had reached the area from Siberia in 1861 in search of their promised land. After a number of years struggling to survive by farming and hunting *khulans* (wild asses) they gave up and, with horses and supplies sent to them by the Chinese in Turfan, set out on the return journey to Siberia. It appears that only a young girl, who was captured by the Bey of Turfan and became his favourite wife, survived the journey – the rest were probably

A magnificent red rock canyon, reminiscent of Central Australia, lies about 40km from Karakol to the south of the south lake road (A363). Turn off the main road after about 25km at the sign to Jety-Oghuz, and continue through the village and up the track to the gorge. The name means 'seven bulls' because of the seven cliffs surrounding the deep gorge. There are lovely walks, friendly people, and great places to camp beside sparkling murdered by rebellious Tungan tribesmen before they reached the Tian Shan. By the end of August Przewalski had re-formed his expedition and, despite deteriorating health, determined to reach Lhasa. The new route took them in an arc to the north before turning south, to avoid the chaotic area around Kashgar. This time they only reached Guchen before Przewalski's health forced them back to Zaysansk early in 1878. While he was convalescing war threatened to break out between Russia and China and the expedition had to be postponed.

Despite the threatening nature of relations between Russia and China, Przewalski set off again, in January 1879, from Zaysansk, even more determined to reach Lhasa. The route took them into the Altai mountains of Mongolia where Khyrgyz hunters brought him the skin of a takhi, which he sent back to St Petersburg; and in May, in the Dzungarian desert, he saw a live specimen of the horse to which he would give his name, *Equus przewalskii*. Despite his reputation as a hunter who shot anything that moved, Przewalski never got close enough to shoot the wary takhi.

The expedition followed the Urungu River to Gasbun Nor and then headed south to Hami, Dzun-dzasak, Tang La and Kuku Nor before turning southeast and entering Tibet. This time, after traversing rugged inhospitable country, crossing mountain passes so high there was not enough oxygen to make a decent fire (water took two hours to boil) and being harried by wild Yograi tribesmen, they reached Nagchu, only 260km from Lhasa.

Alas! The Tibetans refused Przewalski permission to go further and ordered him to leave. After many fruitless arguments and pleas, there was nothing for it but to turn around and head north once more. They reached Urga in October 1880 where Przewalski disbanded the expedition before re-entering Russia at Kyakhta.

However Przewalski did not give up his dream of Lhasa and, in 1883, he set off again. This time he trekked from Kyakhta via Dzun-dzasak, Do Chu and Gas to Polu where he gave up hope of crossing into Tibet – the Chinese had demolished bridges over the Tam Chu River and filled passes with boulders, cutting all routes. This fourth expedition ended at Karakol, on the shores of Issyk-Kul, in 1885; and Przewalski returned to St Petersburg a hero.

The invasion of part of Sikkim in 1886 was seen as a threat to the Empire by the British who began to show an interest in Tibet, which in turn threatened Russia. Who better than Przewalski to lead another Russian expedition to Lhasa?

In August 1888 Przewalski left Moscow for Karakol, travelling via Astrakhan and Samarkand to Pishpek (Bishkek). After an evening spent shooting by the River Chu, Przewalski unwisely drank from the river and a few days later, after reaching Karokol, he became ill and died of typhoid fever on 29 October 1888, aged 49 years. He asked to be photographed in his coffin, wearing his expedition clothes and with his beloved Lancaster rifle at his side, and to be buried beside Issyk-Kul. The rifle was bequeathed to his friend, Roborovsky, who was second-in-command of the expedition.

Nikolai Przewalski was a man of extraordinary talents. Explorer, adventurer, cartographer, botanist, zoologist and hunter; it is surprising he is not as famous as Livingstone and other great 19th-century explorers outside Russia.

streams with a snowcapped mountain backdrop; or you can stay at the Jety-Oghuz Sanatorium and enjoy the hot mineral springs in the company of elderly Kyrgyz.

There are one or two run-down hotels along the south road but camping is preferable beside the red sand beaches or up in the mountains.

BALYKCHY TO UZBEKISTAN

There are a number of different routes from Balykchy to Uzbekistan but whichever one you take be sure to camp beside Lake Song Kel to the west of the Kochkorka–Naryn road. The road via Jalal-Abad and Osh into the Fergana Valley is spectacular but we leave you to explore this area on your own. Be sure you have good maps.

CYCLING IN KYRGYZSTAN
Erik Korevaar

Now that I am back from Kyrgyzstan, China and Pakistan I realise that Kyrgyzstan has made the greatest impression on me. The country is big, wild, rough! Sometimes, when we met people on horses, I felt like a cowboy travelling through Indian country. It is a matter of personal choice whether or not you are attracted to this and if you feel self-confident enough. I would say this is not a country for 'beginners'. It is better to go with four people than with two or alone but you can still have a great experience!

We found out how criminal Kyrgyzstan was on our second day in Bishkek at the exchange office. My companion, Erik, was robbed and lost his wallet with a few hundred dollars. Luckily we had taken precautions and had spread our money in different places. We had two wallets each and I also had $400 in the frame of my bicycle.

After a long search we found a taxi with a roof-rack to take us and our bikes to Lake Issyk-Kul. I liked the way people drive in Kyrgyzstan. Every possible drop of gas is saved by driving slowly and by turning off the engine at traffic lights and when going downhill.

We swam and then slept in a simple house near the water. It belonged to farmers and was built for holidaymakers. In the morning we assembled our bikes. The damage from transport was not so bad and in the afternoon we really started our cycling trip.

The air was clean, the sun strong and there were no clouds to protect our skin so we needed to cover up with clothes. The air was not hot and it was quite pleasant to cycle. The road was better than we expected. Our first day was as a first day should be – easy – and after about 40km we arrived in Balykchy on the western end of the lake. We found it difficult without a translator and had trouble finding food and a room.

When we found the bazaar the sun had already set and people were packing up ready to go home. We bought some biscuits and then focused on the next problem: where to sleep for the night. People frowned when we asked for a hotel, we didn't know if they could not understand us or if they did not know about a hotel. At last we found a young man who understood us. He was a teacher and speaks a little English. He took us to the house of his friend where we were welcomed by an always-smiling electrical worker.

We slept there and in the morning gave a mini-bottle of whisky to the man who had been so hospitable. He did not believe in saving things for a rainy day and immediately fetched glasses. So there we stood, toasting and drinking alcohol at nine in the morning. They wished us a good journey as we cycled off.

Not everyone was this kind and, a few hours later, we were robbed again. We had stopped for lunch at a deserted place when a car pulled up. Four men got out and we shook hands. We were surprised when they asked for narcotics. We said we had none but they would not go away that easily. They started looking in our bags. We didn't know what to do. There was no-one to help us and, because there were four of them and only two of us, we decided to play along. They were very interested in our medicine box and when they found our sterile needles they thought we used them for drugs. They searched our arms for needle holes – as if two heroin addicts would go to Kyrgyzstan for a cycling holiday!

I was afraid they would force us to hand over our money but they didn't even steal our camera. They only took some 'give-away' stuff – small bottles of liquor and perfume. Finally, after one hour, we shook hands as good friends and they left.

After this incident we started believing the stories saying Kyrgyzstan is a rather criminal place and we saw we were helpless in isolated places. We forgot about camping but there were not many hotels in the area. From then on we had to depend on people to help us find places to sleep.

In the small village of Kochkorka we asked a young woman for water. She shyly pointed at a tiny stream that crossed the road. We frowned and tried to explain that we wanted drinking water. She looked at us uncertainly. Then another woman invited us for tea and soon we were sitting at a table with three women rushing to set the table. That is the nice thing about this country – one moment you are robbed, the next you are invited for tea by friendly people. The three women were sisters living with their father. We asked if we could camp in the porch but the father did not trust us and sent us to the hotel.

The hotel is in the 'no star' class: no tap water, no shower and no toilet. If you 'have to go' you must walk 25m to a dirty pit toilet behind the hotel but not at night because of the guard dog. We had a nice long sleep and, after a good breakfast of baked fish, we left for the Dolon Pass.

The pass was the first real climb for us – to 3,030m. The road was not steep and the surface was good but there was a strong head wind. It did not matter if the road turned – the wind turned with it. We took a rest in Sary Bulak and had lunch. Within minutes we attracted a dozen children watching us light our stove. As is normal with demonstrations the bigger the audience the greater the chance of failure but at last it caught alight.

We went on and the wind got stronger. I used all my power to keep going. I did not feel we were climbing, I only felt the wind pulling at me. The last part of the Dolon Pass was sand and stones. We put on goggles and climbed through a sandstorm. The other side of the pass the wind was the same and we bounced down the rocky road.

It started to rain and we sheltered at a farm. Of course the people served us tea. I believe it is a sacred duty to serve tea to strangers until they are sick of it. Other things on the table were bread, sugar, butter, apricots in syrup and *kymys* (Kyrgyz spelling of Mongolian airag, *qymyz* in Kazakstan) made from fermented mare's milk – the strong-tasting national drink of Kyrgyzstan. I drank two bowls but afterwards I didn't feel that good. Then we were able to go on because the rain and wind had disappeared. We were told there was a hotel at Ottuk, 20km down the road.

This turned out not to be correct. We asked for the hotel or if we could sleep in the school or camp in somebody's garden. The answer was no, no and no! It started getting dark and we started to get worried. Then we met a woman who spoke English and promised to help us. She addressed a man who did not look very happy. He kept glancing at us and the more the woman said the less happy he looked. Finally he took a deep breath and invited us to his house. An hour later we moved to a woman's house where we could pay for accommodation. At her house the atmosphere was tense. We did not feel welcome in Ottuk.

Breakfast was simple with tea, raisins and pears. It was striking that there was almost no protein in the diet of the people we met. An important source of protein is *kymys* and everyone says it is a healthy drink but you need a strong stomach for it. It was still freezing as we left and we saw fresh snow on the mountains. The views were not spectacular but the vast landscape made us feel small.

The last real town before the border with China is Naryn, where we shopped. We parked our bikes and again were immediately surrounded. The men were silent, staring at us while the children laughed and tried to touch the bikes. Erik guarded our belongings while I went into the bazaar to buy tomatoes, dried fruit, nuts and biscuits.

Our day ended in At Bashi where the road changed from good asphalt to terrible rocks. This was no welcome for cyclists. We looked at a dead dog lying on the side of the road, surprised that nobody had done anything about it. We asked for a hotel but only got uneasy looks. But there are always kind people. A woman said the hotel was no good and let us sleep in her house. Unfortunately I felt sick; my stomach hurt and I had a temperature. Erik had to take care of the small talk, I fell asleep on the couch.

The next day was August 31, Independence Day. We discussed staying on another day because of my sickness but decided to continue. We had to be at the border on time to meet our Chinese guide. We followed the wide valley, slowly going up towards the border, a little wind at our backs. Now we were close to the Tian Shan range. Cycling was hard that day; I lacked strength and I hardly ate anything for two days. We had to do 80km – half of it not paved.

When we stopped for lunch a strange man on a donkey approached and stopped near us. He looked at us as if we were disgusting insects and I thought about going on without lunch. Then a car stopped and a friendly man got out. A little game started: we called the name of a place, he wrote an amount on his dirty windscreen and then we wrote another amount beneath it. He agreed that he would take us to Tashgorgan, a border post 60km from the actual border, for 450 som.

It was a joy to sit back and enjoy the view for a change. When we reached the unpaved road we created a cloud of dust. Soon, a man on a bicycle came our way and we stopped and asked where he had come from. He was Swiss and had started six months ago with his brother in Bangkok. He had already seen India, Pakistan and China. Quickly we exchanged tips and money and then went on. We looked back as he disappeared in the dust – he seemed incredibly lonely.

Tashgorgan is no more than a fence, a big building with Russian soldiers and a few wagons (like road workers' caravans on wheels, with curved roofs and chimneys). Although Kyrgyzstan is independent the border is still protected by Russia. We slept in the wagon of our 'taxi driver', Mischa. A week ago he had crashed his car and we admired the wreck; he advised us not to drink and drive. Then he tried our bikes and we tried his horse. The sunset that followed was fabulous. It goes quickly here – at seven it was full daylight, then the shadows got longer and at eight it was completely dark.

With care Mischa prepared our beds; it gets cold at an altitude of 3,500m. Before he left for a drink with the soldiers he told us not to open the door to strangers. At night strange things can happen so we were to listen for his special knock and his voice. We had been lying there a few minutes when we heard people outside. Without knocking or speaking they started pulling at the door. We went to the door and held our breaths. Someone pulled the door so hard the hook broke and it swung open. Quickly we jumped at the door and pulled it back. The men started to pull, shouting. We shouted back that they should go away but instead of obeying they pulled harder. I sat on the floor with two hands on the doorhandle and one foot on the wall. My companion held the doorhandle with his shoulder against the wall. Our heartbeat went over 180. They kept pulling and I was not sure I could hold it much longer. It was like a scene from a horror movie and it was certainly an experience.

Finally they went away but a few moments later they were back again, now with our friend Mischa. We recognised his voice and we opened the door. He smiled and said it was all a mistake, we were completely safe in his house. Although he told us we could trust him we had trouble getting to sleep. Until late into the night we heard soldiers laughing and shouting.

In the morning Mischa had a hangover. We wanted to let him sleep but he insisted on making us *chai*. We easily got through the check post and then we entered no man's land. We could not see much because of the fog. Sometimes we saw men on horses. The road was bad and we went slowly.

A little hill made us breathe heavily, feeling the altitude, and we had our first puncture. Eventually we stopped at the other check post, about 6km from the actual border.

We slept in a wagon, again with a complete family. They let us read and talk without interfering, which was relaxing. It's hard to spend a long time with people you cannot properly communicate with. We showed them our guidebook and photos and we smiled a lot but that is all we could manage. I missed having some privacy.

For dinner we had mutton and I was 'lucky' to get the best part – the head. It lay on my plate, looking at me, complete with eyes and ears. I did not know what to do with it so I exchanged plates with another guest at the table. He ate everything, except for the eyes, which were for his wife. That is all she had to eat; the brain was for the children. With the back of a spoon they emptied the skull. We heard that the brain is good for children, as it contains many vitamins.

In the morning the washstand was frozen. One person poured water from a kettle for another to wash. One little boy was alone, with no-one to hold the kettle, but he was smart. He drank from the kettle, spat the water into his two hands folded like a bowl and then he washed his face.

The last Kyrgyz check post posed no problems. Our passports were checked about seven times but we could not find a system. We also showed our fax saying that a guide would pick us up at the Chinese border. We were one day earlier than the day we had arranged but no-one seemed to notice. And so we cycled through the little 'arc de triomphe' that the Chinese people have built at the border and entered a completely different country: China.

Tips

Take a small album with photos of family, home country and town. A photo book about your country is also a good thing to bring. Souvenirs like photos, stickers, pens and key-rings, or whatever small stuff you can bring, are nice to give to people who have been hospitable.

Kyrgyzstan is not completely safe. There is the problem of unemployment and alcoholics and the police are not present everywhere.

The car that robbed us did not have number plates and we saw more cars like that. When you stop try to stay near the road where people can see you. It is sensible to hide some of your money in the frame of your bicycle. Divide your money between different wallets, decreasing the chance of losing all your money at one time.

When you plan on crossing the border with China make sure you get used to the altitude. Read something on altitude sickness before you go.

It is not difficult to leave Kyrgyzstan (with the proper stamps from OVIR in your passport), but to enter China can be difficult. To avoid problems, make an arrangement with a Chinese agency from Kashgar to pick you up with a jeep. At the Chinese border your bags will be checked thoroughly but if your papers are OK and your guide is there, there is no problem and no need to bribe. It is possible to arrange transport from Bishkek but it is easier to arrange it before you go. If you did not arrange transport for the Chinese side they will keep you at the border until there is a tourist bus willing to take you and you have paid a certain amount of money to the officials.

What to take
Repair and maintenance kit
* 10 patches, rubber (to cut more patches), tyre levers (2 plastic and 1 metal)
* cotton clothes, sandpaper, glue
* 3m wire, piece of chain, nuts and bolts, white grease, Teflon spray (for chain), sport tape, nylon wire, elastic cords,
* Spares: tyre, tubes, brake cable, gear cable, rear wheel axle
* Tools: Swiss army knife, file, saw, spanners, pliers, screwdrivers, small scissors, spoke spanner, bearing key

First aid kit
* Sticking plaster, sterile dressings, sterile needles, safety pins
* Paracetamol, malaria prophylactics, oral rehydration salt, arnica gel (for strained muscles), insect repellent, iodine, dental floss, tooth picks, emergency filling for teeth, multivitamin pills

Gear
* Tent, repair patches and seamseal
* Water filter, 4-litre water bag, plastic bottle, cloth to pre-filter, iodine for disinfecting water.
* Stove, fuel bottle, matches, pans, 35m film canisters for salt, herbs etc, plastic bags, plate, mug and dish washing detergent
* Camera, spare battery, film
* *Central Asia* (Lonely Planet)
* Road maps, compass
* Radio

Note that water filters do not kill all bacteria so we used iodine and boiling but the filter was good for improving the taste and reducing chemicals in the water.

Food
* Cookies, herbs, bouillon, ultra sugar, tea, instant coffee, milk powder, 250ml oil

We would have liked to take more food but the bikes took up most of the weight allowance on the plane.

Visas
We had problems getting visas as we were told we had to have an 'invitation'. We used the Internet to make contact with Tina and Fyodor at

the Computer Science Department of Bishkek University who were very helpful. They arranged for an invitation to be sent to the Kyrgyzstan Embassy in Brussels (there is no embassy in the Netherlands) but the telex never arrived. Eventually the embassy in Brussels issued a visa without the invitation. We had no problems getting visas for China or Pakistan.

We organised a Chinese guide to meet us at the Kyrgyzstan/China border with the help of Dostuck Trekking, tel: (3312) 42 74 71; fax: 41 91 29; email: nikolai@dostuk.bishkek.su and a colleague of Dostuck in Kashgar: Wang Xiaojing, Kashgar Mountain Association; fax: (86 0998) 222 957. However, be warned, the guide arrived with a $100 permit for us to cycle the Karakoram Highway – which we bought, but then later discovered was not necessary.

Erik Korevaar and Erik Loeff from the Netherlands brought their bikes with them by plane to Bishkek and then cycled from Lake Issyk-Kul to China over the Torugart Pass and on to Pakistan.

Chapter Eight

Uzbekistan

Uzbekistan, with its ancient Silk Road cities of Samarkand, Bukhara and Khiva, is one of the most romantic countries of Central Asia. With a history going back to the 6th century BC this area has traditionally had a settled population, unlike its nomadic neighbours. It was not until 1924, under Russian domination, that Central Asia was split into ethnic divisions and the state of Uzbekistan was formed.

In 1929 Tajikistan became a separate state and in 1936 Karakalpakstan was added to Uzbekistan. The boundary with Kazakstan was moved several times in the 1950s, 60s and 70s.

FACTS AND FIGURES

Uzbekistan is the third largest and most densely populated of the 'Stans. It is also, perhaps, the most romantic and historically interesting. The golden road to Samarkand may now be black tarmac but Samarkand, Bukhara and Khiva are still magnificent.

Time
GMT +5 hours

Population
23,000,000; population density 51.6 per km^2.

Capital
Tashkent, population 2.3 million.

GEOGRAPHY

With a total area of 447,400km^2 Uzbekistan is similar in size to Sweden and California. It is surrounded by four other CIS republics, Kazakstan, Kyrgyzstan, Tajikistan and Turkmenistan, and also has a short border with Afghanistan. It has a 420km stretch of the Aral Sea coastline.

The most fertile area is the Fergana Valley in the east, with its Syr-

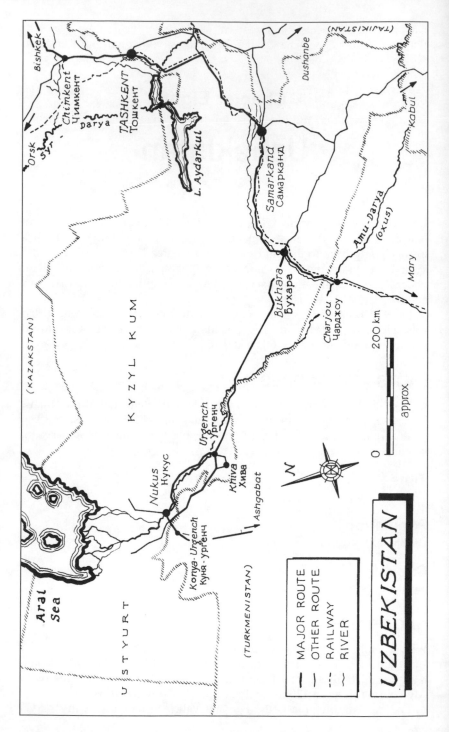

Darya River. The central and western two-thirds of the country is mainly flat desert and steppe. The Chatkal Mountains, which join the Tian Shan range, and the Fan mountain, close to Samarkand, are the main mountain ranges. Beshtor Peak in the east is the highest point at 4,299m.

Huge irrigation schemes, which take vast quantities of water from the Syr-Darya and Amu-Darya rivers for cotton farming, have cut off the water supply to the Aral Sea in the north west creating an environmental disaster of major proportions.

CLIMATE

Uzbekistan has long, hot, dry summers and short, cold winters with some snow, although it rarely settles due to strong winds. The average annual minimum temperature is -14°C, usually in January. From late June until the end of August the average maximum temperature is 32°C or above. Average annual rainfall is 200mm.

NATURAL HISTORY AND CONSERVATION

Forests of wild walnut trees occur in the foothills of the Tian Shan mountain range. The goitred gazelle, ground squirrels and gerbils can be seen in the desert. As in all of Central Asia there are many magnificent raptors in Uzbekistan.

Nature reserves

South east of Bukhara is the Ecocentre Gazelle, a small 45km² reserve funded by the Department of Conservation, with help from the CNRS, France and WWF Central Asia. Established in 1977 to preserve the goitred gazelle, it also has small herds of takhi and khulan.

Baday-Toghay Nature Reserve

This reserve, 30km north of Urgench, has an interesting strip of *toghay* forest – a dense, jungly area of trees, shrubs and creepers. Unfortunately the toghay forest is shrinking rapidly due to the drying-up of the Amu-Darya and Syr-Darya deltas – another result of the cotton irrigation schemes. You might be lucky and see a Karakal desert cat, Bukhara deer, badger, fox, jackal or wild boar. The last Caspian tiger was killed in 1972.

HISTORICAL OUTLINE

In this ancient land, artefacts from the Stone Age and remains of *Homo sapiens neanderthalensis* have been found in the Aman-kutan cave near Samarkand. The country's written history dates back to the first of many invasions of Khorezm (today's northern Uzbekistan) when, in the 6th century BC, it was invaded by the Persians. Over the following 2,500 years the area now known as Uzbekistan was invaded by Alexander the Great,

Kushans (bringing Buddhism), Sassanians (Persians), Turks, Arabs (bringing Islam), Saminids (Persians), Turkic tribes, Genghis Khan and finally the Russians. In 1969 Samarkand celebrated its 2,500th anniversary. In the 5th century BC both Herodotus and Hekates of Miletius wrote of the city of Khorasmiy and the Khorasnians. The first Persian invasion was followed by a visit from Alexander in the 4th century BC on his way to conquer the Scythians north of the Syr-Darya River in present-day Kazakstan. By the 8th century AD it was the turn of the Arabs to overrun the area.

Contrary to romantic belief, the Silk Road was in reality several routes meeting in Uzbekistan which became a centre for merchants from both east and west. In this way the tribes of the area became traders and were some of the first nomads to lead a settled life.

In the 13th century Genghis Khan swept into Uzbekistan seeking retribution for the assassination of a Mongol delegation he had sent to try to establish trade relations. His sacking of Otrar and Khojand was followed by the burning of Bukhara and the conquering of the whole area.

Timur (Tamerlane 'the lame'), whose reputation almost rivalled that of Genghis Khan as a fearless and bloody warrior ruler, conquered a vast area of the Middle East sending back to Samarkand the spoils of his campaigns in Central Asia in the late 1300s. It was with this wealth that he built and decorated the magnificent *madrasahs* (religious schools), mausolea and mosques of Samarkand, his capital.

The establishing of the sea route between Europe and Asia in the 15th century saw the wane of the historic Silk Road.

Modern Uzbeks are descended from Mongolian Shaybani and Turkic tribes who swept back and forth, conquering and being conquered in the Middle Ages. It seems likely that Uzbeks took their name from Uzbek Khan, leader of the Golden Horde, in the first half of the 14th century.

Three despotic khans had divided up the region into the khanates of Bukhara, Khiva and Kokand by the end of the 18th century but they spent much time, energy and wealth fighting each other as well as scrapping with neighbouring Afghanistan, China and Persia.

The Russians appeared on the scene in the 18th century when they signed a pact to 'protect' the Kazaks. Gradually pushing the Kazaks off the land they had roamed for centuries, the Cossacks and Tatars, recently liberated from serfdom, had begun to settle and farm the land by the mid-19th century. In 1865 Russian forces marched on Tashkent and by 1876 had conquered the three khanates.

Russian participation in World War I and the demand for livestock and other commodities from the region created much unrest there. When Russia began conscripting labour, not to fight but to support the army in a non-combatant role, Uzbeks rebelled along with the Kazaks and the

Kyrgyz and in 1916 a general uprising began in Tashkent. Reprisals were swift and severe.

With the Russian October Revolution, people of the 'Stans began to hope for better things; but when a group of Bolsheviks approached Emir Alim Khan of Bukhara asking him to capitulate he responded by slaughtering them and a holy war was declared. Despite the aid of White Russians, and even a small British force, Khiva was soon in the hands of the Bolsheviks. By 1918 the Red Army had overcome the opposition and the Uzbeks became part of the autonomous Turkistan republic although the rebel Muslim Basmachi continued to resist communist rule until 1923.

Like the other Central Asian countries Uzbekistan was created in 1924 and officially became the Uzbek Soviet Socialist Republic within the USSR.

On August 31 1991 Uzbekistan declared its independence and, in December, joined the other 'Stans in the Commonwealth of Independent States.

POLITICS

Russia, under the Tsar, ruled the Uzbeks from 1876 until 1916. With the collapse of the Russian Empire the following year civil war broke out but by 1918 the communists were in control.

After the demise of the USSR Uzbekistan moved uneasily towards democracy. In 1991 the Communist Party of Uzbekistan (CPUz) changed its name to the Popular Democratic Party of Uzbekistan with the communist president, Islam Karimov, as its leader. The Birlik (Unity) People's Movement (BPM), the first opposition party to be formed, was banned from standing a candidate in the first democratic presidential election in December 1991 which Karimov won with 86% of the vote. His only opposition was a poet, Salai Madaminov Muhammed Salih, of the Erk (Freedom) Democratic Party (EDP).

Uzbekistan was admitted to the United Nations in 1992, and, in 1993, to the Asian Development Bank, the IMF and the World Bank.

In 1993 the government accused the EDP of encouraging Islamic fundamentalism and evicted them from their offices. Birlik was banned and a number of the opposition were charged with conspiracy.

The Autonomous Republic of Kara-Kalpak, in the northwest of Uzbekistan, declared its independence with its own constitution and two official languages – Kara-Kalpak and Uzbek – but is still within the borders of Uzbekistan.

As a result of a referendum held in March 1995, President Karimov's term was extended until the year 2000 with 99.6% voting 'Yes'.

The last election for the unicameral Oli Majlis, which has 250 seats, was held in January 1995 when the People's Democratic Party was re-elected. The president is assisted by a cabinet of ministers.

ECONOMY

Despite being the world's third largest producer of cotton and having significant gold, other minerals, oil and natural gas deposits, Uzbekistan is one of the poorest countries in the CIS. Slow to embrace economic reform, the government is, at last, encouraging investment from outside Russia and the CIS. It is also trying to decrease the area of irrigated land under cotton and to replace it with grain, of which enough is not yet produced for home consumption.

PEOPLE

In 1995 the majority (71.4%) were Uzbek with 8.3% Russian, 4.7% Tajik, 4.1% Kazak, 2.4% Tatar, 2.1% Kara-Kalpak and 7% other minorities.

The boundary changes which have taken place since the Revolution have meant that most people label themselves by their place of origin (or that of their forebears) rather than as Uzbek. So Russians whose great-grandparents were born in Tashkent will be likely to answer 'Russian' when asked their nationality.

LANGUAGE

Uzbek is now the official language with most people in the towns speaking Russian as well. Few of the Russian population speak Uzbek and they are uncomfortable about the change in the official language. In fact much official business is carried out in Russian still.

From 1941 the Cyrillic script was used to write Uzbek but the government is changing back to the Roman script, in line with Kyrgyzstan and Turkmenistan, and many signs are now in both scripts.

The Autonomous Republic of Kara-Kalpak has two official languages: Kara-Kalpak and Uzbek.

RELIGION

Nominally, 88% are said to be Sunni Muslim, with 9% Russian Orthodox but, as in all CIS countries, religious claims seem to be allied to ethnicity as much as to belief.

CULTURE AND THE ARTS

Architecture

It is impossible to think of Uzbekistan and not think of the architecture. Without a doubt some of the finest examples of Islamic architecture are to be found here.

Unfortunately one of Genghis Khan's habits was to destroy the towns he conquered so very few buildings erected before the 14th and 15th centuries survive. However, the magnificent mausolea, madrasahs, mosques and minarets of Samarkand, Bukhara and Khiva more than make up for any lack of earlier architecture. Decorated with beautiful majolica, coloured tiles and intricate brick patterns these religious buildings are a joy to explore.

When the 6th–7th-century Afrasiab site near Samarkand was excavated a number of beautiful frescos were found. Similar to early Persian miniature painting they show caravans of merchants using elephants to carry their goods. Again at Penjikent, on the banks of the Zeravshan River, friezes portraying people, fish and monsters were uncovered. However it was about this time that Islam was brought to Central Asia and from then on no living thing could be represented in art although there are one or two notable exceptions in Uzbekistan – for example the Madrasah Nadir Divan-begi in Bukhara.

Art and craft
Jewellery
The earliest jewellery found in Uzbekistan dates from prehistoric times. Lazurite, agate and cornelian were used in the Copper Age; by the Bronze Age, crowns, hairpins, necklaces, bracelets and rings were being crafted.

Over the centuries Central Asian jewellery shows the influence of the invasions and withdrawals of various cultures: Persian, Turkic, Mongolian, Arabic, Islamic and, finally, Russian. Although many Uzbek treasures have found their way to Russian museums some good collections remain in Uzbekistan.

Textiles
Traditional craft in Uzbekistan includes carpet weaving and cotton and silk needlework for wall hangings and bedspreads. Brightly coloured *suzanni* (hand-embroidered wall hangings), were begun by young girls, with their mothers' help, to be taken with them when they married.

Metal work
The invasion of Central Asia by Alexander the Great in the 4th century BC brought an infusion of Hellenistic culture to Uzbekistan and with it the art of metal embossing. The earliest pieces of toreutic art found in Uzbekistan date back to this time and include bronze vessels and hairpins depicting animals. By the 3rd–8th centuries AD gold and silver articles, decorated with myths and heroes, hunting scenes, animals and birds, were being made for the nobility. With the advent of Islam, in the 9th and 10th centuries, the imams pleaded for the use of simple clay jugs and other plain items and people compromised by replacing precious metals with bronze and copper. Engraving began to replace embossing in the 11th century and the style of vessels changed from rather heavy shapes to more elegant forms.

By the 18th century shields, helmets, swords and daggers were being decorated with embossing, engraving and precious metals and stones. Russian influence begins to show in the 19th century with embossed samovars.

Toreutic art still thrives in Uzbekistan and you can see items being engraved for the tourist market in Khiva, Bukhara and Samarkand today.

Music and literature

As in most rural cultures stories and poems were passed from generation to generation by word of mouth rather than in writing. Travelling minstrels sang their stories accompanying themselves on long-necked lutes. Women sang the *sozanda* to the sound of tablas, castanets and bells.

PLANNING AND PREPARATION

See also Chapter One

When to go

The northern summer is best but much will depend on whether you are driving east to west or vice versa. It can be very hot in June/July so April, May and September/October are the best weatherwise if you have a choice.

Maps

The *Automobile Road Atlas* covers the whole of the CIS and is fairly accurate in Kyrgyzstan.

Documentation

Visas

Although, in theory, a visa from one of the CIS automatically allows a three-day transit through the rest of the member states it is probably safer, but more expensive, to get visas for each one. There are serious customs and immigration formalities on the Kazakstan/Uzbekistan border. It took three weeks to obtain Uzbek visas in Almaty but it is doubtful whether we would have been allowed to enter Uzbekistan without them.

Insurance

Take the best medical insurance you can afford. Hospitals are very basic and the means to fly home for medical treatment in an emergency is essential.

Embassy and consulate addresses

Austria Uzbekistan Embassy, Friedrich-Schmidt-Platz 3, 1080 Vienna; tel: (6) 405 0927; fax: 405 0929

France Uzbekistan Embassy, 96 Avenue de Suffren, F-75116 Paris; tel: (1) 43 06 62 98

Germany Uzbekistan Embassy, Deutschherrenstrasse 7, 53177 Bonn; tel: (228) 953 5715; fax: 953 5799

India Uzbekistan Consulate, D 2/5 Vasant Vihar, New Delhi 110057; tel: (11) 673 752, 678 991

Iran Uzbekistan Consulate, Grand Hotel Ozodi, Suite 1301, Tehran; tel: (21) 808 3021

Kazakstan Uzbekistan Embassy, Baribaev koshesi 36, Almaty; tel: (3272)610 235, 618 316; fax: 619 203

Pakistan Uzbekistan Consulate, D 66/1 Block 4, Clifton, Karachi; tel: (21) 572 566

Russia Uzbekistan Embassy, Pogoresky pereulok 12, 113017 Moscow; tel: (095) 230 1301, 230 0076; fax: 230 0032

Turkey Uzbekistan Embassy, Ahmet Rasim Sokak 14, Chamkaya, 06680 Ankara; tel: (312) 439 2740; fax: 440 9222

Uzbekistan Consulate, Cumhuriyet caddesi 39/4, Taksim, Istanbul; tel: (212) 237 1993; fax: 237 3322

United Kingdom Uzbekistan Consulate, 72 Wigmore Street, London W1H 9DL; tel: (0171) 935 1899; fax: 935 9554

United States Uzbekistan Embassy, Suites 619 & 623, 511 K Street NW, Washington DC 20005; tel: (202) 638 4266; fax: 638 4268

Customs and immigration

All the usual things are prohibited imports – guns, explosive items, drugs, pornography.

If you think, or hope, any carpets or other souvenirs are antiques make sure you get a receipt with the dealer registration number on it. Declare these items on entering and leaving each new country to avoid problems when you leave.

Health and safety
Health

Consult your local travellers' health centre about what inoculations they recommend before leaving home.

Prescription drugs – as for other CIS countries, bring all medication you may need. Carry the prescriptions with you in case Customs want an explanation of the drugs you have in your possession.

First Aid – as for other CIS countries, bring a comprehensive first aid Kit with you and restock when necessary in the big cities.

Safety

As Uzbekistan is a tourist destination take all the usual precautions and be extra careful. We let our guard drop and David's wallet was stolen in a crowded metro train. Be particularly cautious about parking the car in city streets. Sometimes it is better, and more fun, to leave it in a security carpark or at the hotel and use public transport.

Police

There are GAI posts on the outskirts of towns, as in the rest of the CIS, but you will not always be stopped. Uzbeks in uniform seem to be friendly, helpful and pleasant to deal with in our experience.

Photography

Make sure your flash unit has new batteries – flash photography is allowed in many of the historic buildings. Fast film for interior shots is useful.

IN UZBEKISTAN

Communications

Country telephone code: 7

Mail

Like the rest of the CIS the mail service is cheap but slow.

Telephone

Calls to Russia and other CIS countries are trunk calls so no country code is used. International calls – in theory, dialling 062 will connect you to an English-speaking operator who will book your call. Inter-city and CIS calls – dial 8, wait for the dial tone, dial area code and number. Only local calls can be made from street phones using zhetons bought from post offices and kiosks. The telephone system is similar to the rest of the CIS – frustratingly bad.

Faxes

These can be sent from most post offices but are expensive because of the poor telephone system – the operator rings the recipient to see if the transmission was legible and if not sends it again (and again, and again).

Email

This is possible when phone connections are possible. When functioning properly, it's the best way to communicate.

Couriers

DHL has an office in Tashkent.

Air connections

International flights go to many countries in Europe and Asia. Internal flights serve most cities.

Roads

There are approximately 67,000km paved and gravelled and 11,400km earth roads.

Railways
There are 3,462km connections between Tashkent and Moscow, Tashkent and Dushanbe, and most major Uzbek cities.

Electricity
220 volt, two-pin European type plugs.

Driving in Uzbekistan
Drive on the right.

Rules of the road
These are as for the rest of the CIS. For some reason Uzbek drivers seem to be more polite and more careful than most.

Road conditions
Roads between major cities generally have a good sealed surface.

Fuel
It's cheap but diesel is not readily available – fill up whenever possible. Unleaded petrol was not on sale in 1996.

Workshops and vehicle agencies
As in the rest of the CIS, sophisticated workshops are rare so take as many spares as you have room for. See *Appendix Two*.

Security parking
Hotels in the bigger cities usually have security parking. In smaller places take local advice but, if in doubt, ask the police.

National holidays
January 1	New Year
March 8	International Women's Day
March 21	Nauroz (Spring Festival)
May 1	International Labour Day
May 9	Victory Day
September 1	Independence Day
December 8	Constitution Day

Money
100 tiyin = 1 sum

National Bank, 23 Okhunbobcov Street, Tashkent, tel: (3712) 33 60 70, fax: 33 32 00, will give cash advances on Visa and will cash travellers cheques. Tourist hotels accept some credit cards.

Shopping
There are several supermarkets and department stores in Tashkent which stock imported goods of every description. Markets and roadside stalls are still the best places to buy fresh fruit and vegetables.

Souvenirs

Silk and cotton quilted coats, bright silk by the metre and traditional Uzbek hats can be found in the markets and also at department stores. Khiva, perhaps because it is more remote and therefore attracts fewer tourists, is a good place to buy traditional hats, carpets, robes and other souvenirs. Bukhara is a good place to buy carpets and rugs.

Food and drink
Water

Bottled water is available in the bigger cities. Boil and/or filter other water for drinking.

Drinks

Choy (tea) is the usual drink and, as in most of Central Asia, there is a customary way of serving it. Tea is poured into a small china cup and then back into the teapot twice before offering it to the guest. The cup is usually only half filled but constantly refilled to make sure the tea is warm.

Coffee, usually instant, is available in tourist hotels.

Pepsi and other bottled drinks as well as mineral water are sold in the towns.

Alcohol

Despite being a mainly Muslim country Uzbekistan makes some quite drinkable wine although much of it is rather sweet. As in other CIS countries vodka is widely drunk. Imported beer from China and Europe is on sale in most towns.

Food

Food served in most hotels and restaurants is the usual CIS fare but small guesthouses in Samarkand, Bukhara and Khiva provide a variety of well cooked and presented meals. Traditional dishes such as *plov* (rice with mutton and, sometimes, diced vegetables), *laghman* (thick noodles, sometimes in spicy soup), and *nan* (flat unleavened bread) are served in cafés and restaurants everywhere.

Accommodation
Camping

As it is largely desert yet more densely populated than other CIS countries, finding campsites away from the crowd in Uzbekistan is not easy. In rural areas it is safest to ask if you can camp close to a farm house.

Hotels

There are the usual Soviet-style high-rise hotels in most of the main towns. They cater adequately for group tours but can be unwelcoming for independent travellers. For instance one hotel in Samarkand charges almost double if you arrive without a booking through an agent.

Guesthouses/Homestays

These are definitely the best bet and are springing up in Samarkand, Bukhara and Khiva. Ask other travellers where they stayed and whether they recommend it. HOFA can arrange homestays in Tashkent, Samarkand and Bukhara. See *Chapter One*, page 30.

Arts and entertainment

Even in summer a variety of opera, ballet and drama is performed at various venues in Tashkent. There is not a lot of nightlife in the smaller cities but who needs it when you can stroll through the streets of ancient towns under a starlit sky?

GETTING THERE AND AWAY

From Kyrgyzstan, either through the Fergana Valley or via the main Bishkek to Tashkent road; from Turkmenistan, either through the desert from Ashgabat to Nukus (conditions unknown) or from Mary and Charjou to Bukhara; or from Kazakstan via Chimkent.

BISHKEK TO TASHKENT

Route M39; distance 448km

The M39, the main Almaty to Tashkent road via Zhambyl (Dzhambyl) and Chimkent, is a sealed highway, much of it dual carriageway, and mostly with a good surface. Approximately 76km from Bishkek the road crosses back into Kazakstan and away from the mountains. After another 200km it passes through Zhambyl, the site of the ancient silk road city of Taraz. Razed by Genghis Khan in the early 13th century it was re-established in the 18th century as the city of Aulie-Ata (Saint Father). After the Russian conquest in 1864 the city was demolished, rebuilt and named Dzhambyl – only the spelling has changed since the fall of the USSR.

A few kilometres along the road towards Chimkent the mausolea of two women, Aisha-Bibi (12th century) and Babadzha-Khatyn (11th century) are well worth a visit.

Although the *Road Atlas* shows the M39 going straight ahead, in fact it turns left a few kilometres from the border. If you reach Saryagach you've gone too far!

At the Uzbekistan border there may well be a long queue of trucks – go to the front and a guard will tell you where to stop. At the sight of your strange documents the guard will take you into the office building and you will be passed from one non-English-speaking official to another until eventually someone will stamp your passport and send you on your way. You would have difficulty getting into Uzbekistan without a visa although nobody noticed ours was not valid until the following day.

TASHKENT Тошкент

Time GMT + 5 hours
Population 2.3 million

Tashkent is the fourth largest city in the CIS – only Moscow, St Petersburg and Kiev have a bigger population. Excavations suggest there was a city on the site 2,000 years ago and certainly by the middle of the 8th century, when it came under Arab influence, it was an important crossroads on the silk route from Russia to India, China to Rome and Persia to Mongolia.

The name Tashkent, meaning 'city of stone', first appeared in manuscripts in the 11th century but in the 13th century Genghis Khan virtually wiped out the city. However Timur began to rebuild it in the late 1300s and during the late 14th and early 15th century, under the Mongols, the city began to prosper once more. By the 16th century Tashkent was thriving again under the Shaybanids. The few historic buildings which have survived date from this period.

The Kokand khanate ruled Tashkent from the beginning of the 19th century to 1865 when the Emir of Bukhara's planned takeover was foiled by the Russians. Soon after General Mikhail Chernyayev captured the city, the Tsar installed a Russian governor, encouraged Russian merchants to settle in Tashkent and declared it the capital of his new Central Asian territory of Turkistan.

By 1889 Russia had pushed the Trans-Caspian Railway through to Tashkent and it was the Russian railway workers who were in the forefront of the 1917 Revolution in Uzbekistan. After a bloody civil war Tashkent became the capital of the Turkistan Autonomous Soviet Socialist Republic in 1918 but in 1924, after a further division, Samarkand was declared the capital of the new Uzbek SSR. In 1930 the seat of government was returned to Tashkent.

The terrible earthquake in 1966 resulted in a whole new modern city being built over the bulldozed ruins, with much help from the USSR. As a result its appearance is much more Russian than Uzbek. The Chorsu district, all that is left of old Tashkent, hides a number of lovely 15th- and 16th-century madrasahs and mosques in a muddle of dusty alleys. Tashkent claims to be the academic and cultural centre of not only Uzbekistan but also Central Asia.

Money

The National Bank, Okhunbobcov 23, tel: 33 60 70, fax: 33 32 00, will give advances on Visa and will cash travellers cheques as well as change cash. All the big hotels have exchange desks and most will cash travellers cheques. There is a thriving black market for US dollars, sterling and Deutschmarks and you may be approached by the women who clean your hotel room. Uzbeks are only allowed to take a small amount of hard currency out of the country and, as many people want to visit friends and family who have left the CIS in recent years, their only way of accumulating cash is by participating in the black market. The rate is much higher than the official rate but be very careful. Avoid dealing with the swarms of people offering to change money around the train and bus stations.

Communications

City telephone code: 3712

Mail The main post office is on the corner of Abdulla Tukay and Aleksey Tolstoy.

Telephone The office at Navoi Avenue 28 is for long-distance and international calls. Be prepared for a long, frustrating wait.
For local calls use telephones on the street which take zhetons sold at post offices and kiosks. The major hotels have business centres with satellite phones and cost anywhere from $6–10 a minute but are quick and clear – perhaps your family will ring you back!

Faxes These can be sent from the telegraph office on Navoi Avenue but, due to the poor phone system, are expensive and unreliable.

Email If you can get a connection that does not constantly drop out this is the best way to communicate.

Air connections International flights go to and from China, Germany, India, Iran, Israel, the Netherlands, Pakistan, Russia and other CIS countries, Thailand, Turkey, United Kingdom and USA.
Internal flights serve Andijan, Bukhara, Fergana, Kokand, Nukus, Samarkand, Termez and Urgench.

Foreign embassy and consulate addresses

Afghanistan Gogol Kuçesi 73; tel: 339 171, 339 189

Canada see *Kazakstan, Foreign embassy and consulate addresses*, page 191.

China Gogol Kuçesi 79; tel: 333 779, 338 088

France Akhunbabayev Kuçesi 25; tel: 335 382; fax: 336 210

Germany Sharaf Rashidov Kuçesi 15; tel: 344 726,391 259, 347 658; fax: 394 359

India Aleksey Tolstoy Kuçesi 3; tel: 338 267, 338 357

Iran General Petrov Kuçesi 20; tel: 688 247/683 847/672 329; fax: 683 739. Women must wear a headscarf when entering the grounds of the embassy. Passport-size photos of women wearing headscarves are necessary for visas. Transit visas issued within 24 hours.

Kazakstan Holida Samatova Kuçesi 20; tel: 335 944, 333 795; fax: 336 022

Kyrgyzstan Mustaqillik Maydoni Kuçesi 5; tel: 394 543, 391 877

Pakistan Chilanzar Kuçesi 25; tel: 776 977, 771 003, 558 589; fax: 779 302

Russia Nukus Kuçesi 83; tel: 543 641, 552 948

Turkey Gogol Kuçesi 87; tel: 332 104, 332 107, 333 525, 323 757; fax: 331 358

Turkmenistan Taroby Kuçesi, local tel: 16, 547 461; fax: 556 478. Transit visas issued within 24 hours but must have visa for next country to be visited.

United Kingdom Gogol Kuçesi 87; tel: 339 847; international tel: 406 288/406 451; international fax: 406 549/406 575

United States Chilonzor Kuçesi 82; tel: 771 407, 771 081, fax: 776 953

Uzbekistan Taroby Kuçesi; tel: 547 461

Where to stay
Inexpensive
Hotel Tashkent, Buyuk Turon 50, tel: 332 735, opposite the Navoi Opera and Ballet Theatre, is very central. The rooms are large with basic furniture, bare floorboards, telephone and TV (BBC). There is hot water but plumbing is uncertain so insist on changing rooms if there are major problems. The Tashkent is very popular and caters mainly for tour groups – if they refuse you a room try getting a travel agent to book you in. There is a change bureau on the ground floor. Even if you don't eat there, do go into the main restaurant – it is an excellent example of Soviet-style pressed metal interior design. A Canadian company is said to have bought the hotel and there are plans to renovate so the prices are likely to rise. Visa accepted.

Hotel Turon, on Abdulla Kodiry between Usmon Yusupov and Abai Streets, tel: 410 705, employs an English-speaking staff member to help foreigners – the receptionists don't speak English and are not very helpful. Very small shabby rooms, no hot water and rather a long way from the centre of town but if you can't get into the Tashkent try here.

Expensive
Hotel Uzbekistan, Khamza 45, tel: 332 773, fax: 335 120, a multi-storey building facing the new Amir Timur Museum and public gardens. The usual Russian-type tiny rooms with basic furnishings and uncertain plumbing. Renovations were under way in 1996. Change bureau, travel agent, news agency, souvenir and chemist shops on the ground floor, business centre with satellite phone link and fax machine on first floor. Credit cards accepted. Every year new, privately owned hotels are opening – many very expensive – but if you have time, shop around and you may find a gem.

Security parking
Most hotels have security parking for a small fee.

Where to eat
Inexpensive
There are lots of *choyhonas* (tea houses) serving plov, laghman, shashlyk, tea and soft drinks, around town. Some also sell beer. **Kafe**

Golubye Kupola (Blue Domes Café) in the park between Sharaf Rashidov Avenue and Buyuk Turon Street serves Uzbek food in pleasant surroundings at very reasonable prices. Self-service at lunchtime, table service at dinner.

Moderate

Beware of the Western-type (usually painted red and white) fast food outlets – badly cooked, poor quality food and not very fast service. The restaurants in the hotels are often booked for weddings or other functions and no provision is made for guests unless you are in a tour group. The **New World Buffet** in the Navoi Theatre opposite the Tashkent Hotel serves a flat price buffet boasting 'over 80 delicious dishes'.

Expensive

The restaurants in the upmarket hotels are often expensive and disappointing but they often have cheaper cafés of varying quality too. There are also several exceptionally expensive restaurants – usually empty – in the centre of town.

Shopping
Supermarkets

Almazar Superstor, an Uzbek-Turkish joint company on Uzbekistan Street, has all sorts of imported foodstuffs at similar prices to Britain. The local shopping centre near the Turon Hotel has imported biscuits at very reasonable prices, local and imported cheeses and lots of tinned food.

Markets

There are four main markets, the three most central being **Eski-Djuva** on Saghbon Street, **Oloy** on Amir Temur Street and **Farkhod** on Chilonzor Massif, Block 12. The fourth is **Kuyluk** on Farghona Yuli Street.

What to see

The **Navoi Theatre**, opposite the Tashkent Hotel, has a repertory programme of ballets and operas all the year round and is very cheap and lots of fun. Performances start early – often at 18.00. The ticket office is in one of the pillars at the front of the building.

The **Museum of Applied Arts**, Shpilkov Street 15, tel: 563 943, in a turn-of-the-century house built by a Russian diplomat has a good collection of decorative folk and applied arts. The house itself is worth a visit with its brightly coloured plaster carving and carved wooden doors. There are collections of hand-embroidered suzanni, ceramics, traditional carpets and fabrics, jewellery, toreutic (metal) art and magnificent musical instruments inlaid with mother-of-pearl.

The **Museum of Fine Arts** and the **Museum of History** have many fine examples of toreutic art and jewellery, although much Uzbek jewellery is now in Moscow and St Petersburg museums.

TASHKENT TO SAMARKAND

Route M39; distance 293km
The M39 from Tashkent to Samarkand is all sealed and in good condition. The drive across flat dry countryside is not very scenic and has some of the worst pollution from factories and power stations in the 'Stans.

SAMARKAND Самарканд

Time as Tashkent
Population 400,000
Deep azure blue is the hallmark of Samarkand. As your eyes travel up the tiled walls to the fluted domes against the sky you wonder at the skill of the architects, artists and builders of the 14th and 15th centuries. The second largest city in Uzbekistan, Samarkand celebrated its 2,500th anniversary in 1969. Like so many Central Asian cities it has a dramatic and often bloody history although it's usually written of in more romantic terms. As the brochure of the Uzbek Havo Yullari Air Company so graphically puts it: 'It either was famous for its picturesque markets, or it was left half-escaped by its inhabitants.'

In recent years excavations have uncovered the ruins of Afrasiab, the name by which the hilly land around the city was known until the 13th century. Three times the city has been held under siege – by Alexander the Great, by the Arab Caliphate and by Genghis Khan.

When Timur made Samarkand his capital the city became a centre for poetry, science, astronomy, music and architecture. Timur's grandson, Ulughbek, whose astronomic tables are still used today, built a very advanced observatory on Chapal-ata Hill where part of the quadrant is on view.

In 1996 extensive road resurfacing and landscaping of the city was undertaken as well as a UN-funded restoration programme of the Registan buildings.

Money

National Bank, Firdavsi Street between Sharaf Rashidov and Mohmud Qoshqari, will give Visa cash advances, cash travellers cheques and change most currencies into sum. Exchange desks at the Hotel Samarkand will cash travellers cheques and change US dollars into sum.

Communications

City telephone code: 3662

Mail The main post office on Pochta Street has the usual facilities. Post code 703011.

Telephone The telegraph offices – long distance and international – are also on Pochta but the phone system is poor. Hotel Samarkand has a satellite phone – quick, efficient, very expensive.

Faxes These can be sent from the telegraph office which has the same problems as Tashkent and most of the CIS.

Air connections There are daily flights to Tashkent. Unfortunately for tourists all flights go through Tashkent so it is not possible to fly on to Bukhara and Khiva direct.

Where to stay
Inexpensive
Furkat, Mullokandova 105, behind Registan Square and the museum; tel: 353 261, is within walking distance of almost all the historic sites. It's a tiny private hotel or, as Furkat Rahmatov the proprietor says, a 'beg and breakfast', where tea or instant coffee is available all day long and you can rest in the heat of the day on a traditional Uzbek day bed in the courtyard under the tree. Definitely a home from home – the bathroom is clean and so are the bedrooms, and the family live in a wing so you'll be entertained by Furkat's three well-behaved school-age children. Dinner (traditional Uzbek cuisine) with Uzbek wine is available in the evening.

Moderate
Hotel Samarkand, an Uzbektourism establishment, corner Universitati and Okhunbobcov, is a Russian-style tourist hotel. With small rooms, tiny bathrooms and uncertain plumbing, it caters mainly for groups and charges 40% extra if you have not booked through a travel agent.

Security parking
Available in a locked courtyard at the Samarkand – if you have a camper-van or similar you might persuade the manager to let you camp there. Depending on the height of your vehicle you can either park at Furkat or in the school yard round the corner.

Where to eat
There are many choyhonas around town where you can choose what you want to eat from the open kitchen. The tourist hotels have restaurants – often over-priced and it is irritating to watch groups being served better food than you can order. Furkat will serve you dinner even if you are staying somewhere else.

Shopping
The main market is off the Tashkent Road and has excellent quality vegetables. Stock up here with bread, lentils, rice and other staples. There is a bakery around the corner from Furkat where you can buy bread hot from the tandoori oven.

Samarkand, Bukhara and Khiva are all good places to buy souvenirs, silk and carpets.

What to see

Everything! In particular, don't miss **Shakh-i-Zinda**, the Street of the Living King. Although some restoration has been undertaken it has been sympathetically done. This is a place to spend some time sitting quietly, absorbing the atmosphere. At the top of the hill the new cemetery meets the beautiful old mausolea. Shiny black marble tombstones, with photographs of solemn old men and women, nudge the grave of the cousin of Muhammed, Qusam ibn Abbas, who brought Islam to Samarkand.

Guri Amir, where the tombs of Timur, his son Ulughbek and two grandsons lie below the beautiful blue fluted dome.

The **Registan**, amazingly difficult to photograph unless you are lucky with the light, decorated with brilliant majolica. It was once the centre of the city where courts of justice met, merchants traded and young people attended religious schools.

Ulughbek's Observatory, on Chapal-ata Hill, where the lower part of the curved track of the quadrant can be seen. A small museum has been built beside it housing an interesting exhibition of the history of astronomy.

The **Samarkand Museum of History Architecture and Art** has some fine examples of 19th-century amulets and other jewellery.

SAMARKAND TO BUKHARA

Route M37; distance 268km
The road surface is good throughout.

BUKHARA   Бухоро
Time as Tashkent
Population 255,000
If the colour of Samarkand is blue then Bukhara is brown – clay-burnt-by-the-sun-brown. Set downstream of Samarkand on the Zeravshan River, Bukhara is an oasis city at the edge of the Kyzylkum desert on the Silk Route. The name, Bukhara, comes from the Sanskrit for monastery and the place was first mentioned in the 2nd century BC.

Like so many cities of Central Asia, Bukhara has a colourful and often bloody history. The Arabs brought Islam to the city in the 8th century but it was not until the 9th and 10th centuries that the Samanid dynasty made Bukhara its capital and thus the cultural and religious centre of Central Asia – by the 10th century it was known as Bukhoro-i-sharif (Noble Bukhara).

Such luminaries as historian Narshakhi, poet Rudaki and philosopher/scientist Avitsenna (Ibn Sina) were all born and educated in Bukhara.

At the beginning of the 13th century Genghis Khan conquered the city and 150 years later Timur ousted the rulers, plundering not only the works of art but also the artists and taking them to his capital, Samarkand. In the 16th century Bukhara came under the influence of the Uzbek khans when the Shaybanids made it their capital.

Money
National Bank, Sorok Let Uzbekistan 10, will change dollar travellers cheques and dollars. Most of the tourist hotels have change bureaux.

Communications
City telephone code: 36522

Mail The main post office is on Anbar, opposite Samarkand junction. Postcards sent from here took four to six weeks to reach Australia.

Telephone As in most of the CIS, the telephone system is not good. If you are staying at Sasha and Lena's you can use their satellite phone at very reasonable rates.

Faxes Facilities in the the post office.

Email It depends on the telephone connection.

Health
Until early this century people living in Bukhara drew their water from stone cisterns, called *hauz*, fed by a series of canals. Unfortunately the water was often stagnant and bred disease – the average life-span last century was said to be about 30 to 35 years. After the Revolution the water system was modernised and it is about as good – or bad – as most CIS cities.

Where to stay
Inexpensive
Sasha and Lena's B & B, Molodyozhnaya 13, tel: 3 38 90, is highly recommended although it is a fair way from the centre of the old town. It has three doubles and one three-bed room, clean, modern shared bathrooms but unreliable hot water pressure. Breakfast is included in the tariff and an excellent dinner with Uzbek wine can be served if you order at breakfast time. Sasha was due to open a new hotel close to Labi-hauz early in 1997 with even better facilities at the same price. Sasha and Arthur, the young manager, are very helpful and can book accommodation for you at your next destination, help you find diesel and introduce you to carpet dealers.

Moderate
Hotel Bukhoro, Sorok Let Oktyabrya 6, tel: 3 22 76, fax: 3 57 50, is the usual unappealing Soviet design but the rooms have en suite bathrooms and the lifts sometimes work.

Security parking
Guarded parking at Hotel Bukhoro and an enclosed courtyard at Sasha and Lena's.

Where to eat
Inexpensive
The area around Labi-hauz has a number of choyhonas which serve shashlyk, laghman and plov in a picturesque setting but they close early

– around 19.00 – and we were dismayed to see the water for tea and washing-up being drawn from the hauz. **Hotel Bukhoro** serves the usual Russian-type food and caters mainly for groups who seem to get better meals than those served up to independent travellers. Sasha and Lena's is the best bet if you are staying there and it's worth asking if you can have dinner even if you're not.

What to see

Wander around the **Labi-hauz**, take a look at the statue of Hoja Nasruddin, the Sufi wise-fool, visit the 17th-century Nadir Divanbegi Madrasah and Khanaka and the Kukeldash Madrasah. The **Ismail Samani Mausoleum** (9th–10th century) is one of the earliest and most beautiful buildings in Uzbekistan. This apparently delicate structure, built of burnt brick in elegant patterns which appear to vary in texture as the light changes from early morning to dusk, has walls 2m thick which have survived unrestored since it was built.

The **Ark** is a must with fine views over the city and a history stretching back to the 5th century. It was lived in until 1920 when it was bombed by the Bolsheviks during the Revolution. The Registan below the Ark was the scene of many bloody executions. It was here that two British army officers, Colonel Charles Stoddart and Captain Arthur Conolly, were put to death in 1842 by Emir Nasrullah Khan – victims of British political arrogance and the murderous (he had already killed his brothers and numerous other members of his family) Emir's hurt pride.

Stroll around the covered bazaars to the northwest of Labi-hauz. Here you can see the Taqi-Sarrafon (money-changers), Taqi Telpak Furoshon (cap-makers) and Taki-Zargaron, the centre of the jewellery trade during the 17th–19th centuries, where 21 jewellers had their workshops.

Buy star aniseed and nutmeg at the spice shop, browse through the rugs in the covered market and visit the Abdullah Khan and Modari Khan Madrasahs.

Don't miss the old wooden Bolo-hauz mosque on the way to the main markets or the little Chasma-Ayub Mausoleum with its waterworks exhibition beside the markets.

Around Bukhara

The Ecocentre Gazelle Nature Reserve is about 40km southwest of Bukhara on the M37 to Turkmenistan. It is a small reserve dedicated to preserving the Persian gazelle (*gazella subgutturosa subgutturosa*), a subspecies of the goitred gazelle. It also has two small breeding herds of 21 khulan and 11 takhi. The director, Natalia Soldatova, is breeding the Houbara bustard and some turtles. All these animals and birds are listed in the *Red Book* of endangered species.

Watch for the boundary fence; the entrance gate is on the northwestern side of the road. It is a long narrow reserve, approximately 15km x 3km.

Officially it is open only to organised groups so try to contact Natalia Soldatova before you visit, but communication is difficult so you may have to chance it. We were given a very warm welcome and a guided tour for about $20.

BUKHARA TO KHIVA

Route A380; distance 467km
Take the A380 for approx 439km westward to Urgench then turn off and head 28km southwest to Khiva.

KHIVA Хива

Time as Tashkent
Population 40,000
Khiva is one the oldest cities of the ancient land of Turkic Khorezm whose recorded history covers 2,500 years. The old city has been preserved and restored while a new one has sprung up outside the city wall. Most of the mausolea, mosques and madrasahs have been turned into museums but many families still live within the old city.

Communications

City telephone code: 36237

Where to stay

Inexpensive

Hotel Orkanchi, tel: 5 22 30, is a family-run hotel with spotlessly clean rooms and shared bathrooms, hot water and friendly service. In the old town, the Orkanchi has a big veranda spread with mattresses ideal for relaxing between forays up the minarets, to the museums and into the markets.

Moderate

The only other hotel in the old town is the **Uzbektourism Hotel Khiva**; tel: 5 27 75/5 49 45, the Muhammed Amin Khan Madrasah opposite the Orkanchi. In 1996 it was only intermittently open and guests walked across to the Orkanchi for meals.

Security parking

This seemed to be unnecessary so park in the 'street' outside the Orkanchi – the owner sleeps on the veranda on the ground floor.

Where to eat

The food at the **Orkanchi** is excellent – some of the best in Uzbekistan – and independent travellers were not discriminated against.

Shopping

The market in the old town is very good – fresh eggs and meat, fruit and vegetables, sweets and nuts, bread and soft drinks, rice and tea are all set out for you to inspect before you buy. The Sunday market is the biggest of the week.

Khiva is also a good place to buy wild hats, local silk and rugs at reasonable prices.

What to see

Everything – and when you've finished walk around again in the early morning and yet again at sunset. There are magnificent views over Khiva to the surrounding desert from the Aqshih bobo tower of the Kukhna Ark. A visit to the **Juma Masjid** (Friday) mosque with its 218 beautifully carved ancient wooden columns is a must. Climb the 118 steps of the Islamhuja minaret beside the Islamhuja Madrasah for another magnificent view – and be warned: going up the steep uneven steps is easy compared to the descent, but it is well worth the effort. If you are in a ghoulish frame of mind visit the medical museum where you can see Siamese twins preserved in formaldehyde.

The **Ichan-kala State Museum** has some excellent examples of 19th-century jewellery and ornaments.

KHIVA TO NUKUS

Route A380; distance 191km
Return to Urgench and take the A380 northwest to Nukus. We would welcome more information from readers on this route.

NUKUS   Нукус

Time as Tashkent
Population 180,000
Nukus is the capital of the Kara-Kalpak Republic of Uzbekistan, founded in the early 1930s, and is the largest town in the west. It has borne the brunt of the environmental disaster of the draining of the Aral Sea by irrigation schemes.

Money

There are exchange bureaux at the bank on Gharezsizlik Street, Hotel Tashkent and the airport.

Communications

City telephone code: 36122

Mail Post and telegraph office, Qaraqalpaqstan Street

Where to stay
Inexpensive
There are two hotels in Nukus – the **Tashkent**, corner Berdakha and Qaraqalpaqstan; and the **Nukus**, Lumumba Street, opposite the post office.

Chapter Nine

Turkmenistan

The third largest country of the CIS after Russia and Kazakstan, Turkmenistan (Turkmen, Turkmenia) borders Afghanistan, Iran, Kazakstan, Uzbekistan, and the Caspian Sea. Despite being the world's tenth biggest producer of cotton Turkmenistan is mainly desert, sparsely populated with traditional nomadic cattle breeders.

FACTS AND FIGURES

Time
GMT +5 hours

Population
4,000,000

Capital
Ashgabat

GEOGRAPHY

Turkmenistan covers 488,100km^2 and has a 1,768km coastline along the Caspian Sea. Much of the country is flat-to-rolling desert with mountainous sand dunes in the south and the low Kopetdag mountain range forming the boundary with Iran. The Karakum (Black Sand) Desert is one of the largest sand deserts in the world. The only river of any size, the Amu-Darya, flows from southeast, in the mountains of Afghanistan, northwest to the Aral Sea close to the Uzbek boundary. The construction of the Karakum canal, which takes water for irrigation from the Amu-Darya, has contributed to the drying up of the Aral Sea.

CLIMATE

Turkmenistan has a subtropical desert climate, hot in summer and cold in winter, but not the sub-zero temperatures of Siberia except in the mountains on the Afghan border. Karakum Desert daytime temperatures reach up to

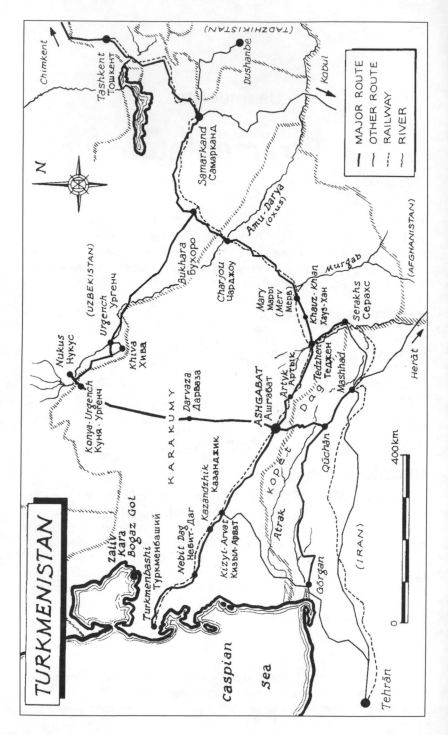

50°C in summer with an average of 35°C. The coldest area is around Kushka and the mountainous border with Afghanistan where the temperature may drop to −33°C. Being mainly desert terrain Turkmenistan has very little rain.

NATURAL HISTORY AND CONSERVATION

Nature reserves

The **Repetek Desert Research Centre** established in 1928 to study the flora and fauna of the Karakum Desert is situated 70km south of Charjou on the Mary road. Try ringing Repetek Tours at Charjou (37822) 4 44 70 to organise a tour, but it is worth calling in on your way through if you haven't managed to connect.

The **Kugitang Reserve**, in the far eastern corner between Afghanistan and Uzbekistan, is set in spectacular mountainous countryside. A rocky plateau covered with hundreds of dinosaur footprints dates back to the Jurassic period.

In the winter, flamingos, pelicans and other water birds take refuge from the northern winter at **Krasnovodsk Bay Reserve** on the eastern coast of the Caspian Sea, not far from Turkmenbashi.

HISTORICAL OUTLINE

The history of the region dates back several centuries BC. The ancient city of Margiana, now named Merv, is known to have existed in 500BC. In the 4th century BC Alexander the Great chose Margiana as his centre on his route to India. It remained an important trading place as a crossroads on the Silk Route until the 13th century when Genghis Khan's army destroyed the city and massacred all its inhabitants.

At the foot of the Kopetdag Mountains lies the historic Akhaltekin oasis, centre of the Parthian Kingdom from the third century BC. The capital, Nisa, met the same fate as Merv at the hands of Genghis Khan. Its ruins are a few kilometres west of Ashgabat.

It appears that the first Turkmen reached the area around the 11th century, perhaps from as far afield as the Altai Mountains. They were wild and splendid horsemen who sallied forth from the oases along the edges of the Karakum Desert to harass caravans and raid Persian villages for slaves. Unfortunately for them they also captured thousands of Russians to sell as slaves and by 1877 the Russians had had enough. Using Krasnovodsk (Turkmenbashi) on the Caspian Sea as a base, they fought their way southeast. After a number of battles they took Geok-Tepe and slaughtered thousands of people. From here the Russians continued east, taking Ashgabat and Merv with little resistance and by the 1880s the whole of Trans-Caspia was under the rule of the Tsar.

The Russians lost no time in establishing a railway between Krasnovodsk and Charjou on the Uzbek border and by 1888 the link from the Caspian Sea to Tashkent, capital of Uzbekistan, had been completed.

The Bolsheviks eventually established a Communist government in 1919 and, on October 27 1924, the Turkmen Soviet Socialist Republic came into being.

Sixty-six years later, on August 22 1990, the Supreme Soviet of the Turkmen SSR proclaimed the republic's sovereignty. Fourteen months later, after a national referendum, Turkmenistan was declared an independent state. On May 18 1992 a new constitution was adopted.

POLITICS

One of the most reluctant members of the USSR to embrace independence and democracy, Turkmenistan is still a one-party state with its president, Saprmurad Niyazov, having been re-elected unopposed, in 1992 for a ten-year period. Shortly afterwards President Niyazov adopted the title Turkmenbashi (Chief of all Turkmen) and the government appears to endorse this personality cult. The president is also prime minister and chairman of the Democratic Party of Turkmenistan (former Communist Party of Turkmenistan). All other political parties are banned.

There are two parliamentary bodies – Halk Maslahaty (People's Council) and Majlis (Assembly). All candidates for members of these bodies have to be approved by the president.

ECONOMY

Potentially Turkmenistan is a very wealthy country with the world's fifth largest reserves of oil and natural gas, exported through the USSR/Russia until the mid-1990s. In 1994 Russia refused to continue exporting Turkman gas to hard-currency markets and, due to the failing economies of its traditional markets in the CIS, Turkmenistan went into a recession. There is now a big push to construct a new gas pipeline through Turkey and Iran.

Exports include cotton (Turkmenistan is the world's tenth largest producer), natural gas, petroleum products, textiles, carpets and electricity, but Turkmenistan must find new markets before its economy stands a chance of recovery.

PEOPLE

In 1993 the population comprised approximately: Turkmen 73%, Russian 10%, Uzbek 9%, Kazak 2%, other 6%. There are many 'tribes' in Turkmenistan and for the majority of Turkmen tribal loyalty overrides all other allegiances.

LANGUAGE

Turkmen is the official language and is spoken by the majority of the population. In the cities Russian is widely spoken, particularly by officials and business people.

RELIGION

Sunni Muslim 87%, Eastern Orthodox 11%.

CULTURE AND THE ARTS

Horses and carpets

The old Turkmen saying: 'Water is a Turkmen's life, a horse is his wings, and a carpet is his soul' sums up the most important elements in the lives of Turkmen.

Most of the beautiful carpets offered for sale in the 'Stans are made in Turkmenistan. For nomads, carpets are a vital part of life and the art of Turkmen carpet-making dates back to at least the 6th century BC. Used to line yurt walls for insulation, hanging on walls for storage, covering yurt and wagon floors, as donkey and camel bags and for many other purposes, Turkmen carpets are not just utilitarian but also decorative. The patterns used tell the story of an ancient but continuing tradition.

According to Agamurad Akhmedov, the chairman of Turkmenkhaly (the state carpet manufacturers' association), 15 carpet-making factories employ about 10,000 people and produce 41,000m² of carpets a year. Like their Turkmen ancestors, carpet makers use natural dyes and smooth Sargin sheep wool for the best carpets although chemical dyes are being used more and more.

Akhaltekin horses are known to have been bred by Turkmen since the 4th century BC and probably much longer. Famous, but only to the cognoscenti, since the time Alexander the Great declared Bucephalus to be his favourite horse, Akhaltekins are faithful, hardy and fast. Nowadays they are sold for millions of dollars to horse breeders all over the world. Since 1991, when Turkmenistan claimed independence from the USSR, a breeding programme has seen the number of pure-bred Akhaltekins in Turkmenistan more than double from 1,250 to 2,600.

Literature

The 18th-century poet and philosopher Makhtumkuli is revered by all Turkmen. His work was published in English for the first time in 1995.

PLANNING AND PREPARATION

See also Chapter One

When to go

As with the rest of the 'Stans, May to September are the pleasantest months. If you are driving west to east you will be likely to arrive in spring but if your route is east to west you will probably arrive in autumn – either way you will avoid the hottest months of summer.

Maps

The *Road Atlas* covers Turkmenistan but, if this is your first CIS country, you may have difficulty getting a copy before you reach Ashgabat where it should be available.

Documentation

Visas

Transit visas can be issued in Tashkent only if applicants already have visas for the country they plan to enter after leaving Turkmenistan. This can be difficult as there is no Azerbaijan diplomatic representation in Uzbekistan. In theory, a visa valid in any of the CIS countries automatically gives a three-day transit visa in the others but, as the member states of the CIS become more independent, it is not advisable to bank on it. No photographs are required for Turkmenistan visas.

Insurance

Try to arrange third party insurance before you leave home. It is not available at the border.

Take out the best medical insurance you can afford. Hospitals are very basic and the means to fly home for medical treatment in an emergency is essential.

Vehicle documentation

As in Russia and the CIS but a charge is made at the border for a 'visa' for vehicles – US$36 for our LandCruiser in 1996. Payment is in manat but there is a bank in the same building and a receipt is given.

There are frequent traffic police checks, sometimes involving filling in forms, but no real problems.

Embassy and consulate addresses

Austria Turkmenistan Embassy, Friedrich-Schmidt Platz 3/3 30/39, 1080 Vienna; tel: (1) 407 3190

France Turkmenistan Embassy, 13 Rue Picot, F-75116 Paris; tel: (1) 4755 0536; fax: 4755 0568

Iran Turkmenistan Embassy, Kheyabun-e Maleka 8, Tehran; tel: (021) 761 015. Also Consul at Mashad

Russia Turkmenistan Embassy, Filippovsky pereulok 22, 21019 Moscow; tel: (095) 291 66 36; fax: 291 09 35

Turkey Turkmenistan Embassy, Rabat Sokak 22, Gaziosmanpasa, 06700 Ankara; tel: (312) 446 85 63; fax: 446 83 78. Turkmenistan Consulate, 2 Tasocegi caddesi, Altan Erbulak Sokak 4, Medidiyekoy, Istanbul; tel: (212) 272 70 20/1; fax: 275 39 93

United States Turkmenistan Embassy, 1511 K Street NW, suite 412, Washington DC 20005; tel: (202) 737 4800; fax: 737 1152

Uzbekistan Turkmenistan Embassy in a lane off Nukus Street on the right just before the T-junction with Bobur Street, Tashkent. Look for the security guards.

Customs and immigraton

Entry by road into Turkmenistan is taken seriously. Visas are required, a fee is charged for vehicles (see above), and there are immigration, police and customs checks at the border. Make sure you enter any carpets, artefacts, computers, cameras and other items of value on your customs declaration – this will speed processing when you leave the country.

Health and safety

As for other CIS countries, no immunisations are required but it is sensible to keep the usual ones – diphtheria, tetanus, typhoid and polio – up to date. Visit your local travel medical centre before leaving home and take their advice about hepatitis A and B, tick-borne encephalitis and rabies.

First aid and prescription drugs – do not forget to replenish your first aid kit in capital cities. Most large hotels in Central Asia have pharmaceutical counters in the foyer selling antibiotics as well as bandages, dressings and so on. Carry prescriptions with you as proof of need for medication.

Take similar safety precautions to those in other CIS countries.

Police

The usual GAI posts are there as you enter towns, slightly more serious than in the rest of the CIS but we did not find them a problem.

IN TURKMENISTAN

Communications

Country telephone code: 7

Mail, telephone and fax

Post and telegraph offices are sometimes in the same buildings, sometimes separate, and are about as efficient as the rest of the CIS.

Air connections

International flights go to and from UAE, India, Iran, CIS, Russia, Syria and Turkey. Internal flights serve Charjou, Dashkhovuz, Mary and Turkmenbashi.

Electricity

220 volt, two-pin European-type plugs.

Driving in Turkmenistan

Drive on the right.

Rules of the road
These are as in other CIS countries. See *Chapter Three*, page 57.

Road conditions
Road surfaces are not as good as in Uzbekistan – less maintenance, more potholes.

Fuel
It is cheap and readily available.

Workshops and vehicle agencies
As in Russia and the CIS, sophisticated workshops are rare. None of the major 4WD manufacturers have agencies in Turkmenistan as yet.

Security parking
Take local advice but, if in doubt, ask the police.

National holidays
January 1–2	New Year
January 12	Remembrance Day, 1948 earthquake
February 19	National Flag Day
March 8	International Women's Day
March 21	Novruz (Spring festival)
May 1	International Labour Day
May 9	Victory Day (WWII)
May 18	Day of Revival & Unity
October 27	Independence Day

Money
100 tenge = 1 manat
   Expensive hotels and restaurants in Ashgabat will take credit cards but otherwise they are not accepted.

Shopping
There are a few department stores in Ashgabat. They are not as well stocked as in Almaty and Tashkent but most things are available if you are prepared to shop around. The **Tolkuchka Bazaar** on the road past the airport is a great market and sells traditional clothing, jewellery and livestock as well as good quality fruit and vegetables.
   Markets and street stalls in the country sell fresh fruit and vegetables in season. Turkmenistan melons come in all shapes and sizes and flavours. Bought very cheaply on the side of the road they are deliciously refreshing in hot weather.

Food and drink
Water
Although the water in Ashgabat is probably safe to drink, boiling and filtering water or buying bottled water is the safest way to go.

Drinks
Tea, served without milk, is the usual drink. Locally bottled soft drinks are very cheap and fairly nasty.

Alcohol
Despite it being nominally a Muslim country, Turkmen are not teetotal. Beer, wine and spirits from various sources are available. If you have acquired a taste for kumys then you should definitely try the Turkmen equivalent, *shubat*, which is made from fermented camel's milk.

Food
Turkmen food is similar to that eaten in most of the other 'Stans: nothing to get excited about. However, there are plenty of good fresh fruit and vegetables for sale so cook your own whenever possible.

Tips and tipping
Tipping is not traditional in Central Asia, except in tourist-type hotels, although 'service charges' are beginning to appear on some restaurant bills.

Accommodation
Camping
Unless you can find somewhere to camp away from the road it is probably best to ask if you may camp beside someone's house in a village or at a farmhouse.

Hotels
Most towns have a hotel of a standard similar to those in Russian country towns and the rest of the CIS but often much more expensive.

GETTING THERE AND AWAY
NUKUS (UZBEKISTAN) TO ASHGABAT

Distance 538km
According to the *Road Atlas* a road runs west-southwest for 58km from Nukus to Konya-Urgench and then almost directly south across the Karakum Desert for 230km to Darvaza. It is another 159km south through the desert to Bakhardok and then 91km to Ashgabat, the capital of Turkmenistan. We did not meet anyone who had driven this route so conditions are unknown. Ask for local knowledge before setting off across the desert. There were rumours that this border was not an 'international' crossing but we could not confirm this.

BUKHARA TO TURKMENBASHI

Route M37; distance 1,311km
This is the more usual route into Turkmenistan from Uzbekistan. The M37 runs from Samarkand to Turkmenbashi on the Caspian Sea. Take the M37

from Bukhara to Charjou, approximately 146km. There is a floating pontoon toll bridge over the Amu-Darya River at Charjou – costs about US$4 so be sure to have some local currency (lads wave bundles of manat at the border – we changed our remaining few tenge there). Continue to Mary, approximately 239km, then Ashgabat is another 352km to the west. Ashgabat to Turkmenbashi (Krasnovodsk) is 574km.

BUKHARA TO MASHHAD, IRAN

Distance 692km
Drive from Bukhara to Mary, as above. Then there are two roads south to the border crossing at Sarakhs but the Ambassador in Tashkent told us to take the second road approximately 122km from Mary if we went that way. (The first turn-off is at Khauz-Khan, approximately 66km from Mary.)
   Sarakhs to Mashhad is approx 185km on route 22.

Our route was as follows:

BUKHARA TO QUCHAN (IRAN) VIA ARTYK

Distance approx 822km
Drive from Bukhara to Mary, as above. Continue to Artyk, approx 288km from Mary, where you turn left to cross into Iran at Artyk/Lotf Abad border crossing. Take route 224 to Dargaz, Kabkan and Emam Qoli. Turn south on to route 875 to Quchan.

CHARJOU   Чарджоу
Time as Ashgabat
Population 164,000

Where to stay
All we can say is keep going unless you must stay here. The hotels are grossly over-priced.

Expensive
Hotel Amu-Darya, Saprmurada Niyazov 5; tel: 2 24 34.

MARY   Мары
Time as Ashgabat
Population 95,000
An industrial and agricultural centre, Mary is the second largest city in Turkmenistan and produced 9% of the total gas output in the former USSR. Established in 1884 when Russia set up a garrison close to Merv, it was, in fact, called Merv until 1937 when it was renamed Mary.

Money
The Hotel Sanjar has an exchange bureau.

Communications
City telephone code: 37022

Mail The main post office is on ul Mollanepesa.

Telephone and fax The main telephone office is on ul Pervomayskaya.

Air connections Flights go to Ashgabat and Dashkhovuz.

Where to stay
Moderate
Hotel Sanjar, ul Mollanepesa 58; tel: 5 76 44.

Where to eat
Not much choice. There is a café and restaurant next to the Hotel Sanjar and a *stolovaya*.

What to see
The main reason for staying in Mary is to explore Merv.

MERV   Мepв
History
The written history of Merv, an oasis in the Karakum Desert, goes back to the 5th century BC when the Achaemenian king, Darius the Great, recorded the putting-down of a revolt in the province of Merv in an inscription on the mountain at Bisitun. In the 3rd century BC approximately 360 hectares around Merv became a fortified area called Erk Kala; and a walled city, Gyaur Kala, under the rule of Antiochus, the Seleucid ruler.

Merv continued to prosper as a principal trading centre on the Great Silk Route until AD1221 when Genghis Khan, infuriated by the murder of his tax inspectors – the tax was in the form of grain and beautiful young women – invaded and razed the city, killing all the inhabitants.

By the beginning of the 15th century Merv had been re-established under the rule of Tamerlane's descendents but it never recovered the prosperity or glory of the 11th and 12th centuries.

For a brief period in the 18th century Merv struggled to regain its importance but problems with the Persians prevented it. In 1884 the Russians annexed Merv, building their garrison a few kilometres away by the Murgab River but still calling it Merv. It was not until 1937, when the Russians changed the name of the town to Mary, that Merv regained its name.

The International Merv Project, set up in 1991, is a joint venture between academics from the Institute of Archaeology, the University of London, the

Academy of Sciences of Turkmenistan and Russian archaeologists from St Petersburg and Moscow, together with the Margiana Project, which aims to map, record and assess the earliest cities of Merv. They hope to publish two books in 1997, *Merv, Forgotten City of the Silk Road* and *Ancient Merv*, both written by Turkmen for the public rather than for specialists. At one time Merv covered about 640 hectares and it has recently been chosen by UNESCO to take part in its Space Archaeology Program. Archaeologists hope that Merv will be given World Heritage listing before long.

ASHGABAT Ашхабат

Time GMT + 5 hours
Population 517,000
About 2,000 years ago the Parthians established Nisa, 10km from Ashgabat, as a capital city. Around this time mention was made of Ashgabat as a wine-making area. In the 1st century BC the town was destroyed by an earthquake but, because of its importance as a Silk Road centre, it was re-established and flourished until the Mongols flattened it in the 13th century.

Nothing much happened in Ashgabat for the next six centuries until the Russians conquered Turkmenistan in 1881. They decided to establish their capital at Ashgabat in preference to Merv.

On October 6 1948 Ashgabat was devastated by another massive earthquake. The city was quickly rebuilt and is now a totally modern place.

Money
The Savings Bank of Turkmenistan, Makhtumkuli 86, has an exchange bureau as has the Hotel Ashgabat.

Communications
City telephone code: 3632

Mail The main post office is on ul 50 let TSSR, open weekdays 08.00–12.00 and 13.00–19.00, closed 12.00–13.00, Saturdays until 17.00 and Sundays until noon.

Telephone International and long-distance calls can be made from the telegraph office at Karla Libknekhta 33, open 08.00–19.00.

Fax Can be sent from the telegraph office.

Air connections International flights go to and from Abu Dhabi (UAE), India, Iran, Kazakstan, Russia, Syria, Turkey and Uzbekistan. Internal flights serve Charjou, Mary, Dashkhovuz and Turkmenbashi.

Foreign embassy and consulate addresses
Afghanistan Hotel Kolkhozchy, ul Azadi 78; tel: 257 087, 257 4354

Canada see *Kazakstan, Foreign embassy and consulate addresses*, page 191.

China ul Sankt Pazina 2; tel: 474 980, 474 676

France Hotel Jubileynaya, ul Tehranskaya 6; tel: 244 906

Germany prospekt Makhtumkuli, Pobedy Park, ul Dzerjinsky, 744000
Ashgabat; tel: 512 144/5-8; fax: 510 923

Iran ul Tehranskaya 3; tel: 244 611, 249 707. This embassy will issue an
Iranian transit visa in 24 hours.

Kyrgyzstan prospekt Saparmurada Turkmenbashi 13; tel: 468 804, 292 539

Pakistan ul Kemine 92; tel: 512 287, 512 317, 512 388, 510 667; fax: 512 304

Russia prospekt Saparmurada Turkmenbashi 11; tel: 510 262, 253 957;
fax: 298 466

Tajikistan prospekt Saparmurada Turkmenbashi 13; tel: 251 374

Turkey ul Shevchenko 9; tel: 354 118, 353 467, 355 595

United States ul Pushkina 1; tel: 350 045, 350 046

Where to stay
Moderate
Hotel Turist, ul Gorogly 60; tel: 25 41 19, 24 40 17

Expensive
Ak Altin Plaza Hotel, prospekt Makhtumkuli, tel: 51 21 81, fax: 51 21
77, 51 21 79, a Turkish owned and run establishment, has all mod cons
and accepts credit cards.

There are a number of small hotels at Berzengy, out in the desert about
10km from town – the **Hotel Independent** and the **Gara Altin** accept
credit cards.

Security parking
Ask at the hotel for the nearest reliable carpark.

Where to eat
There are plenty of cafés and restaurants to choose from, including
Lebanese, Turkish and Russian. The **Florida**, above the take-away Florida
at ul Shevchenko 8, serves quite good food and accepts credit cards.

What to see
The **Carpet Museum** is worth a visit. Pride of place is taken by the huge
Turkmen Kalby (Turkmen's soul) carpet. It is the biggest hand-woven
carpet in the world and: '40 weavers working in shifts, non-stop, finished
the carpet in seven months: from July 1941 to February 1942. The
Turkmen's Soul has 48,300,000 knots!' according to Agamurad
Akhmedov, the chairman of the state association, Turkmenkhaly.

Horseracing is big in Turkmenistan and the **Hippodrome** is the place
to go. Race meetings are held every weekend from late March to May and
from the end of August to mid-November.

The **Tolkuchka Bazaar**, on the road past the airport, is one of the great markets of Central Asia – don't miss it.

Ask at your hotel for directions to the **Akhaltekin Stud-Farm**.

NISA Hecca

The ruins of Nisa, in the foothills of the Kopet Dag about 10km west of Ashgabat, are all that remains of the Parthian capital. The Parthian nomads proved to be a match for the mighty armies of Alexander the Great and commanded a huge empire for 15 centuries. In the 13th century the Mongols invaded Nisa and razed it to the ground.

TURKMENBASHI Туркменбаши

Time as Ashgabat
Population 65,000

A settlement was established briefly in the early 18th century during an unsuccessful campaign by the Russian army; but it was not until 1869 that the Russians appeared on the scene again. Landing from the sea, they built a fort and named it Krasnovodsk. The name stayed until 1993 when it was renamed in honour of the president.

Communications

City telephone code: 43243

Air connections International flights go to and from Baku and Tashkent, internal flights to and from Ashgabat and Dashkhovuz.

Ferry connections Ferries which will take vehicles to Baku in Azerbaijan are scheduled to run several times a week. The trip takes about 12 hours.

Where to stay
Inexpensive
Hotel Khazar, ploshchad Pobedy; tel: 70 46 33.

Appendix One

Language

ALPHABET

Cyrillic	Russian transliteration	Russian pronunciation
А, а	a	farther
Б, б	b	bet
В, в	v	vet
Г, г	g	get
Д, д	d	dog
Е, е	ye	yet
Ё, ё	yo	yonder
Ж, ж	zh	measure
З, з	z	zebra
И, и	i (long, stressed)	seek
И, и	i (short, unstressed)	sit
Й, й	y	toy
К, к	k	king
Л, л	l	link
М, м	m	mad
Н, н	n	nut
О, о	o	pot
П, п	p	pink
Р, р	r	roll (roll the r)
С, с	s	sat
Т, т	t	tap
У, у	oo	moon
Ф, ф	f	fat
Х, х	kh	loch or Bach
Ц, ц	ts	lots
Ч, ч	ch	child
Ш, ш	sh	shut
Щ, щ	shch	fresh chops
Ъ, ъ	no symbol	hard sign

Ы, ы	y	did
Ь, ь	no symbol	soft sign
Э, э	e	hell
Ю, ю	yu	union
Я, я	ya	yard

USEFUL PHRASES

Greetings

Good morning	dobraye ootrah	Доброе утро
Good afternoon	dobriy dyen	Добрый день
Good evening	dobriy vyechyer	Добрый вечер
Good night	spahkoynigh nochee	Спокойной ночи
Goodbye	dasvidanya	До свидания
Hello!	zdrahstvooytyeh	Здравствуите!

Polite phrases

Please	pazhalsta	Пожалуйста
Thank you	spahseebah	Спасибо
Thank you very much	bal'shoye spahseebah	Большое спасибо
Sorry	prastitye, pazhalsta	Простите, пожалуйста
That's all right	nichyevo	Ничего!
Excuse me, please...	izveeneetye, pazhalsta	Извините, пожалуйста...

Questions

Do you have...?	u vas yest...?	У вас есть?
Tell me, please...?	skahzhityeh pazhalsta	Скажите, пожалуйста...?
How much/how many?	skol'ka?	Сколько?
What time is it?	katoriy chas?	Который час?

Complaints

| The toilet won't flush | slivnoy bachok isportilsa | Сливной бачок испортился |
| The ... doesn't work | ...nye rabotayet | ...не работает |

Language problems

| Please write it down | nahpeeshityeh pahzhalsta | Напишите, пожалуйста |
| Please speak more slowly | gavaritye pamyedlyenyeye pahzhalsta | Говорите помедленее, пожалуйста |

I don't understand	ya nye pani**ma**yu	Я не понима.
I understand	ya pani**ma**yu	Я понимаю
Can you show me, please?	paka**zhi**tye, pah**zhal**sta	Покажите,
		пожалуйста?
I will show you	ya vam paka**zhu**	Я вам покажу
Do you speak...?	vi gava**ri**tye...	Вы говорите
English	pa **ahn**gleeys**kee**	по-английский?
French	pa fran**tsu**ski	по-французский?
German	pa nye**mye**tski	по-немецкий?
Spanish	pa is**pan**ski	по-испанский?

Addresses

boulevard	bool**vahr**	бульвар
prospect	**pro**spekt	проспект
square	**plo**shcheed	площадь
street	**oo**leetsah	улица
suburb	prygorod	прйгород
district	**Rai**on	Район
region	**O**blast	Область

Directions

Where is the road to...?	gdye dah**rog**a...?	Где дорога ...?
Where to...	koo**dah**	Куда
How do I get to...?	kak mnye do**brat**'sa...?	Как мне
		добраться...?
Where is the hotel?	gyde gas**tee**nitsa?	Где гостиница?
Is it far?	dal**ye**ko?	Далеко?
Is it close?	**blee**ska?	Близко?
Can you show me on the	paka**zhi**tye mnye na	Покажите
map?	**kar**tye, pa**zhal**sta	мне на карте,
		пожалуйста?
Can I walk there?	**mozh**na iti too**da**	Можно идти
	pyesh**kom**	туда пешком?
Go straight ahead	**idi**tye **prya**ma	Идите прямо
Turn right	pavyer**nit**ye na**pra**va	Поверните
		направо
Turn left	pavyer**nit**ye na**lye**va	Поверните
		налево
At the traffic lights	u svyeta**fo**ra	у светофора
Next to	**rya**dam s	Рядом с
Opposite	na**pro**tif	Напротив·
What is this ...?	kak naziv**a**yetsa...?	Как
		называется...?
street	eta **u**litsa	эта улица
suburb	etat ra**yon**	этот район

What street number is this?	**Ka**koy **e**tat **no**myer?	Какой этот номер?

Parking

Where can I park?	gdye **mozh**nah mah**shi**noo?	Где можно поставить машину?
Is there a car-park nearby?	Yest lee zdyes pah**blee**zahstee aftasta**yan**ka?	Есть ли здесь побизости автостоянка?

Road signs

STOP	СТОП
NO OVERTAKING	ОБГОН ЗАПРЕЩЕН
ONE – WAY TRAFFIC	ОДНОСТОРОННЕЕ ДВИЖЕНИЕ
DIVERSION/DETOUR	ОБЪЕЗД
REDUCE SPEED	ОГРАНИЧЕНИЕ СКОРОСТИ
DANGEROUS BEND	ОПАСНЫЙ ПОВОРОТ
NO THROUGH ROAD	ПРОЕЗД ЗАПРЕЩЕН
NO PARKING	СТОЯНКА ЗАПРЕЩЕНА

Useful words

Car	ma**shi**na/aftomo**beel**	машина/ автомобиль
Light	svyet	свет
Lift	lift	лифт
Lock	za**mok**	замок
Passport	**pas**part	паспорт
Post Office	**po**chta	почта
main P O	pahch**tahmt**	почтамт
Room	**no**myer	номер
Shower	dush	душ
Tap	kran	кран
Telephone	tyelye**fon**	телефон
Toilet	tua**lyet**	туалет
Toilet paper	tua**lyet**naya bu**ma**ga	туалетная бумага
Water	va**da**	вода
hot water	ga**rya**chaya va**da**	горячая вода

Appendix Two

Vehicle Agency Addresses

Mitsubishi motors authorised agents
Russian federation
Moscow, 2/3 ShubinskyPerevlok, Rolf Company Ltd; tel: 241 7810; fax: 948 1938, 486 5214

Nissan Motor Co
Russian Federation
Ul Vorodzinskaya 46 – 50, Vladivostok; tel: (4232) 324 966

Azerbaijan
36 Khaatai Avenue, Baku; tel: 99 (412) 980 561

Iran
SAIPA Corporation, KM13 Special Road, Tehran; tel: 98 (21) 602 6560; fax: 602 6563/6564

Pars Khodro Co, Karaj Road KM7, Tehran; tel: 602 4711/4614

Kazakstan
Nissan Kazakstan, 240 Dostyk Avenue, 480051 Almaty; tel: 7 (3272) 641 708

Poland
Nissan Poland Ltd, Farbiarska 73, 02862 Warsaw; tel: 48 (226) 449 191; fax: 448 989

Ukraine
Nissan Ukraine, Geroev Obornory 4, Kiev 252022; tel: 380 (44) 263 2810; fax: 267 5601

Toyota authorised service stations
Russian Federation
Moscow, ul Gorbunova 14, Toyota Center Kuntsevo; tel: (095) 448 4138; fax: 448 6727

Moscow, Toyota Center Bitsa, Balaklavsky Av 26; tel: (095) 310 7345; fax: 310 7154

Irkutsk, Toyota Center Irkutsk, ul Polyamaya 199A, Irkutsk;
tel: (3952) 421 417; fax: 350 677

Kemerovo, ul Zheleznodorozhnaya 4A; tel: (3842) 258 798; fax: 287 877

Khabarovsk, Toyota Center Khabarovsk, ul Montazhnaya 42;
tel/fax: (4212) 526 891

Kholmsk, Toyota Center Kholmsk, ul Markarov 1, Sakhalin 694620;
tel/fax: (42433) 60 752

Nakhodka, Toyota Center Nakhodka, ul Sakhalinskaya 6; tel: (42366) 43 323;
fax: 43 637

Perm, Toyota Center Perm, ul Promishlennaya 4A; tel: (3422) 279 898;
fax: 531 2403

St Petersburg, Toyota Center St Petersburg, ul Balkanskaya 57;
tel: (812)101 6148; fax: 101 6426

Vladivostok, Toyota Center Vladivostok, ul Snegovaya 13A;
tel: (4232) 295 861; fax: 462 971

Belarus
Minsk, Toyota Center Minsk, vul Mogilyovskaya 43A; tel: (0172) 218 295;
fax: 218 296

Kazakstan
Almaty, Astana Motors, Toyota Center Almaty, Tyuljkubasskaja 2, corner
Suyunbaja Ave; tel: (3272) 302 996, 304 587; fax: 304 567

Ukraine
Kiev, Toyota Center Kiev, 179 Kharkovskoe Shosse; tel: (044) 562 7302;
fax: 562 7301

Odessa, Toyota Center Odessa, 76 Chkalova Shosse, 19th km of Ovidiopol
Shosse 272062; tel: (0482) 262 627; fax: 615 150

Uzbekistan
Samarkand, Toyota Center Samarkand, Oblastnoi Mechanicicheski Masterskie,
ul Karla Marksa 1, Djuma; tel: 5 17 22 (through the operator); no fax

Tashkent, Toyota Center Tashkent, pr Druzhba Narodov 118; tel: (3712) 768
715; fax: 456 567

Tashkent, Toyota Uzinavtoservice, 118 Khalklar Dustligi, 1 Firkat Street; tel:
761 715, 768 715, fax: 451 473, work on Toyota vehicles but have a very limited
stock of spare parts. They do have some Shell motor oils.

Appendix Three

Further Reading

CIS

History

Bobrick, Benson, *East of the Sun*, London: Mandarin Paperbacks, 1992. ISBN 0 7493 0612 2. A very readable history of Russia from the 16th century to post-perestroika.

Cronin, Vincent, *Catherine, Empress of All the Russias*, Collins Harvill, 1989. ISBN 0 00272035 3

Essays on Uzbek History, Culture, & Language, edited by Bakhtiyar Nazarov and Denis Sinor, Indiana University Research Institute for Inner Asian Studies. 1993, ISBN 0-933070-29-2

Glazebrook, Philip, *Journey to Khiva: A Writer's Search for Central Asia*, Kodansha America. ISBN 1-56836-074-6

Hopkirk, Peter, *Foreign Devils on the Silk Road: the search for the lost treasures of Central Asia*, OUP, 1980. Most of Hopkirk's books are rattling good true (mostly) stories of derring-do in the 19th century with rarely a mention of the female of the species. This one tells of the European heroes/villains, depending which side you're on, who found and removed thousands of ancient treasures along the Silk Road.

Hopkirk, Peter, *The Great Game*, OUP. The fascinating story of the struggle for power and influence between Russia and Britain in the 19th century.

Hopkirk, Peter, *On Secret Service East of Constantinople*, OUP, 1994

Hopkirk, Peter, *Setting the East Ablaze*, OUP, 1984. Continues where *The Great Game* leaves off.

Hosking, Geoffrey, *Russia, People and Empire 1552–1917*, Harper Collins

Khiva, introduction by Andrei G Nedvetsky, UK: Garnet Publishing, 1995 (Great Photographic Archives Ser. *Caught in Time*. ISBN 1 873938-27-6

Mowat, Farley, *The Siberians*, New York: Penguin Books, 1972, ISBN 0 14 00 3456 0. An interesting and often amusing account of two journeys covering 29,000 miles through Siberia and the Russian Far East in the 1960s. Farley Mowat is also the author of *People of the Deer* and has written with great empathy of the lives of minorities in the United States and the USSR.

Negus, George, *Across the Red Unknown: a journey through the New Russia*, photographs by Peter Solness, Sydney: Weldon Publishing, 1992. Negus and a team of four 4WDs, laden with TV cameras and satellite communications, drove from Vladivostok to Moscow in 1991. They were on the train between Shimanovsk and Chernishevsk when the Communists attempted to oust Gorbachev. Great photographs.

Olcott, Martha B, *The Kazakhs*, Hoover Institution Press, 1995, 2nd ed. ISBN 0-8179-9352-5

Pipes, Richard, *The Russian Revolution 1899–1919*, London: Fontana, 1992 (1990). A massive – almost 1,000 pages – well documented history of the Revolution, written in a very readable style.

Pipes, Richard, *Russia under the Old Regime*, 2nd ed London: Penguin, 1995. ISBN 0 14 02 4768 8. In case you think the communists started the idea of 'sending enemies of the state' to Siberia, read a good history of Russia under the Tsars.

Reed, John, *Ten Days that Shook the World*, exciting eyewitness account of the Revolution in 1917.

Schwarz, Henry G, *Mongolia and the Mongols*, ISBN 0 914584 88 X

Yevtushenko, Yevgeny, *Don't Die Before Your Death: an almost documentary novel*, translated by Antonina W Bouis, Melbourne: Heinemann, 1994. This novel by the well known poet gives an insight into life in Russia after the 'thaw' – sometimes funny, often moving and always very Russian.

Nature guides

Birds of Russia by Algirdas Knystautas, forward by Peter Scott, Harper Collins, 1993. Includes all the CIS but not Mongolia. ISBN 000 219913 0

Durrell in Russia by Gerald Durrell, New York: Simon and Schuster, 1986. Written to accompany a television series. Slightly irritating as it does not name the plants shown in photographs.

Field Guide to the Birds of the USSR, Princeton, NJ: Princeton University Press.

Politics

Kulchik, Yury et al, *Central Asia after the Empire*, London: Pluto Press, 1996. Overview of the 'Stans since 1991 by Russians from the Ministry of Nationalities and Regional Politics and the Russian Academy of Sciences.

Hiro, Dilip, *Between Marx and Muhammed*, London: Harper Collins, 1994. Discusses relevance of models of Turkey's secular democracy versus Islamic fundamentalism of Afghanistan and Iran to the 'Stans.

Russian phrase books and dictionaries

Berlitz *Russian Phrase Book & Dictionary*, Oxford. ISBN 2 8315 0910 6

Lonely Planet language survival kit *Russian Phrasebook*, Melbourne. ISBN 0 86442 307 1

Collins Gem *Russian Dictionary*, ISBN 0 00 458665 4 (true pocket dictionary)

The Pocket Oxford Russian Dictionary, Oxford: OUP, 1994. ISBN 0 19 864526 0 (very large pocket needed)

Travel guides

Central Asia, a travel survival kit, by John King et al, Melbourne: Lonely Planet, 1996. ISBN 0 86442 358 6

Central Asia by Giles Whittle, London: Cadogan Guides, 1996, 2nd ed

The Insider's Guide to Russia, Gleb Uspensky, Hong Kong: CFW Publications, 1993. ISBN 962 7031 69 0. An amusing guide written by a Russian but already rather out of date (eg: internal visa restrictions no longer apply.) Concentrates on the European Russia – Siberia and the Far East merit only five pages plus five pages of photographs each.

The Russian Far East, Erik Azulay, New York: Hippocrene Books, 1995. A useful guide to the Far East which includes walking tours of the cities. Photographs in B/W only.

Russia, Ukraine & Belarus travel survival kit, by John Noble et al, Melbourne: Lonely Planet Publications, 1996. ISBN 0 86442 320 6. Comprehensive travel guide for the independent traveller. Includes area and city maps.

Siberian BAM Railway Guide: The Second Trans-Siberian Railway, by Athol Yates, Trailblazer Publications 1995, ISBN 1 873756 06 2.

Travel

Burnaby, Fred, *Ride to Khiva: Travels & Adventures in Central Asia*, Ayer Company Publishers: 1970. ISBN 0 405 03010 X

Farson, Negley, *Caucasian Journey*, London: Penguin Travel Library, 1951

Whittell, Giles, *Blowing Hot and Cold through Central Asia*, London: Indigo, 1996 ISBN 0 575 40006 2

Classics

Chekov, Anton, *Lady with Lapdog and Other Stories*

Dostoyevsky, Fyodor, *The Brothers Karamozov, Crime and Punishment, The Idiot*

Gogol, Nikolai, *Dead Souls, Diary of a Madman and Other Stories*

Gorky, Maxim, *My Childhood, My Apprenticeship, My Universities*

Lermontov, Mikhail, *A Hero of Our Time*

Pushkin, Alexander, *Eugene Onegin*

Tolstoy, Leo, *Anna Karenin, War and Peace*

Turgenev, Ivan, *Fathers and Sons, A Month in the Country*

All the above are published in Penguin Classics editions, many translated by David Magarshack.

Sholokov, Mikhail, translated by Robert Daglish, *And Quiet Flows the Don*, *Virgin Soil Upturned*, Moscow: Progress Publishers.

MONGOLIA

It is difficult to find anything written about Mongolia since the demise of communism but the following titles make interesting reading.

Bawden, C R, *Modern History of Mongolia*, Kegan Paul International, 1989

Berger, Patricia and Bartholomew, Terese Tse, *Mongolia, the legacy of Chinggis Khan*, Thames and Hudson, 1995. ISBN 0 500 23705 0

Blanch, Lesley, *Journey into the Mind's Eye*, London: Century-Hutchinson, 1968.

Field Guide to the Birds of the USSR, Princeton, NJ: Princeton University Press. Includes most of the birds seen in Mongolia.

MacGrath, Amy, *Free from all Curses: the story of Kublai Khan*, Sydney: Wolseley House, 1983. ISBN 0 9591879 0 1

Martyn, Norma, *The Silk Road*, Sydney: Methuen Australia, 1987. ISBN 0 454 00836 8

Middleton, Nick, *Last Disco in Outer Mongolia*, Phoenix, 1993. ISBN 1 85797 012 9

Mongolia's Wild Heritage, Mongolia Ministry for Nature and the Environment, United Nations Development Programme/Global Environment Facility – Mongolian Biodiversity Project, WorldWide Fund for Nature, 1996. ISBN: 0-937321-04-4

Pozdneyev M (sometimes A Pozdneev), *Mongolia and the Mongols*, Indiana University Publications – Uralic and Altaic series – v.1: 1971, v.2: 1977. Fascinating account of life in Mongolia in 1892–3 but only of interest to real students of Mongolia. Unfortunately does not include maps, and place-names have changed since the 19th century.

Severin, Tim, *In Search of Genghis Khan*, London: Century-Hutchinson

The Travels of Marco Polo, New York: The Orion Press

MAPS

Almaty, Toksan Sayingy Tourist Kartasy (Quarterly Guide Map), tel/fax: (7 3272) 426 196, index in English, no scale shown.

CIS – Commonwealth of Independent States with places of interest, German transliteration, Kümmerly and Frey, scale 1:12,000,000, European part 1:5,000,000, the 'Stans 1:5,000,000

CIS – Commonwealth of Independent States, German transliteration, Hallwag, index in Roman script, scale 1:7,000,000

Iran Foreign Drivers' Manual, Ministry of Roads & Transportation, Transportation and Terminals Organization, PO Box 15875 – 6538, Tehran; fax: 6400648

Kyrgyzstan, map and facts, International Foundation, 'Discovery of Kyrgyzstan', 6, Kamskaya Str., Bishkek, Kyrgyz Republic 720020; tel: (3312) 427 615; fax: 225 432, 427 615; Stichting, 'Ontdekking van Kirgizie', Postbus 65742, 1070 AS Amsterdam, Netherlands; tel/fax: (3120) 6862103; scale 1:1,300,000

Mongolia, Map of Mongolia, 1:3,000,000

Moscow, city map, Freytag and Berndt, index in Cyrillic and Roman, scale: 1:20,000

Moscow Map, includes metro map, Visitor Guide Publishing Inc. Boston, Mass. USA, tel (617) 542 5283; Moscow (095) 923 7354, 928 0151

Moscow North, 'The Golden Ring', Euro Map, GeoCenter International, scale 1:300,000

St Peterbourg, city map, Freytag and Berndt, with Cyrillic and Roman index, scale: 1:20,000/1:53,000

Tashkent, Business Map of Tashkent, Tashkent Cartographic Factory, 6 Colonel Asom Mukhiddinov Str, Tashkent 700170; index in English, lots of information including map of metro, enlarged central city section, scale 1:28,000

NOVGOROD STREET NAMES
all ulitza except where stated

Old name	New name (B = Bolshaya)
Mstinskaya	Andreevskaya
Leningradskaya	B St Peterburgskaya
Gertsana	B Dvortsovaya
Chemyshevskovo	B Vlasevskaya
Bolshevikov	Boyana
Yakovlevsakaya	Danslavnya
Musy Dzhalilya	Dukhovskaya
Yuria Gagarina	Fyodorovsky Ruchey
Cheremnova	Konyukhova
Sovetskaya	Lyudogoschaya
Litvinova	Lyukina
Kirovskaya	Mikhailova
Mstinskyi by	Nikitin by
Suvorovskaya	Nikolskaya
T Frunze	Olovyanka
Nekrasova	Predtechenskaya
Zhelyabova	Prusskaya
Telegina	Ryadyatina
Slavny by	Slavkov by
ploshchad Pobedy	ploshchad Sofiyskaya
Lermentova	Stratilatovskaya
Komarova	Tikhvinskaya
Proletarskaya	Troitskaya-Proboynaya Frolovskaya
Krasnaya	Tsitnaya
Dmitreyskaya	Velikaya
Lukinskaya	Vozdvizhenskaya
Pankratova	Zapolskaya
Chemyakhovskovo	Zavainaya-Koitsevaya
Krasilova	Znamenskaya
Bredova	Zverinskaya

Index

main entries in **bold**
entries in *italics* indicate maps

Abbreviations

CA	Central Asia
Ir	Iran
Kaz	Kazakstan
Kyr	Kyrgyzstan
Mong	Mongolia
Rus	Russia
Tur	Turkmenistan
Uz	Uzbekistan

accommodation 29-31
 see also individual countries
Afrisiab (Uz) 227
Akademgorodok (Rus) 102
Akayer, Askar, President (Kyr) 198
Akmola *see* Aqmola
Ala-Too mountains (Kyr) 197
Almaty 179, **190-193**, 195
 accommodation 192-3
 communications 190-1
 food and drink 192
 foreign embassies and consulates 191
 money 190
 security parking
 what to see 193
Altai (Mong) 165-6
Altai Mountains (Rus, Mong) 38, 103,
 141, 167, 247
Altai-Sayan (Rus) 40
Altanbulag (Mong) 157-8, 173
Amu-Darya River (Tur) 223, 245, 254
Amur River (Rus) 123, 129
Amursky Gulf (Rus) 130
Angara River (Rus) 105
Aqmola (Kaz) 180
Aqsu-Zhabaghly (Aksu-Dzhaballinskiy)
 Nature Reserve (Kaz) 180

Aral Sea 144, 180, 221-2, 245
Arguz (Kaz) 189
Arkhara (Rus) 118
Artyk (Tur) 254
Arshan (Rus) 111
Arvaiheer (Mong) 163
Ashgabat (Tur) 253-4, 256-8

Baday-Toghay Nature Reserve (Uz) 223
Bakhardok (Tur) 253
Balykchy (Kyr) 208-9, 211
Barguzinka Nature Reserve (Rus) 41
Barhardok (Tur) 253
Barnaul (Rus) 103, 188
Bayanhongor (Mong) 164
Baydrag River (Mong) 164-5
Beshtor Peak (Uz) 223
Biluu (Mong) 172
Birobidzhan (Rus) 118, 122-3
Bishkek (Kyr) 194-5, 197, **206-8**, *206*,
 213-14, 233
 accommodation 207-8
 food 208
 communications 207
 foreign embassies and consulates 207
 food and drink 208
 fuel 207
 money 206
 security parking 208
 what to see 208
Blagoveshchensk (Rus) 5, 120-2
books and maps 18
Boz-Uzuur (Mong) 168
Bratsk (Rus) 137
Bukhara (Uz) 221, 227, 240-2, 253-4,
Buryatia (Rus) 112
Buyant Gol (river) (Mong) 169

camping 12-14
  see also individual countries
Caspian Sea 23, 38, 40, 51, 137, 180,
  245, 247, 253
Chadan (Rus) 138
Charjou (Tur) 247, 251, 254
Chatkal Mountains (Uz) 223
Cheboksary (Rus) 90
Chelyabinsk (Rus) 96
Chernyshevsk (Rus) 5, 59, 117-18, 136,
  137
China 168, 177, 180, 218
Chinggis Khaan 139
Chita (Rus) 116-17
Cholpon-Ata (Kyr) 210
Chu River (Kyr) 198, 213
CIS (Commonwealth of Independent
  States) 3, 35, 179, 181, 199, 226, 248
clothing 16
communications
  see individual countries
computers 15
consulates
  see embassies and consulates *and*
  individual countries
customs and immigration 24-5
  see also individual countries
customs agents 25
cycling 60-2, 214-20

Dargaz (Iran) 254
Darhan (Mong) 159-60
Darvaza (Tur) 253
Dashkhovuz (Tur) 256
documentation 18-24
  see also individual countries
Dolon Pass (Kyr) 215
Dzhambyl *see* Zhambyl

e-mail
  see communications *under individual*
  countries
Ekaterinburg (Sverdlovsk) (Rus) 87, **92-6**,
  94
  accommodation 93-95
  food 95-6
  communications 93
  connection with Romanovs 93
  consulates 93
  security parking
  what to see 96
  U2 spy plane 93
electricity
  see individual countries

Emam Qoli (Ir) 254
embassies 19-20
  see also individual countries
equipment
  first aid 26-27
  general 16-17
  security 6
  vehicle 4, 5-8

Fan mountain (Uz) 223
fax
  see communications *under individual*
  countries
Fergana Valley (Uz) 198, 205, 214, 221-3,
  233
film 14-15
first aid 26
food and drink
  see individual countries
foreign embassies and consulates 19-21
  see also individual countries

Gaivoron (Rus) 41, 130
Genghis Khan 224, 226, 234, 240
  see also Chinggis Khaan
gift giving 17
  see also individual countries
Golden Ring (Rus) 86
Great Silk Route 221, 255

health and safety 25
  see also individual countries
homestay 30
  see also individual countries and
  towns
hospitals 26

insurance 21-2
marine 22
medical 22
  see also individual countries
Intourist 105, 157, 172
Iran 16,177, 254
Irkum River (Rus) 111
Irkutsk (Rus) **105-11**, *106*
  accommodation/food 109-10
  communications 105-9
  consulates 109
  excursions from 110-11
  money 105
  what to see 109
Ivolginsk Datsan (Rus) 114

Jety-Oghuz (Kyr) 212-3

Karakol (Kyr) 205, **210-11**, 213
Karakum Canal (Tur) 245
Karakum Desert (Tur) 6, 245, 253, 255
Karimov, Islam, President (Uz) 225
Kara-Kalpak,
    Autonomous Republic of 225-6
    language 226
Kazak (Qazak) language 182
Kazakstan 176, **178-95**, *178*
    accommodation 188
    borders 177, 179-80
    climate 180
    communications 185
    culture 183
    customs and immigration 185
    driving and maintenance 186
    economy 182
    embassies and consulates 184-5
    food and drink 187
    foreign embassies and consulates 191
    geography 179-80
    getting there and away 186, 188
    health and safety
        see Chapter One 25-7
    history 181
    language 182
    maps 183
    media 185
    money 187
    national holidays 187
    natural history and conservation 180
    people 182
    planning and preparation 183-6
    police 186
    politics 182
    population 182
    religion 183
    shopping 187
    spelling of place names 179
    time zones 179
    visas and other documents 184, 195
Kazan (Rus) 90-1
Kemerovo (Rus) 103
Khabarovsk (Rus) **123-9**, *126*
    accommodation 124-5
    food 125
    communications 124
    embassies and consulates 124
    money 124
    what to see 125-9
Khandyga (Rus) 137
Khangayn Nuruu Mountains (Mong) 141
Khentii Nuruu Mountains (Mong) 141
Kherlen Gol (Mong) 141

Khiva 221, **243-4**
Khovd (Mong) 168-70
Kochkorka (Kyr) 215
Kokand Khanate 198
Kopet Dag mountains (Tur) 258
Korevaar, Eric 214-20
Kosh Agach (Rus) 138
Krasnovodsk *see* Turkmenbashi
Krasnovodsk Bay Reserve (Tur) 247
Krasnoyarsk (Rus) 104-5
Kronotsi Zapovednik Nature Reserve 41
Kugitang Reserve (Tur) 247
Kuibishev (Rus) 98-9
Kurgan (Rus) 97
Kurgaizhino Nature Reserve (Kaz) 180
Kyakhta (Rus) 115, 157-8
Kyrgyz language 199
Kyrgyzstan *196*, **197-220**
    accommodation 205
    borders 197
    climate 214-20
    communications 201-2
    culture 198
    customs and immigration 201
    driving and maintenance 203
    economy 199
    embassies and consulates 200-1
    food and drink 204
    foreign embassies and consulates 207
    geography 197
    getting there and away 205-6
    health and safety 201
    history 198
    languages 199
    maps 200
    media 203
    money 204
    national holidays 203
    people 199
    planning and preparation 200-1
    politics 198-9
    population 197
    religion 199
    shopping 204
    time zones 197
    visas and other documents 200,
        219-20
Kyzylkum Desert (Uz) 240

Lake Baikal (Mong) 38, 40, 41, 105,
    110-12, 137, 141
Lake Dalai (Mong) 141
Lake Hanka (Rus) 130
Lake Khar-Us (Mong) 168

Lake Khovsgol (Mong) 173
Lake Ladoga (Rus) 41
Lake Issyk-Kul (Kyr) 208-9, 214
Lake Qapchaghay (Kaz) 190
Lake Song-Kel (Song-Kol, Song-Kul)
    205
Lake Song-Kol, *see* Lake Song-Kel
Lake Song-Kul, *see* Lake Song-Kel
Lake Tenghiz (Kaz) 180
languages
    English 51
    German 51
    Kara-Kalpak 226
    Kazak (Qazak) 182
    Kyrgyz 199
    Mongolian 146
    Turkmen
    Russian 51, 182-3, 199, 226, 248,
        259-62
language books and tapes 51, 267
Lapland Nature Reserve (Rus) 41
Lena River (Rus) 38, 137
Leningrad *see* St Petersburg
Lensk 138 (Rus)
Listvyanka (Rus) 110-11
Loeff, Erik 214-220
Loft-Abad (Ir) 254

Magadan (Rus) 136-8
Magdagachi (Rus) 120
mail
    see communications *under individual*
        countries
Manas (Kyrg epic poetry)199
maps 17-18
    see also individual countries
Margiana (Merv) (Tur) 247
Markovo (Rus) 138
Mary (Tur) 233, 254
Mashad (Iran) 254
McGonigal, David 8-12
Medeu (Kaz) 193
medical centres 25-6
Merv (Tur) 254-6
Mirny (Rus) 138
Moldo-Too mountains (Kyr) 205
money 28-9
    see also individual countries
Mongolia **139-73**, *140*, 181
    accommodation 156-7
    borders 157, 168
    climate 141, 149
    communications 152
    culture 147-9

Mongolia *(continued)*
    customs and immigration 151
    driving and maintenance 153-4
    economy 145-6
    electricity 153
    embassies and consulates 151
    food and drink 155-6
    foreign embassies and consulates 161
    geography 141
    getting there and away 157, 171-3
    health and safety 151-2
    history 143-5
    languages 146
    maps 149-50
    media 152
    money 154
    national holidays 149, 154
    natural history and conservation 142-3
    people 146
    planning and preparation 149
    population 139
    police 153
    politics 144
    religion 146-7
    shopping 154-5
    spelling of place names 139
    time zones 139
    travel agents 150
    visas and other documents 150
motorcycles 8-12
    choice of 9
    security 10-12
    spares 9-10
Moron (Mong) 173
Moscow **79-86**
    accommodation 84
    communications 84
    food and drink 85
    foreign embassies and consulates 84
    metro 80-3, 80-1
    money 79, 84
    population 79
    security parking 85
    what to see 86

Naadam (Mong festival) 149, 154-5
Nagarbayer, Nursultan, President (Kaz)
    182
Naushki (Rus) 115, 157-8
Naryn (Kyr) 205, 216
Naryn River (Kyr) 198
Naryn River (Mong) 165
national holidays
    see individual countries

natural history and conservation and
nature reserves
see individual countries
Nevada-Semipalatinsk Movement (Kaz)
179
Nisa (Tur) 256, 258
Niyazov, Saparmurad, President (Tur)
248
Nizhneudinsk (Rus) 105
Nogoonuur (Mong) 171
Novgorod (Rus) 74-9, *76-7*
Novosibirsk (Rus) 98-102, *100*
Novovoznesenovka (Kyr) 205
Nukus (Uz) 233, **244**, 253

Ob River 38, 98-100
Ochirbat, Punsalmaagiyn, ex-President,
Mongolia 145
Olgii (Mong) 170-2
Omsk (Rus) 97-8
Osh (Kyr) 206, 214
Ovoo 147

Penjikent (Tajikistan) 205
Penjikent (Uz) 227
people
see individual countries
Perm 91-2
Petrodvorets (near St Petersburg) 74
Petrograd *see* St Petersburg
photography 14-15
Pigott, Rohan 60-2
Pik Pobedy (Kyr) 198
Pishpek now Bishkek (Kyr) 206
planning and preparation 1-31
see also individual countries
police
see individual countries
politics and government
see individual countries
population
see individual countries
post
see mail *under* communications *under*
individual countries
Przewalski horse 165
Przewalski, Nikolai 213
public holidays
see national holidays *under individual*
countries

Qazaqstan (Kazakstan) 179
Quchan (Iran) 254

religion
see individual countries
Repetek Desert Research Centre (Tur)
247
roads and rules of the road
see individual countries
Russian Federation 35-138, *36-7*
accommodation 66-7
administrative districts 35
borders 38
climate 38-9
communications 55
culture 52-4
customs and immigration 24
driving and maintenance 57-60
economy 49-50
embassies and consulates 19-21
food and drink 64-6
foreign embassies and consulates *see*
individual towns
geography 38
getting there and away 23
health and safety 25-7
historical chronology 48-9
history 41-9
insurance 21-2
languages 51
maps 17-18
money 28-9
national holidays 63
natural history and conservation 39-41
people 50
police 58-9
politics 49
population 35
religion 51-2
shopping 64
time zones 35
visas and other documents 18-19

safety 27-8
Samarkand (Uz) 221-3, 227-8, 232-3,
238-40
Sangyakhtakh 137
Sary Bulak (Kyr) 215
Saryagach (Uz) 233
security equipment 6
security parking
see individual countries and towns
Semey (Semipalantisk) (Kaz) 177,
179-80, 188-9
Shamanism 50, 52, 147
Sharga (Mong) 166
shipping 23-4

shopping and souvenirs
  see individual countries
Shymbulaq (Kaz) 193-4
Skovorodino 118-19, 137
spares,
  bicycle 219
  motorcycle 9
  vehicle 7
St Petersburg **68-74**, *68*, *70-1*
  accommodation 73
  communication 72
  food and drink 73
  foreign embassies and consulates 72-3
  metro 70-1
  money 72
  population 69
  security parking 73
  what to see 73-4
Suhbaatar (Mong) 157-8, 173
Sutai Mountain (Mong) 166
Susuman (Rus) 137-8
Suzdal (Rus) 86-9, *88*
Svobodny (Rus) 136
Syr-Darya River (Uz) 221-3

Tajikistan 205-6
Takhi (Przewalski horse) 167-8, 242
Takhi Reintroduction Centre 167-8
Takhiin Tal (Mong) 167
Taldan (Rus) 119-20
Taldy-Qorghan (Taldy-Kurgan) (Kaz)
  189-90, 205
Tamchi (Kyr) 209-10
Tamerlane *see* Timur
Taraz (Uz) 233
Tashanta (Rus) 171-2
Tashgorgan (Kyr) 217
Tashkent (Uz) 205, 230-1, 233, **234-8**
  accommodation 236
  communications 235
  food and drink 236-7
  foreign embassies and consulates
    235-6
  money 234-5
  security parking 236
  shopping 237
  what to see 237
telephone
  see communications *under individual
    countries*
Terskey Ala-Too (Kyr) 209
Tian Shan mountain range (CA) 180,
  197-8, 206, 211, 216, 223
Timur 224, 234, 238

Togrog (Mong) 167
tools 7
Torugart Pass (Kyr) 157, 177, 205
travellers cheques 29
Tsagaanuur (Mong) 171
Tsetseg Nuur (Mong) 168
Tsetseg (Mong) 168
Turkmenbashi 253, 256, 258
Turkmenistan **245-58**, *246*
  accommodation 253
  borders 245
  climate 245-6
  communications
  culture and the arts 249
  customs and immigration 251
  economy 248
  embassies and consulates 250-1
  food and drink 252-3
  foreign embassies and consulates
    256-7
  geography 245
  getting there and away 177
  health and safety 251
  history 247-8
  insurance 250
  languages 248
  maps 250
  money 252
  national holidays 252
  natural history and conservation 247
  people 248
  police 251
  politics 248
  population 245
  religion 249
  shopping 252
  time zones 245
  visas and other documents 250
Turpan (China) 177

Ulaan Sunduy uul (Mong) 168
Ulaanbaatar 5, 139-41, 150, 153-4, **159-
  63**, 173, *160*
  accommodation 161-2
  communications 159
  food and drink
  foreign embassies and consulates 161
  money 159
  security parking 162
  what to see 162
Ulaangom (Mong)171
Ulan Ude (Rus) 112-14, 157
Urumqi (China) 177
Ust-Kut (Rus) 137-8

Ust-Nera (Rus) 137-8
Ust-Taata (Rus) 137
Uyench (Mong) 168
Uzbekistan *222*, **221-44**
  accommodation 232-3
  borders 222
  climate 223
  communications 230
  culture and the arts 226-8
  customs and immigration 229
  driving and maintenance 231
  economy 226
  embassies and consulates 228-9
  food and drink 232
  foreign embassies and consulates 235-6
  geography 221-3
  getting there and away 233
  health and safety 229
  history 223-5
  insurance 228
  languages 226
  maps 228
  money 231
  national holidays 231
  natural history and conservation 223
  people 226
  police 230
  politics 225
  population 221
  religion 226
  shopping 231
  time zones 221
  visas and other documents 228

vehicles
  agencies 59, 263
  choice and preparation 4-7
  documentation 22
Veseloyarsk (Rus) 177
video cameras 15
visas 18-19
  see also individual countries
Vladivostok (Rus) 5, 23-5, **130-6**, *132-3*
Volkov River (Rus) 74
Volga River 180
Vyborg (Rus) 69, 136

Wescott, Gary and Monika 136-8
Western Tian Shan (Kaz) 180
Winter Palace (St Petersburg) 74
workshops
  see vehicle agencies

Xianjing Province (China) 157, 177, 197, 205, 212

Yakutsk (Rus) 136-8
Yeltsin, Boris 47-9
Yenisei River (Rus) 198
Yenisei-Angara River (Rus) 38
Yesik River (Kaz) 181
Yudin, Lena 130
Yudin, Victor 130

Zeravshan River (Uz) 227, 240
Zhambyl (Uz) 233
Zhungar Ala-Too Mountains 180, 189

COMPLETE LIST OF GUIDES FROM BRADT PUBLICATIONS

Africa by Road   Bob Swain/Paula Snyder   £12.95
Albania: Guide and Illustrated Journal   Peter Dawson/Andrea Dawson/Linda White   £10.95
Antarctica: A Guide to the Wildlife   Tony Soper/Dafila Scott   £12.95
Australia and New Zealand by Rail   Colin Taylor   £10.95
Belize, Guide to   Alex Bradbury   £10.95
Brazil, Guide to   Alex Bradbury   £11.95
Burma, Guide to   Nicholas Greenwood   £12.95
Central America, Backpacking in   Tim Burford   £10.95
Central and South America by Road   Pam Ascanio   £12.95
Chile and Argentina, Backpacking in   Hilary Bradt et al   £10.95
Cuba, Guide to   Stephen Fallon   £11.95
Eastern Europe by Rail   Rob Dodson   £9.95
Ecuador, Climbing and Hiking in   Rob Rachowiecki/Betsy Wagenhauser   £10.95
Eritrea, Guide to   Edward Paice   £10.95
Estonia, Guide to   Ilvi Cannon/William Hough   £10.95
Ethiopia, Guide to   Philip Briggs   £11.95
Greece by Rail   Zane Katsikis   £11.95
India by Rail   Royston Ellis   £11.95
Laos and Cambodia, Guide to   John R Jones   £10.95
Latvia, Guide to   Inara Punga/William Hough   £10.95
Lebanon, Guide to   Lynda Keen   £10.95
Lithuania, Guide to   Rasa Avizienis/William J H Hough   £10.95
Madagascar, Guide to   Hilary Bradt   £12.95
Madagascar Wildlife   Hilary Bradt/Derek Schuurman/Nick Garbutt   £14.95
Malawi, Guide to   Philip Briggs   £10.95
Maldives, Guide to   Royston Ellis   £11.95
Mauritius, Guide to   Royston Ellis   £11.95
Mexico, Backpacking in   Tim Burford   £11.95
Mozambique, Guide to   Philip Briggs   £11.95
Namibia and Botswana, Guide to   Chris McIntyre/Simon Atkins   £10.95
North Cyprus, Guide to   Diana Darke   £9.95
Peru and Bolivia, Backpacking and Trekking in   Hilary Bradt   £10.95
Philippines, Guide to   Stephen Mansfield   £12.95
Poland and Ukraine, Hiking Guide to   Tim Burford   £11.95
Romania, Hiking Guide to   Tim Burford   £10.95
Russia and Central Asia by Road   Hazel Barker   £12.95
Russia by Rail, with Belarus and Ukraine   Athol Yates   £13.95
South Africa, Guide to   Philip Briggs   £11.95
Spain and Portugal by Rail   Norman Renouf   £11.95
Spitsbergen, Guide to   Andreas Umbreit   £12.95
Sri Lanka by Rail   Royston Ellis   £10.95
Switzerland by Rail   Anthony Lambert   £10.95
Tanzania, Guide to   Philip Briggs   £11.95
Uganda, Guide to   Philip Briggs   £11.95
USA by Rail   John Pitt   £10.95
Venezuela, Guide to   Hilary Dunsterville Branch   £12.95
Vietnam, Guide to   John R Jones   £11.95
Zambia, Guide to   Chris McIntyre   £11.95
Zanzibar, Guide to   David Else   £10.95

Bradt Guides are available from bookshops or by mail order from:
Bradt Publications, 41 Nortoft Road, Chalfont St Peter, Bucks SL9 0LA, England.
Tel/fax: 01494 873478. Email: bradtpublications@compuserve.com
Please include your name, address and daytime telephone number with your order and
enclose a cheque or postal order, or quote your Visa/Access card number and expiry date.
Postage will be charged as follows:
UK: £1.50 for one book; £2.50 for two or more books
Europe (inc Eire): £2 for one book; £4 for two or more books (airmail printed paper)
Rest of world: £4 for one book; £7 for two or more books (airmail printed paper)